POVERTY AND SOCIAL EXCLUSION IN THE UK

Volume 1 – The nature and extent of the problem

Edited by Esther Dermott and Gill Main

First published in Great Britain in 2018 by

Policy Press
University of Bristol
1-9 Old Park Hill
Bristol
BS2 8BB
UK
t: +44 (0)117 954 5940
pp-info@bristol.ac.uk
www.policypress.co.uk

North America office:
Policy Press
c/o The University of Chicago Press
1427 East 60th Street
Chicago, IL 60637, USA
t: +1 773 702 7700
f: +1 773-702-9756
sales@press.uchicago.edu
www.press.uchicago.edu

© Policy Press 2018

British Library Cataloguing in Publication Data
A catalogue record for this book is available from the British Library

Library of Congress Cataloging-in-Publication Data
A catalog record for this book has been requested

978-1-4473-3215-2 hardback
978-1-4473-3217-6 paperback
978-1-4473-3216-9 ePdf
978-1-4473-3218-3 ePub
978-1-4473-3219-0 Mobi

The rights of Esther Dermott and Gill Main to be identified as editors of this work has been asserted by them in accordance with the Copyright, Designs and Patents Act 1988.

Cover design by Hayes Design.
Front cover image: Jess Hurd/Report digital
Printed and bound in Great Britain by CPI Group (UK) Ltd, Croydon, CR0 4YY
Policy Press uses environmentally responsible print partners

This book is dedicated to Peter Townsend who developed the relative deprivation method for measuring poverty.

Contents

List of tables and figures

Tables

Figures

List of tables and figures

Notes on contributors

Nick Bailey is Professor of Urban Studies based in the School of Social and Political Sciences at the University of Glasgow. He has published in the fields of housing and urban policy, as well as in poverty, and has advised national and local government on the analysis of poverty and social exclusion.

Jonathan Bradshaw, CBE FBA, is Emeritus Professor of Social Policy at the University of York. His research is focused on child poverty, child benefits and comparative social policy and he is a Trustee of the Child Poverty Action Group and a Fellow of the British Academy.

Esther Dermott is Professor of Sociology and Head of the School for Policy Studies at the University of Bristol. Her research examines the culture, practices and policies associated with contemporary parenthood, including interrogating how 'good' parenting is related to poverty and inequality. She is Co-editor of the Policy Press book series on Children and Families.

Eric Emerson is Professor of Disability Population Health at the University of Sydney and Emeritus Professor of Disability and Health Research at Lancaster University. He has written widely about the well-being of people with disabilities and was founding Co-director of England's specialist Public Health Observatory on learning disability.

Eldin Fahmy is a Senior Lecturer in the School for Policy Studies at Bristol University and Head of the Centre for the Study of Poverty and Social Justice. His current research focuses on poverty and social exclusion in the UK and understanding the social impacts of UK climate change policies.

Maria Gannon is a Research Associate in Urban Studies at the University of Glasgow. Her current research focuses on the impact of local authority funding cuts on vulnerable groups. She has experience in estimating hidden or hard-to-reach populations and has applied modelling techniques to provide estimates of problem drug use for Scotland, England and Northern Ireland.

David Gordon is Professor of Social Justice and Head of the Bristol Poverty Institute at the University of Bristol. He was the Principal Investigator of the ESRC-funded Poverty and Social Exclusion in the UK project. He has acted as an external expert for the European Union and United Nations on poverty measurement.

Pauline Heslop is based at the University of Bristol's Norah Fry Centre for Disability Studies where she is Professor of Intellectual Disabilities Studies. She is currently the Programme Lead for the national Learning Disabilities Mortality Review (LeDeR) Programme.

Saffron Karlsen is based at the Centre for Ethnicity and Citizenship at the University of Bristol where she is a Senior Lecturer in Social Research. Her work explores the different ways in which ethnicity has meaning and relevance in people's lives, both as a form of potential group affiliation and as a driver of socioeconomic, health and other inequalities.

Gill Main is a University Academic Fellow in Young People and Precarity at the University of Leeds. Her research interests include child and youth poverty, social exclusion, and well-being. She is Co-editor of the *Journal of Poverty and Social Justice*.

Christina Pantazis is Reader in Zemiology in the Centre for the Study of Poverty and Social Justice in the School for Policy Studies at the University of Bristol. Her research interests include poverty, social exclusion and inequalities, and crime, social harm, and criminalisation.

Demi Patsios is a Senior Research Fellow in the School for Policy Studies at the University of Bristol. He has maintained a primary interest in the effects of an ageing population on policy development and on the capacity of the health and welfare systems to respond to these needs.

Marco Pomati is a Lecturer in the School of Social Sciences at Cardiff University. His recent research focuses on the measurement of poverty and the impact of poverty on parents.

Mike Tomlinson is Emeritus Professor of Social Policy at Queen's University Belfast. His main research interests lie in the causes and consequences of economic and social marginalisation for communities, families and children. He focuses particularly on Northern Ireland and has published on child poverty, suicide, austerity and the measurement of well-being.

Acknowledgements

The PSE-UK research project was funded by the Economic and Social Research Council (ESRC) from 2010 to 2014 and we thank the ESRC panel for choosing to support the UK's largest ever research project on poverty, social exclusion and living standards, and offering their support throughout.

The research project was a major collaboration between the University of Bristol (lead), Heriot-Watt University, the Open University, Queen's University Belfast, the University of Glasgow and the University of York. The research project involved not only those who are contributing authors to this volume but many other colleagues involved in research and dissemination. David Gordon was the Principal Investigator. Nick Bailey, Jonathan Bradshaw, Glen Bramley, Mary Daly, Esther Dermott, Eldin Fahmy, Pauline Helsop, Paddy Hillyard, Ruth Levitas, Joanna Mack, Christina Pantazis, Demi Patsios, Simon Pemberton, Sarah Payne, and Mike Tomlinson were Co-Investigators on the project.

The other UK team members were: Tammy Alexander, Karen Bell, Kirsten Besemer, Jamie Daniels, Glen Darby, Maria Gannon, Saffron Karlsen, Grace Kelly, Gabi Kent, Stewart Lansley, Sasha Laurel, Mark Livingston, Gill Main, Shaileen Nandy, Jennifer Nockles, Kirsty McLaughlin, Pete Mitton, Beverley Parker, Marco Pomati, Ronan Smyth, Eileen Sutton, Sharon Telfer, David Watkins, Lisa Wilson, Steve Yates and Hong Yu. Nikki Hicks was invaluable as the project manager.

The research was supported by Joanne Maher and Emma Drever from NatCen, which conducted the survey under their supervision in Britain, and Dermot Donnelly from the Northern Ireland Statistics and Research Agency, which was responsible for the Northern Ireland survey. Others who supported the data collection, analyses and project management were: Tracy Anderson, Clare Tait, Colin Setchfield, Keven Pickering, Andrew Shaw, Eleanor Taylor, Liz Clery, Kirby Swales, Kevin Palmer, Jo Goddard, Paul Meller, Bruce Jackson, Mary Hickman, Julie Sullican, Vekaria Rupesh, David Evans, Gemma N Thomas, Steven Dunstan, Simon Hudson and Jackie Shelton.

The PSE team would like to thank all of the members of the national and international advisory boards who provided advice and help on the design and implementation of the research. The UK board members and advisory group were: June Burrough, Samantha Coope,

Tim Crosier, Danny Dorling, Rosalind Edwards, Alison Garnham, Nuala Gormley, Mike Harmer, Stephen Jenkins, Jane Lewis, Jean Martin, Peter Matejic, Anne MacDonald, David McLennan, Monica McWilliams, Jill Morton, Polly Toynbee, Paul Tyrer and Robert Walker. The international board members were: Aya Abe, Petra Böhnke, Julio Boltvinik, Madior Fall, Björn Halleröd, Daniel Hechiun Liou, Brian Nolan, Bryan Perry, Veli-Matti Ritakallio, Pedro Sáinz, Peter Saunders, Melissa Wong and Gemma Wright. The most recent PSE research also relies on its predecessors, conducted in 1983, 1990, 1999 in Britain and 2002/3 in Northern Ireland. Details of past research can be found on the poverty.ac.uk website.

We would also like to acknowledge our colleagues at Policy Press, in particular Laura Vickers and Jess Mitchell for their patience and advice in getting the book to completion. Finally, personal thanks from Esther and Gill are due to Richard Stubbings, Ronan Dermott and Ewan, Chris and Carolyn Main for their support during this research.

Introduction: poverty and social exclusion in the UK

Esther Dermott

Poverty and social exclusion in the UK

The results of the Poverty and Social Exclusion 2012 survey (PSE-UK 2012) present a staggering picture of poverty in the UK today. There is little disagreement that in the 21st-century poverty is a serious social problem in one of wealthiest countries in the world. Over one hundred years since Rowntree wrote that 'in this land of abounding wealth, during a time of perhaps unexampled prosperity, probably more than one fourth of the population are living in poverty, is a fact which may well cause great searchings of heart' (1901, p 304), the problem of poverty in the UK has not been solved. As Julia Unwin, ex-chief executive of the Joseph Rowntree Foundation, has written 'current levels of poverty are neither acceptable nor inevitable' (Derbyshire, 2013, p 5).

A third of households are deprived of three or more items that are necessary for an adequate standard of living. Significant proportions of the population lack the most basic items – adequate housing, food and clothing. Our main findings show that:

- 10% of households (2.7 million) live in a damp home;
- 9% of households (2.3 million) cannot afford to heat the living areas of their home;
- 8% of adults (3.5 million) cannot afford two meals a day, fresh fruit and vegetables once a day, and or meat, fish or vegetarian equivalent every other day;
- 4% of children (0.5 million) do not have three meals a day, fresh fruit and vegetables once a day, and or meat, fish or vegetarian equivalent every day because their families cannot afford them;
- 9% of adults (4 million) cannot afford either or both a warm, waterproof coat and two pairs of all-weather shoes;
- 9% of children (1 million) go without necessary clothing (warm winter coat, new properly fitting shoes, some new clothes, four pairs of trousers) because of a lack of money.

Very large numbers of people cannot afford basic social activities and are financially insecure. Almost 12 million people are too poor to engage in common social activities and almost half of all adults (30 million) lack one of the four financial necessities (being able to pay an unexpected cost of £500; saving £20 a month for a rainy day; make regular payments into a pension; afford household insurance).

Views on *why* poverty is a cause for concern range across the political spectrum. For some, improving the material lives of individuals is important simply to reduce the harm of living in poverty; for others, eradicating poverty is part of a wider project to reduce inequalities in a programme of redistributive progressive politics; for others again, the concern to be addressed is that having significant numbers of the population excluded from mainstream society is a loss of economic and social potential. Responses to how poverty should be tackled reflect these diverse philosophical and political positions; focusing on structural, familial or individualistic solutions. In examining the situation of various social groups, the chapters in this edited collection reflect the importance of structural influences and in many cases actively challenge individualistic discourses. However, even those with a different perspective will be able to benefit from the statistics on the nature and extent of poverty that are presented here since 'shining an honest light on reality in the poorest parts of our society is a contribution social scientists can continue to make' (Glennerster et al, 2004).

The PSE-UK 2012 survey

The PSE-UK 2012 survey extends our knowledge of national poverty and social exclusion by providing the most comprehensive study ever undertaken in the UK.[1] Capturing the nature and extent of poverty across a population is expensive and time-consuming task. This explains why governments and researchers have often relied on survey measures of indirect poverty, most prominently low income. The PSE-UK 2012 instead adopts a definition of poverty based on the consensual approach, that is, a minimum standard of living based on majoritarian public opinion. This was first developed by Mack and Lansley in *Poor Britain* (1985) and built on Peter Townsend's (1979) earlier work on relative deprivation, which proposed that poverty should be defined as having a living standard that placed individuals and families outside of ordinary activities and practices.

There were two survey stages.[2] The first was an attitudes survey which involved asking people about the items and activities they considered to be necessities (as well as those that are desirable but should not be classed as necessities). Choices over the items and activities to include in the initial list took into account: the need to provide some degree of continuity with previous studies in order to compare changes in attitudes; a desire to update the list to reflect recent social and technological shifts (for example, the question on having access to a CD player was dropped); and the decision to cover a wider range of living standards. In addition to a literature review and drawing on the views of international experts from the advisory board, 14 focus groups were used to check public perceptions of necessities (Fahmy et al, 2015). Separate questions were included for adults and children. The final set of questions had 32 items and 14 activities for adults and 22 items and 8 activities for children. The Necessities of Life survey was carried out in May and June 2012 with a sample of 1,447 adults aged 16 or over in Britain and 1,015 in Northern Ireland. 'Shuffle cards' were used to randomise the question order. Each card has one item or one activity listed and the cards are shuffled by the interviewer before being given to the respondent to ensure that the order is different. For adults, respondents were asked:

> On these cards are a number of different items which relate to our standard of living. I would like you to indicate the living standards you feel all adults should have in Britain today by placing the cards in the appropriate box. BOX A is for items which you think are necessary – which all adults should be able to afford and which they should not have to do without. BOX B is for items which may be desirable but are not necessary.

Respondents were then asked to do the same exercise thinking about necessities for children and using the child-specific items and activities. In the Northern Ireland survey half of respondents used shuffle cards and half a personal digital assistant (PDA) system so that the techniques could be compared.

In line with the consensual method approach, items and activities that over half of the population viewed as necessities were classified as such; 25 of those included on the list for adults were viewed as necessities by over 50% of the population and 24 of those listed for children. As with previous surveys, there was general consensus among the population as a whole over what should count as necessities. However, the public have become less generous in their assessment of a minimum standard of living, especially with respect to social engagement. For example, in the four surveys conducted since 1983, being able to afford to give presents to family and friends once a year (such as on birthdays or at Christmas) was considered a necessity by the majority of people, but in 2012 this item failed to reach the required 50% threshold. This hardening of attitudes perhaps reflects the tougher economic climate in which individuals were making their decisions about consumption and social participation (see Mack et al, 2013 for further analysis of the necessities survey).

The second, main PSE survey asked individual respondents about whether they had access to the list of consensually defined necessities. If they did not have any of the items or activities they were asked whether this was due to preference or inability to afford it, with only those who lacked necessities because of affordability classed as deprived. The wording of the questionnaire was trialled using 20 cognitive interviews conducted in June and July 2011 in order to reduce measurement error (see Fahmy et al, 2011). The final annotated questionnaire is available through the project website (PSE, 2013). The main PSE-UK 2012 survey was carried out between March and December 2012 and re-interviewed respondents to the 2010/11 Family Resources Survey (FRS) who said they could be contacted again, with every adult living at each address interviewed. The sample size achieved was 5,193 households (4,205 in Britain and 988 in Northern Ireland) in which 12,097 people were living (9,786 in Britain and 2,311 in Northern Ireland). This was much larger than the previous PSE-GB 1999 survey, which consisted of a total of 1,534 respondents. The detail of the sampling frame is outlined in Gordon (2011). The method of calculating a poverty line combining a deprivation element (lacking necessities) with a low income is described in detail by David Gordon in chapter one. It is this 'PSE poverty' measure which is used as the basis for most of the analysis in the following chapters.

Social groups

This edited volume answers the question of who falls below a publicly agreed minimum standard of living: *who* is poor in the UK?[3] Social characteristics are important because we know that they make a difference to how vulnerable individuals and families are to poverty. Characteristics such as gender, ethnicity and disability are associated with differential access to resources that impact on living standards, as do life course transitions such as family formation. While critical events, such as changes to employment, health or relationship status, can trigger entry into poverty (Smith and Middleton, 2007). Poverty analysis increasingly recognises the importance of capturing both the structural and biographical risk factors for poverty (for example Vandecasteele, 2011). Further, measures to reduce poverty and social exclusion tend to be targeted at sections of the population and understanding both the extent and nature of living standards among high-profile groups is an essential first step if policy interventions are to be successful.

Decisions over who to focus on in this collection reflect a combination of rationales: a straightforward academic desire to expand knowledge about the circumstances of particular groups, including examining the situation of subgroups of the population that are possible now through improvements in the quality of data collected, and an interest in providing analyses that can be used as evidence in political debates on the nature of poverty and social exclusion among specific population groups. This book therefore includes information about the extent of poverty and social exclusion among: young adults; older people; men and women; ethnic groups; children; parents; disabled people; those living in different regions of the UK; and in urban and rural locations. It captures the current situation of social groups over whom there has been longstanding concern about levels of poverty and social exclusion, such as pensioners, children, disabled people and women. As such, it is valuable for noting changes and continuities in the situation of these populations over time. The chapters also explore the circumstances of those who have risen to prominence in popular discussions quite recently, such as young adults and parents. The impact of recession and austerity has been highlighted as perhaps being especially damaging for young people, while parents have been given a renewed focus in government discourse as an important factor in children's experience of poverty. In addition, this volume includes social groups for whom meaningful analysis of levels of consensual poverty and social exclusion is possible for the first time because of a larger survey. Authors have provided detailed analysis of different ethnic minority and national groups, those living in urban and rural locations, and regional variation within the UK.

Chapters two and three respectively deal with the fortunes of younger and older people in UK society. In the previous PSE survey, conducted in 1999, a focus on younger people was prompted by concern over the existence of group of 'disaffected' young adults who were at risk of being socially excluded from education and the labour market (Fahmy, 2006). By the time of the PSE-UK 2012 survey, commentaries about the precarious nature of life as a young person in the UK had increased significantly. 'Millennials' are increasingly depicted as being unable to achieve the living standards of previous generations and as losing out in terms of housing, career and financial stability as a result of vulnerability to austerity. For example, unemployment rates reached 22.5% among 16–24-year-olds in late 2011; the highest level since comparable records began in 1992 (ONS, 2016). Eldin Fahmy's chapter highlights that young people have indeed witnessed a huge increase in social and material deprivation and argues that, as a consequence, social policy needs to address youth disadvantage more seriously.

Pensioner poverty has been high on the political agenda for the last twenty years. Statistics from the turn of the century showed that older people were a particularly poor group; the results of the 1999 PSE survey indicated that 40% of pensioners were poor using 'blunt' income measures (Patsios, 2006). In the context of an ageing population which could exacerbate this trend – and perhaps more cynically the view that pensioners are more likely to vote – successive governments have intervened on the issue. The £11 billion annual increase on benefits for pensioners by the Labour governments between 1997 and 2010 did have a significant impact in reducing the numbers of older people living in poverty (Joyce and Sibieta, 2013). The focus on older adults continued under the Coalition government which, in 2010, introduced the 'triple lock' for UK state pensions by guaranteeing that they would rise at whichever was highest: earnings, inflation or 2.5%. Again, this has had an noticeable effect, with the Institute for Fiscal Studies concluding that these measures, combined with cuts to other parts of the welfare budget, have resulted in current pensioners being better off than previous generations *and* having higher incomes than the working-age population (Johnson, 2015).[4] Demi Patsios' chapter in this volume (chapter three) shows that large numbers of those in pensioner households do indeed have adequate access to material resources, but also that a significant portion of the 'oldest old' still suffer from impoverishment and 'deep' social exclusion.

Chapters four, five and eight focus on gender, ethnic groups and disabled people respectively. The gendered nature of poverty has long been recognised in feminist literature, with women facing lower living standards and more responsibility for managing household finances in straitened circumstances. The PSE-GB 1999 survey results on poverty confirmed this finding, with the precarious circumstances of lone mothers and older single women highlighted as special cause for concern (Levitas et al, 2006; Pantazis and Ruspini, 2006). Esther Dermott and Christina Pantazis's chapter on men and women's experiences of poverty and social exclusion (chapter four) highlights that today women in general are not significantly worse off than men.

However, this broad finding disguises significant variations based on age and life stage, which means that subgroups of women, and also some men, face significant disadvantage and social isolation. A key message is that intersectional analysis, which looks at the cross-cutting dynamics of impoverishment and social disadvantage, is necessary in order to better understand the living standards of specific social groups.

Poverty research based on income measures has shown that ethnic minorities in the UK have higher poverty rates than the ethnic majority (Platt, 2007; JRF, 2017). The previous PSE survey, which captured poverty and social exclusion as multidimensional rather than based solely on income measures, also noted higher levels of poverty among the non-white population, albeit based on a small sample of ethnic minorities (Gordon et al, 2000). Research for the Joseph Rowntree Foundation, which looked at the impact of the relationship between ethnicity and poverty in the context of the recent period of recession and austerity, concluded that ethnic minorities felt greater effects (Fisher and Nandi, 2015). However the experiences of different ethnic minority groups also varied widely; Chinese, Indian, and Black African groups saw the largest falls in income, with persistent poverty most prevalent among Pakistani and Bangladeshi groups (Fisher and Nandi, 2015). In the PSE-UK 2012 survey, a larger initial sample size and a further 'ethnic booster' sample meant that much more detailed and rigorous analysis was possible. Chapter five, on ethnicity, by Saffron Karlsen and Christina Pantazis, is therefore able to describe levels of disadvantage for particular ethnic groups that have previously gone largely unreported, such as the circumstances of white minority Poles, and Black Africans.

The living standards of disabled people have been relatively ignored in studies of poverty in the past, perhaps partly as a consequence of difficulties over meaningful definitions of disability that are appropriate for use in large-scale surveys (see chapter eight). However, debate over the implications of the austerity measures introduced between 2010 and 2013 drew attention to the inadequate living standards of many disabled people, most prominently over the scrapping of Disability Living Allowance and its replacement with the Personal Independence Payment (Cross, 2013). Further, research has suggested that local authority cuts have made it harder for disabled workers to remain in employment (Harwood, 2014) thereby potentially impacting on their levels of poverty and social exclusion. Pauline Heslop and Eric Emerson's chapter (chapter eight) outlines disabled people's levels of poverty and social exclusion compared to those who are non-disabled, arguing that disabled people appear to be 'among the poorest of the poor', are excluded from a range of aspects of contemporary life and continue to face negative discriminatory attitudes.

Chapters six and seven deal with the linked circumstances of children and parents. Childhood poverty continues to be viewed as a significant social problem that should not exist in a just society. Even among those who are reluctant to attribute poverty to social circumstances rather than poor individual choices, children tend to be positioned as the 'innocent victims' who should not bear the brunt of their parents' mistakes; hence 'Eradicating child poverty is an absolute priority for this government' (Duncan Smith, 2015). A range of policy interventions introduced at the end of the 1990s resulted in declining poverty rates for children. However, the effects of the economic recession and austerity measures since then have ensured that the pledge made under Tony Blair's Labour government that child poverty would be eradicated by 2020 will fail (Social Mobility and Child Poverty Commission, 2014). Chapter six, by Gill Main and Jonathan Bradshaw, confirms that progress in reducing child poverty rates has stalled and, significantly, that most poor children live in households in which at least one adult is in paid work.

Analysis of children's poverty also shows that children would be significantly poorer if their parents did not engage in 'parental sacrifice', cutting back on their own needs to prioritise the needs of their children. This runs counter to claims made by some politicians that it is the profligacy of parents which results in poverty for their children. The role of parents has taken an especially high profile in recent government claims about how poverty should be addressed as what parents do is increasingly viewed as the most important element in determining outcomes for children (Dermott, 2012; Jensen and Tyler, 2012), with parents living in poverty chastised as being bad parents (Dermott and Pomati, 2016). Esther Dermott and Marco Pomati's chapter on parents and parenting (chapter seven) undermines these views. It shows that parents as a whole have higher rates of poverty than the general population, and that lone mothers have exceptionally high levels of poverty. However, there is no indication of an association between living in poverty and a failure to engage in parent–child activities that are often used as markers of good parenting.

The final two substantive chapters consider the spatial location of poverty by comparing levels of poverty between rural and urban locations (chapter ten) and across regions within the UK (chapter nine). This is the first time that PSE analysis has been able to explore inequality in this way. This is partly due to the expanded sample size, which allows for more fine-grained analysis. In addition, the inclusion of a Northern Ireland sample moves this iteration of the PSE to a fully UK study, allowing analysis of the regions and countries within the UK. Further, an additional Scottish booster sample permits statements about Scotland to be more robust and is important for capturing a larger number of rural communities across the UK as a whole. Political discussion of regional economies has increased, with the promotion of the 'Northern Powerhouse' and 'Midlands Engine'. Mike Tomlinson's analysis of income and deprivation across regions within the UK (chapter nine) shows that Wales, the North of England, Northern Ireland and London have noticeably higher rates of poverty than the South of England and Scotland. Assessments of the spatial distribution of poverty have documented inequalities within countries and cities, and suggested that the unequal distribution of incomes and wealth within the UK has increased over recent decades (Dorling et al, 2007). Nick Bailey and Maria Gannon's chapter (chapter ten), which contrasts the fortunes of rural and urban populations, finds that urban areas are slightly worse off but that social exclusion effects both, albeit in different ways. They argue that this means variations in policies between urban and rural populations are justified.

Next steps

In addition to providing an overview of the nature and extent of poverty and social exclusion in contemporary UK society, the research findings of the PSE-UK 2012 help in extending the conceptual and methodological thinking of poverty researchers. The findings take us beyond measures based solely on income, beyond the household as the only meaningful unit of analysis, beyond a focus on standard and undifferentiated population groups and beyond a static view of poverty and inequality.

The PSE-UK 2012 analysis confirms the limitations of focusing solely on income as an indicator of poverty. As is evident in the chapters on young people, older people, men and women, and urban/rural comparisons, it is essential to also capture deprivation and social exclusion to give a more complete picture of living standards. Income is of some use in capturing levels of material deprivation but it is insufficient on its own. The standard example to highlight this in the UK is that while older people have substantially lower incomes than younger age groups they also tend to have lower household costs, especially on housing. A focus on income alone therefore leads to misleading conclusions about the nature and extent of intergenerational inequality. An additional limitation to having a measure of poverty solely based on income is the way it frames the policy response to the problem of poverty. If poverty equals a lack of income then the obvious solution is to supplement the income of those with least. This ignores other forms of benefits that can be offered by the state that could significantly influence living standards (such as good quality child or elder care, or transport) in favour of an individualised approach.

The PSE poverty measure combines income with a deprivation measure to provide an assessment of how many people are living in poverty. It also classifies those in borderline categories: those who may be rising out of poverty due to having an adequate income even while they are currently deprived of necessities, and those who are vulnerable to poverty because their incomes are below what is required even though they currently do not lack necessary items and activities. Given political debates about the measurement of poverty it is pertinent to note that this is not about shifting assessments to indicators that may be either the causes or consequences of poverty, but is about accounting for the reality of material circumstances in a robust way that reflects everyday understandings.

Perhaps the most significant new development within the PSE-UK 2012 survey was the decision to interview all individual adult members of surveyed households rather than relying on a single household representative. The assumption in conventional poverty analysis has been that family members share equally in the distribution of resources that are available to the household and therefore that taking the household as the unit of analysis is adequate to capture the living standards of everyone within it. Feminist researchers have long critiqued the view that women's best interests necessarily equate to those of the larger family unit (for example, Nussbaum, 2000) and research projects exploring intra-household inequalities have begun to emerge (see Bennett, 2013 for an overview). However, up to now there have been no large-scale quantitative analyses of within-household living standards and social exclusion in the UK. This is particularly important when assessing the role of gender (chapter four) but also the differential experience of adults and children within the same household (chapter seven). Other publications drawing on the PSE-UK 2012 research have reflected how informal transfers *between* households impact on living standards; Daly and Kelly's (2015) qualitative account of the significance of sharing resources across households for poor families in Northern Ireland and Dermott's (2016) analysis of non-resident fathers, which highlighted the potential role of intra-household obligations for living standards. The PSE-UK 2012 research therefore indicates the limits of household-level analysis and shows how different approaches can be taken forward.

The analysis of the PSE-UK 2012 survey presented in the following chapters highlights variations within sub-populations and the interrelationships between socio-demographic characteristics. At a political level it is tempting to make statements that claim disadvantaged status for sub-populations according to a single social characteristic and to direct policy initiatives on this basis. However, more detailed analysis *within* social groups – possible because of the larger sample size across the PSE survey as a whole and targeted booster samples – problematises some of these generalisations and gives us a more nuanced and useful picture of poor groups in the UK today. So, for example, no previous surveys in this country on consensual poverty, including previous versions of the PSE, have been able to disaggregate the situation of different ethnic minority groups (see chapter five) or detail the differences between older groups – the 'young old' and 'old old' – that is documented in chapter three. In policy terms this should lead to the development of more useful measures. Looking at relationships *between* social characteristics also reveals findings that would otherwise remain hidden, for example, taking age and life stage into account in relation to gendered poverty (see chapter four). This edited collection encourages us to move beyond thinking about individual social characteristics to look within standard population groups and to the interrelationships between social groups, in order to better capture the dynamics of poverty.

A comparison between the PSE-UK 2012 and previous iterations of the survey shows that the face of poverty is not static, even over a single decade. Some of those who were most disadvantaged in the past, such as lone mothers, continue to lose out as policies have not significantly improved their circumstances. Others, though, have seen a change in fortunes, either with improving living standards or emerging as poor (see Pantazis et al, 2006 for details of findings from the PSE-GB 1999 survey). While a popular depiction of poverty may be of a consistent 'underclass' who are adrift from mainstream society in terms of their ability to consume and engage with majority culture, our analysis presents a different picture. Poverty is dynamic for two reasons. Individuals and households may become more or less well off through life transitions and changes in personal circumstances, but also social policies and broader social and economic transformations result in changes to the population groups who become at risk or are relatively protected.

The PSE-UK 2012 results therefore allow us to make some comments about government policy. Reflections on policy implications for different population groups and for reducing poverty and social exclusion are taken up more fully in the concluding chapter. However, in line with the theme of how the empirical results of the PSE study can help academics and policy makers move beyond previous thinking, the analysis presented in the following chapters indicates that policy decisions should not be viewed as 'once and for all', but need to be defined, redefined and refined within changing economic and social circumstances. Social policy initiatives can fail to lead to significant transformations in people's material circumstances – the situation of lone parents for example remains parlous (chapter seven) – as they depend on a complex set of economic circumstances, social norms and the moral rationality of individual decision making. On a more encouraging note, there is also evidence that policy initiatives really can make a difference in a positive way. If we are to adopt a note of optimism in the face of our findings about the ongoing existence of severe and widespread poverty that currently exists in the UK, perhaps it is that a high public and political profile (Glennester et al, 2014) combined with robust scientific findings may establish the need to make progress on this issue.

Notes

[1] The study was funded by a large grant from the Economic and Social Research Council (ESRC) that ran between 2010 and 2014. ESRC Grant RES-060-25-0052.

[2] The surveys were conducted by the National Centre for Social Research (NatCen) in Britain and the Northern Ireland Statistics and Research Agency (NISRA). Details of the survey instruments are detailed in the technical appendix.

[3] See Bramley and Bailey (2017) for a thematic analysis of the PSE-UK 2012 survey.

[4] The Conservative manifesto in the 2017 general election suggested reducing this to a 'double lock' after 2020.

References

Bennett, F. (2013) 'Researching within-household distribution: overview, developments, debates and methodological challenges', *Journal of Marriage and Family* 75:3: 593–610.

Bramley, G. and Bailey, N. (eds) (2017) *Poverty and social exclusion in the UK: vol. 2 – The dimensions of disadvantage*, Bristol: Policy Press.

Cross, M. (2013) 'Demonised, impoverished and now forced into isolation: the fate of disabled people under austerity', *Disability and Society*, 28:5, 719–23.

Daly, M. and Kelly, G. (2015) *Families and poverty: Everyday life on a low income*, Bristol: Policy Press.

Derbyshire, J. (ed.) (2013) *Poverty in the UK: Can it be eradicated?* London: Prospect Ltd.

Dermott, E. (2012) 'Poverty versus parenting: an emergent dichotomy', *Studies in the Maternal* 14:2, 1–13.

Dermott, E. (2016) 'Non-resident fathers in the UK: living standards and social support', *Journal of Poverty and Social Justice* 24:2, 113–25.

Dermott, E. and Pomati, M. (2016) 'The parenting and economising practices of lone parents: policy and evidence', *Critical Social Policy*, 36:1, 62–81.

Dorling, D., Rigby, J., Wheeler, B., Ballas, D., Thomas, B., Fahmy, E. et al (2007) *Poverty, wealth and place in Britain, 1968 to 2005*, Bristol: Policy Press.

Duncan Smith, I. (2015) 'Government to strengthen child poverty measure', Press release, 1 July, www.gov.uk/government/news/government-to-strengthen-child-poverty-measure

Fahmy, E. (2006) 'Youth, poverty and social exclusion', in C. Pantazis, D. Gordon and R. Levitas (eds) *Poverty and social exclusion in Britain: The Millennium Survey*, Bristol: Policy Press.

Fahmy, E., Pemberton, S. and Sutton, E. (2011) 'Cognitive testing of the UK Poverty and Social Exclusion Survey', PSE Working Paper Methods Series 17, www.poverty.ac.uk

Fahmy, E., Sutton, E.J. and Pemberton, S.A. (2015) 'Determining the "necessities of life" in the 2012 PSE-UK survey', in L. Camfield and K. Roelen (eds) *Mixed methods in poverty research: Advancing the art*, London: Palgrave.

Fisher, P. and Nandi, A. (2015) *Poverty across ethnic groups through recession and austerity*. York: Joseph Rowntree Foundation; Colchester: University of Essex.

Glennerster, G., Hills, J., Piachaud, D. and Webb, J. (2004) *One hundred years of poverty and policy*, York: Joseph Rowntree Foundation.

Gordon, D. (2011) 'Main PSE UK sampling frame', Working Paper Methods Series 21, www.poverty.ac.uk/

Gordon, D., Adelman, A., Ashworth, K., Bradshaw, J., Levitas, R., Middleton, S. et al (2000) *Poverty and social exclusion in Britain*, York: Joseph Rowntree Foundation.

Harwood, R. (2014) '"The dying of the light": the impact of the spending cuts, and cuts to employment law protections, on disability adjustments in British local authorities', *Disability & Society* 29:10, 1511–23.

Jensen, T. and Tyler, I. (2012) 'Austerity parenting: new economies of parent-citizenship', *Studies in the Maternal* 4:2, 1–2.

Johnson, P. (2015) 'High levels of income for current retirees shouldn't blind us to future challenges', Press release 20 October, www.ifs.org.uk/publications/8026

Joyce, R. and Sibieta, L. (2013) 'An assessment of Labour's record on income inequality and poverty', *Oxford Review of Economic Policy* 29:1, 178–202.

JRF (2017) 'Poverty rate by ethnicity', Data, 22 March, www.jrf.org.uk/data/poverty-rate-ethnicity

Levitas, R., Head, E. and Finch, N. (2006) 'Lone mothers, poverty and social exclusion', in C. Pantazis, D. Gordon and R. Levitas (eds) *Poverty and social exclusion in Britain: The Millennium Survey*, Bristol: Policy Press.

Mack, J. and Lansley, S. (1985) *Poor Britain*, London: Allen and Unwin.

Mack, J., Lansley, S., Nandy, S. and Pantazis, C. (2013) 'Attitudes to necessities in the PSE2012 survey: are minimum standards becoming less generous?', PSE Working Paper Analysis Series 4, www.poverty.ac.uk

Nussbaum, M. (2003) *Women and human development: A capabilities approach*, Cambridge: Cambridge University Press.

ONS (2016) *Statistical bulletin: UK labour market: February 2016*, London: Office for National Statistics, www.ons.gov.uk/employmentand labourmarket/peopleinwork/employmentandemployeetypes/bulletins/uklabourmarket/february2016#young-people-in-the-labour-market

Pantazis, C. and Ruspini, E. (2006) 'Gender, poverty and social exclusion', in C. Pantazis, D. Gordon and R. Levitas (eds) *Poverty and social exclusion in Britain: The Millennium Survey*, Bristol: Policy Press.

Pantazis, C., Gordon, D. and Levitas, R. (eds) (2006) *Poverty and social exclusion in Britain: The Millennium Survey*, Bristol: Policy Press.

Patsios, D. (2006) 'Pensioners, poverty and social exclusion', in C. Pantazis, D. Gordon and R. Levitas (eds) *Poverty and social exclusion in Britain: The Millennium Survey*, Bristol: Policy Press.

Platt, L. (2007) *Poverty and ethnicity in the UK*, Bristol: Policy Press.

PSE (2013) *PSE UK 2012: Living standards questionnaire with top-level results*, www.poverty.ac.uk/pse-research/questionnaires

Rowntree, S. (1901) *Poverty: A study of town life*, London: Macmillan and Co.

Smith, N. and Middleton, S. (2007) *A review of poverty dynamics research in the UK*, York: Joseph Rowntree Foundation.

Social Mobility and Child Poverty Commission (2014) *State of the nation 2014: Social mobility and child poverty in Great Britain*, London: Social Mobility and Child Poverty Commission.

Townsend, P. (1979) *Poverty in the United Kingdom*, London: Allen Lane and Penguin Books.

Vandecasteele, L. (2011) 'Life course risks or cumulative disadvantage? The structuring effect of social stratification determinants and life course events on poverty transitions in Europe', *European Sociological Review* 27:2, 246–63.

ONE

Measuring poverty in the UK

David Gordon

'While our population during the last century increased three and a half times, the wealth of the community increased over six times. But one factor in our national life remained with us all through the century, and is with us still, and that is that at the bottom of the social scale there is a mass of poverty and misery equal in magnitude to that which obtained 100 years ago. I submit that the true test of progress is not the accumulation of wealth in the hands of a few, but the elevation of a people as a whole.' (Keir Hardie, Labour Party leader, House of Commons, 23 April 1901)

'The word poor is one the government actually disputes.' (Mr Hickey, DHSS Assistant Secretary for Policy on Family Benefits and Low Income, Evidence to House of Commons Social Security Select Committee, 15 September 1989)

'Where is the fairness, we ask, for the shift-worker, leaving home in the dark hours of the early morning, who looks up at the closed blinds of their next door neighbour sleeping off a life on benefits? When we say we're all in this together, we speak for that worker. We speak for all those who want to work hard and get on.' (George Osborne, Chancellor, 8 October 2012)

'That means fighting against the burning injustice that if you're born poor you will die on average nine years earlier than others. If you're black, you're treated more harshly by the criminal justice system than if you're white. If you're a white working class boy, you're less likely than anybody else in Britain to go to university. If you're at a state school, you're less likely to reach the top professions than if you're educated privately. If you're a woman, you will earn less than a man. If you suffer from mental health problems, there's not enough help to hand. If you're young, you'll find it harder than ever before to own your own home.... The Government I lead will be driven, not by the interests of the privileged few, but by yours.' (Theresa May's first speech as Prime Minister, 13 July 2016)

Introduction: the political context

Poverty in the UK is a strange phenomenon, as the quotes above demonstrate. It is something that all politicians agree upon yet it is also highly politically contested. All politicians from all parties agree that poverty in general, and child poverty in particular, are 'bad' things which should be reduced/eradicated. There is political unanimity about this in the UK – no politician, as far as I am aware, has ever said that the UK should have or needs more poverty. The aspects of poverty that are the subject of often passionate contestation are the causes of and solutions to poverty and, in particular, who is to blame for poverty.

The 21st century has witnessed rapid and dramatic changes in UK government policy towards poverty. In 1999, Tony Blair committed the Labour government to the eradication of child poverty within a generation[1] (that is, by 2020) and this goal was actively pursued, to a greater or lesser extent, for the first ten years of the century, culminating in the passage through Parliament of the Child Poverty Act 2010.[2] The Child Poverty Act received cross-party support and wrote the goal of eradicating child poverty into legislation – along with specific and time-limited targets, four measures of child poverty[3] and independent monitoring by a Child Poverty Commission.[4]

The fact that most Conservative MPs voted for the Child Poverty Act shows how much their rhetoric concerning poverty changed during their 13 years in opposition. During the 1970s, 1980s and the early 1990s, successive Conservative governments denied that poverty existed in the UK. For example, in the 1970s, a widely publicised argument by Keith Joseph (who was Secretary of State for Education in Margaret Thatcher's first government) claimed that 'A family is poor if it does not have enough to eat.... By any absolute standard there is very little poverty in Britain today' [Joseph and Sumption, 1979, pp 27–8]). Similarly, in 1989, John Moore (then Secretary of State for Social Security) proclaimed 'The end of the line for poverty' and argued that absolute poverty had been eradicated, relative poverty did not exist and claims that there were many poor people in the UK were 'bizarre' and 'absurd'. Furthermore, people who criticised the government's policies were:

'not concerned with the actual living standards of real people but with pursuing the political goal of equality.... We reject their claims about poverty in the UK, and we do so knowing that their motive is not compassion for the less well-off, it is an attempt to discredit our real economic achievement in protecting and improving the living standards of our people. Their purpose in calling "poverty" what is in reality simply inequality, is so they can call western material capitalism a failure.' (Moore, 1989)

During the 1980s and most of the 1990s, with the exception of Boddy et al (1995), no report published by the government included the word 'poverty'. The Conservative government's policy appeared to be that poverty eradication could be achieved by removing the word 'poverty' from the dictionaries – they contested the very existence of the word 'poverty' (see quote from Mr Hickey above). Unsurprisingly, this policy failed and was in part responsible for Conservatives getting a reputation as the 'nasty party'.[5]

Modernisers in the Tory party, particularly Ian Duncan Smith, saw the past rhetoric about poverty as a problem for the electability of a Conservative government. One response was to discreetly send Baron Chilver (who had been the Vice Chancellor of Cranfield University) to various university departments with a poverty research reputation to see if they would be willing to help the party solve the Tories 'poverty problem'. In the end, this job fell to the Centre for Social Justice (CSJ), a think tank founded by Ian Duncan Smith in 2004. In 2007, the CSJ produced a report entitled *Breakthrough Britain*,[6] which purported to have identified the five primary 'causes of poverty/barriers families face' as: (1) family breakdown; (2) economic dependency and worklessness; (3) educational failure; (4) drug and alcohol addiction; and (5) serious personal debt. A follow-up project, *Breakthrough Britain II*, produced individual reports on these five topics in 2013 and 2014. No other researchers in the UK or elsewhere have ever identified these five factors as the main causes of poverty nor does there appear to be any scientific basis for the CSJ's claims that these *are* the primary causes of poverty.

None of the reports included credible scientific evidence that would support the CSJ's claims about these being the main causes of poverty. For example, the 'addiction' reports include no evidence that addiction is a major cause of poverty. Addiction is, of course, a bad thing and a problem that needs to be tackled but problem drinking and gambling may be just as likely to affect the 'rich' as the 'poor'.

'Problem drinking' has repeatedly been found to have a clear social gradient in analyses of the UK GHS/GLS/CHS[7] data, that is, the richer the household, the more alcohol they consume on average.[8] The *Breakthrough Britain* reports outline social policies which emphasise tackling 'welfare dependency and addiction' (linked together) and thereby falsely located drug addiction as a 'problem' of the disreputable poor (MacGregor, 2013).

The *Breakthrough Britain* report was based on the results from a consultation process: 'Over the past 18 months, there have been more than 3,000 hours of public hearings and over 2,000 organisations have made submissions to the working groups' – and were used to produce policy recommendations for the Conservative Party (Duncan Smith, 2007). Although this may sound impressive, it appears to be pseudo-research rather than real research, that is, there is no evidence of a rigorous sampling frame or of any analytical methodology. The reports have been largely ignored by the academic community but have been very influential on the approaches to anti-poverty policy taken by the recent Coalition and Conservative governments – with ministers frequently stating that the pathways to poverty are family breakdown, educational failure, worklessness and dependency, addiction and serious personal debt. Their aim has been 'to move the poverty debate away from a simple fixation with a single "poverty line"'.[9]

In particular, there have been repeated and, so far, unsuccessful, attempts since 2010 to sideline or abolish the four official Child Poverty Act measures, which all include low-income elements. After the May 2010 general election, the new Coalition government lost no time in trying to change the child poverty measures its MPs had voted for a few months previously. It also named the independent policy monitor (established by the Child Poverty Act) the Social Mobility and Child Poverty Commission (instead of the Child Poverty Commission).

In June 2010, the Coalition government launched an Independent Review on Poverty and Life Chances: Consulting on a New Approach (Field, 2010), with the Labour MP Frank Field as chair. The first aim of this review was to 'examine the case for reforms to poverty measures, in particular for the inclusion of non-financial elements'. In 2012, the Coalition government then issued a consultation on *Measuring child poverty* (DWP, 2012).

Both these consultation documents were of extremely low quality. They were 'conceptually completely inept and confused' and failed 'to recognise the fundamental distinction between measures of poverty and the characteristics of poor children and the associations and the consequences of poverty' (Bradshaw, 2013, p 2). The Review on

Poverty and Life Chances seemed to represent an attempt to revive the discredited cultural deficit theories of the 1960s. For example, the report included statements that were pejorative, anecdotal and unsupported by any evidence:

> I no longer believe that the poverty endured by all too many children can simply be measured by their parents' lack of income. Something more fundamental than the scarcity of money is adversely dominating the lives of these children. Since 1969 I have witnessed a growing indifference from some parents to meeting the most basic needs of children, and particularly younger children, those who are least able to fend for themselves. I have also observed how the home life of a minority but, worryingly, a growing minority of children, fails to express an unconditional commitment to the successful nurturing of children.... Even if the money were available to lift all children out of income poverty in the short term, it is far from clear that this move would in itself close the achievement gap. (Field, 2010, p 16)

Cultural deficit theory is a prejudiced 1960s idea that underachievement among poor/working-class students was a result of deficiencies with the students, their families and communities (Gordon, 2012). The cultural deficit models argued that, since working-class/poor parents failed to embrace the educational values of the dominant middle/upper classes and continued to transmit to their children values which inhibited educational achievement/mobility, then the parents/working-class culture are to blame if low educational attainment continues into succeeding generations. This idea is derived from a misrepresentation of Oscar Lewis's (1964, 1968) work in Mexico, Puerto Rico and New York on the adaptation of the migrant 'rural' poor with 'traditional' ways to their 'marginal' status. In fact, Lewis argued that poverty was primarily a result of structural causes not cultural or behavioural causes. Thus, the Independent Review on Poverty and Life Chances recommended measures largely ignoring the structural reasons for the persistence of poverty and educational underachievement, for example inadequate school funding in poor areas, social class segregation in the education system, low-quality teaching, exclusions, schools' failure to prevent bullying, teacher prejudice/bias/lack of respect and so on (Gordon, 2012). Similarly, the *Measuring child poverty* consultation report (DWP, 2012) failed to acknowledge most of the research on measuring child poverty and even quoted a crude online poll from MoneySuperMarket.com – completed by self-selecting respondents who were highly unlikely to be representative of the UK population – as evidence for the need to change the way poverty is measured (Bradshaw, 2013).

The Coalition government's aim of developing poverty measures which did not include financial indicators received virtually no support. The Prime Minister's Office asked Demos if they could develop a multidimensional poverty measure which did not include low income or expenditure but Demos researchers argued that such a measure would lack credibility (Matt Barnes, pers. comm., 2013). In 2014, Alan Milburn (Chair of the Social Mobility and Child Poverty Commission) concluded that: 'The government's draft child poverty strategy is a missed opportunity. The farce of ministers proving unable to agree on how to measure poverty after rubbishing existing measures is particularly lamentable.'[10]

On being elected in May 2015, one of the first announcements of the new Conservative government was their intention to amend/ repeal the Child Poverty Act to become the Life Chances Act. The four Child Poverty Act 2010 income-based targets would be abolished and replaced with two new measures of children living in workless households in England and the educational attainment of children in England at the end of Key Stage 4. This plan was announced in a government press release with the Orwellian title of 'Government to strengthen child poverty measure'.[11] These 'new' measures had been included in the previous Labour government's *Opportunity for All* annual child poverty reports, as part of a large suite of 24 indicators (DWP, 2005). However, by themselves, they are clearly a partial and inadequate measure of child poverty.

Despite having just won a general election, the new Conservative government failed to persuade the governments of Scotland, Northern Ireland and Wales to abandon the Child Poverty Act targets and child poverty measures, and also failed to persuade the UK Parliament. At the Report Stage on 25 January 2016, the government suffered a defeat on an amendment tabled by the Bishop of Durham which required the Secretary of State to continue to report annually the number of children living in poverty under each of the four existing poverty measures specified in the Child Poverty Act 2010. The amendment was agreed by 290 votes to 198 (Kennedy et al, 2016). The evidence given to the Public Bill Committee[12] was extraordinary in that it was overwhelmingly hostile to the government's proposals, for example, both the Institute of Economic Affairs (IEA) and the Child Poverty Action Group (CPAG) were united in their condemnation of the proposed new child poverty measures. So both the four Child Poverty Act 2010 measures and the two new Life Chances measures are currently published by the UK government but it is far from clear what will happen in the future to the way poverty is 'officially' measured in the UK.

Austerity: the policy context

Governments do not usually spend so much time, effort and political capital on technical issues such as poverty measurement. The reason was that the Coalition government's response to the financial crisis was to implement austerity policies with substantial cuts to the public sector and welfare benefits. The blame for the mounting public debt was put on the imagined profligacy of previous Labour governments rather than on the huge losses made by UK banks which then required a government-funded bailout.

In reality, public sector debt was relatively low (by historical standards) prior to the 2008 financial crash (see Figure 1.1). According to Blyth (2013, p 47): 'What happened was that banks promised growth, delivered losses, passed the costs onto the state and then the state got the blame for generating the crisis in the first place, which of course, must be paid for by expenditure cuts.'

The cuts to benefits and services were targeted at poor and disabled people whom government ministers and much of the media sterotyped

Figure 1.1: UK public sector debt as a % of GDP: 1993–2015[13]

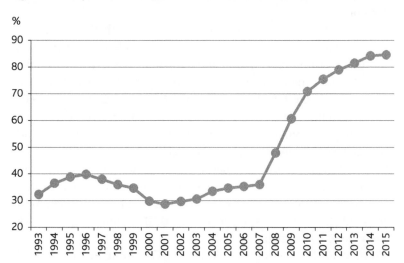

Source: ONS Public Sector Finances time series dataset (PUSF)

as 'workshy', 'scroungers', 'lazy wasters' 'burdens', and even as 'stupid' and 'parasites' (Briant et al, 2011; Baumberg et al, 2012; Taylor Gooby, 2013). Both the Chancellor, George Osborne and the Prime Minister, David Cameron, repeatedly talked about 'welfare scroungers', 'skivers' and benefit receipt as a 'life choice' (see Walker, 2014) and this is consistent with the 'broken Britain' rhetoric popularised by Ian Duncan Smith (then Minister for the Department for Work and Pensions) and the CSJ (Mooney, 2011).

Jones (2011) has documented the increased negative stereotyping of the working class in general and the poor in particular as 'Thick. Violent. Criminal. Scum of the earth' in the media and in politics. The past five years have witnessed a rise in 'poverty porn', with numerous *Jeremy Kyle*, *Benefits Street* and *Gypsies on Benefits and Proud*-style programmes on television, which particularly highlight '"the skiver", a figure of social disgust who has re-animated ideas of welfare dependency and deception' (Jensen, 2014).

Levitas (2005) argued that political debates about social exclusion and poverty in the UK could be grouped into three overlapping and competing discourses; Redistributionist Discourse (RED), Moral Underclass Discourse (MUD) and Social Integrationist Discourse (SID). The prime concern of RED is poverty and it draws upon the work of Townsend (1954, 1962, 1979), who argued that, when income and resources fall below a certain level, people are excluded from the normal activities of their society. The solution for RED is redistribution of income in the form of higher, non-means tested benefits, a minimum wage, financial recognition for unpaid work and so on.

By contrast, the prime concern of MUD is with the moral and behavioural delinquency of the excluded. The underclass is perceived as culturally distinct from the mainstream and is associated with idle, criminal young men and single mothers dependent on welfare (see also Macnicol [1987] 2009; Bagguley and Mann, 1992; Mann, 1994). Welfare dependency on the state is problematic but the economic dependency of women and children on men is not – as women and marriage have a 'civilising' impact on men.

Finally, SID is primarily concerned with inclusion through paid work and is a predominant discourse of the European Union. It focuses on unemployment and economic inactivity, and social integration is pursued through inclusion in paid work. It ignores unpaid work (largely done by women).

Thus, if RED is about no money, MUD about no morals and SID about no work, the political rhetoric and policy options adopted by the Coalition and Conservative governments have clearly focused squarely on MUD and SID, rather than RED.

The Coalition government cut government spending, with the sharpest cuts falling in the poorest areas, affecting some of the poorest groups of people (Edwards, 2012; Reed and Portes, 2014; Innes and Tetlow, 2015). For example, the Campaign for a Fair Society estimated that '2% of the population – the people with the greatest needs – will bear the burden of 25% of all the cuts'[14] (Duffy, 2014). The most deprived local authorities saw cuts of more than £220 per head compared with under £40 per head for the least deprived (Hastings et al, 2015). Real wages and incomes fell and about 1 million people[15] had to use food banks, often as a result of welfare cuts, delays in receiving benefits and increased use of benefit sanctions (Lambie-Mumford and Dowler, 2014; Perry et al, 2014). The Coalition government's policies resulted in income changes that 'were regressive' and that 'the bottom half lost (with the poorest groups losing most as a proportion of their incomes) and the top half gained' (De Agostini et al, 2014). The Institute for Fiscal Studies estimated that real incomes in 2014/15 were, on average, about 2% lower than in 2009/10 (Cribb et al, 2015).

Standing on the shoulders of giants

Given the highly politicised debates about the measurement of, causes of and solutions to poverty, high-quality social science research is of considerable importance, otherwise ineffective and inefficient policies based upon false premises may be pursued and considerable public monies will be wasted. Fortunately, there has been over 400 years of research into British poverty and UK social scientists are arguably the world leaders in this field.

Every decade or so since the late 1960s, UK social scientists have attempted to carry out an independent poverty survey to test out new ideas and incorporate current state-of-the-art methods into UK poverty research. Thus, the 1968–9 Poverty in the UK survey (Townsend, 1979), the 1983 Poor Britain and 1990 Breadline Britain surveys (Mack and Lansley, 1985; Gordon and Pantazis, 1997) and the 1999 Poverty and Social Exclusion survey (PSE-GB 1999; see Gordon et al, 2000; Pantazis et al, 2006) and its 2002 counterpart in Northern Ireland (Hillyard et al, 2003), introduced new methods, ideas and techniques about poverty measurement and helped to keep UK academic research at the forefront of poverty measurement methodology. It is important for social science to build upon the results of the 400 years of research into British poverty. The lessons from this research can be summarised as follows:

- *Poverty is not a behaviour* – since the work of Booth (1902–03), Rowntree (1901) and their Victorian and Edwardian contemporaries (for example Webb and Webb, 1909a, 1909b), repeated studies have shown that the primary cause of poverty is not the 'bad' behaviour of the poor. Poverty in the UK is primarily caused by structural factors such as low wages, a lack of jobs, the lack of state provision to adequately compensate those engaged in unpaid work – particularly caring work – and so on. Despite intensive research by often highly partisan researchers, as far as I am aware, there are no credible scientific studies which show that any significant group of people are poor as a result of indolent, feckless, skiving or criminal behaviour.

- *Poverty is not a disease* – it is not like syphilis – a curse across the generations – you cannot catch poverty from your parents nor pass it onto your friends, relatives or children. Research has shown that poor adults and children in the UK do not have a 'culture of poverty' and tend to have similar aspirations to the rest of the population (Lupton, 2003). The UK welfare state is reasonably effective and there is virtually no one who is born into poverty, grows up living in poverty and remains poor for their entire lives. There are also virtually no families where members have not been in any paid employment over two or more generations. For example, Shildrick et al (2012, p 3) found that, 'Despite dogged searching in localities with high rates of worklessness across decades we were unable to locate any families in which there were three generations in which no-one had ever worked.' Poor children are, of course, more likely than their richer peers, to become poor adults, but this is largely due to structural reasons rather than any 'cycle of poverty' or 'transmission' of poverty (Townsend, 1974; Schoon et al, 2012).

- *The underclass is a persistent myth* – the fruitless search for the underclass is the *Hunting of the Snark* of UK social science research. Over one hundred years of searching has failed to discover any significant group which could be identified as an underclass. The terms used for this group have changed over time, from the Victorian *residuum*, the 'unemployables' of the Edwardian era, the Social Problem Groups of the 1930s Depression era, the Problem

Families of the 1940s, through the culture of poverty and cycle of deprivation of the 1960s and 1970s, the underclass of the 1980s and 1990s to the Troubled Families of the present day (Blacker, 1937, 1952; Welshman, 2013). More research monies and effort have probably been wasted searching for the underclass than in any other area of UK social science research. For example, the Transmitted Deprivation Programme of the 1970s lasted over 10 years, commissioned 23 empirical studies and cost over £5 million at 2016 prices. The Pauper Pedigree Project of the Eugenics Society lasted over 20 years (1910–33), the Social Survey of Merseyside Study lasted five years and the Problem Families Project started in 1947 and eventually petered out in the 1950s (see Lidbetter, 1933; Caradog Jones, 1934; Brown and Madge, 1982; Mazumdar, 1992). Neither these studies, nor any other British study, have ever found anything but a small number of individuals whose poverty could be ascribed to fecklessness or a 'culture/genetics of poverty/dependency' (Gordon and Pantazis, 1997).

- *Redistribution is the only solution to child poverty* – the economics are very simple and are entirely concerned with redistribution: where sufficient resources are redistributed from adults to children there is no child poverty; where insufficient resources are redistributed from adults to children, child poverty is inevitable (Gordon, 2004). Children cannot and should not do paid work to generate the resources they need to escape from poverty. This is the job of adults. Numerous laws since the Factory Act 1833 have restricted and prevented child labour in the UK. Children should be spending their time playing and learning not working at paid labour (Gordon and Nandy, 2016).

The extent of poverty in the UK

The PSE-UK 2012 project conducted an in-depth investigation into the extent and nature of poverty in the UK using a broad range of measures. The project had three primary aims:

- to improve the measurement of poverty, deprivation, social exclusion and standard of living;
- to assess change in the nature and extent of poverty and social exclusion over the past ten years;
- to conduct policy-relevant analyses of outcomes and causal relationships from a comparative perspective.

The chapters in this book focus on the nature and extent of poverty in the UK among different social groups and the policies that are needed to reduce and eradicate it. The remainder of this chapter will focus on the first aim – the development of new measures of poverty, deprivation, exclusion and standards of living. Rigorous qualitative and quantitative methods were used in developing and analysing the survey questionnaire. The methods used included:

- systematic literature reviews
- focus groups
- expert review
- cognitive interviews
- survey pilots
- behaviour coding

Details of this survey development process can be found in the methods development working papers available on the PSE website.[16] As far as possible, comparability was maintained in the PSE-UK 2012 surveys with UK and EU official poverty measures.

The theoretical basis for the PSE-UK 2012 measurement of poverty was Townsend's (1979) theory of relative deprivation.

> Poverty can be defined objectively and applied consistently only in terms of the concept of relative deprivation. [...] Individuals, families and groups in the population can be said to be in poverty when they lack the resources to obtain the type of diet, participate in the activities and have the living conditions and amenities which are customary, or at least widely encouraged or approved, in the societies to which they belong. Their resources are so seriously below those commanded by the average individual or family that they are, in effect, excluded from ordinary living patterns, customs or activities. (Townsend, 1979, p 31)

Townsend defined 'poverty' as a lack of command of sufficient resources over time and 'deprivation' is an outcome of poverty. For Townsend, deprivation is also a relative phenomenon which encompasses both a lack of necessary material goods and social activities:

> Deprivation takes many different forms in every known society. People can be said to be deprived if they lack the types of diet, clothing, housing, household facilities and

fuel and environmental, educational, working and social conditions, activities and facilities which are customary, or at least widely encouraged and approved, in the societies to which they belong. (Townsend, 1987, p 126)

The theory of relative deprivation is a scientific concept in that it can be used to measure poverty in all societies during all periods of history, that is, it is a sociological concept of poverty which is universally applicable (Gordon and Pantazis, 1997; Townsend and Gordon, 2002). It is based on the idea that there are fundamental human needs that all people everywhere require, for example, the need for food, clothing, shelter and so on. In addition, in all societies people have social obligations as parents, children, siblings, friends and so on which they must fulfil. For example, there is a need to give presents on certain occasions and to attend ceremonies marking major life stages (for example birth, marriage, death, coming of age and so on). The way these necessary material and social needs are met varies across both time and place but the underlying categories of material and social needs remain fundamental. Therefore, poverty can be defined as the non-fulfilment of these universal needs due to a lack of resources – rather than for some other reason, such as discrimination. Thus, deprivation can be the result of causes other than poverty (for example, exclusion due to gender, religious, class, caste or ethnic prejudice) but multiple deprivation is often the result of poverty.

The 50 years of research which followed the development of the Poverty in the UK survey in the early 1960s has resulted in the development of a measurement framework and methodology for producing multidimensional deprivation indices which are suitable, valid, reliable and additive, and which can be combined with measures of low income/resources to produce robust multidimensional poverty measures (Gordon, 2000; Pantazis et al, 2006; Fahmy et al, 2011; Guio et al, 2012; Guio et al, 2016).

Multidimensional poverty measures which combine low income and deprivation, such as the UK's combined Low Income and Deprivation measure required by the Child Poverty Act 2010, the Consistent Poverty measure used by the Irish government or CONEVAL's[17] multidimensional poverty measure used in Mexico, produce robust estimates of poverty by combining both the cause (low resources) and effect (deprivation) of poverty into a theory-based single measure.

Some economists (Brewer and O'Dea, 2012) have argued that it would be better to measure poverty using consumption rather than a combined low-income and deprivation measure as low levels of consumption might provide a better estimate of permanent income, that is, consumption is 'considered a better proxy than income for lifetime resources and for current living standards' (Browne et al, 2013).

This is a fantasy. There has never been a consumption survey and there probably never will be. What national statistical offices measure is expenditure (as a part of the Household Income and Expenditure Surveys – HIES) but expenditure is not consumption. Nor is it feasible to use household expenditure data to produce estimates of individual or household consumption without introducing significant measurement errors. For example, even using food expenditure diaries to estimate food consumption requires literally hundreds of 'heroic' assumptions such as how much food wastage occurs for each food item (for example people rarely eat the bones of a chicken or the outer leaves of a cabbage) and how much food is consumed outside the household (Deeming, 2011). In addition, most expenditure surveys only ask households to keep a detailed expenditure diary over a two-week period and this is highly unlikely to be representative of the household's expenditure over an entire year, for example expenditures during the two weeks before Christmas are likely to differ from expenditures during the first two weeks in August. There is no internationally agreed statistical definition of consumption, no agreed method to measure consumption nor a single example of where consumption has been successfully measured. Consumption remains a theoretical concept not a practical measurement option for estimating poverty.

Deprivation measurement framework

Many deprivation indices unfortunately consist of a collection of items the authors think are 'bad', grouped into seemingly arbitrary domains and added together using unsubstantiated weights (Gordon, 1995). There is no good reason why anyone should accept that such indices are good or useful measures. A methodology is required that allows the testing and selection of an optimum set of deprivation indicators which form a consistent theory-based measure of deprivation. To ensure a robust selection of deprivation items it is important to consider four aspects:

- The *suitability* of each deprivation item. The PSE-UK 2012 checked that there was a majority (50% or more) of respondents in a random Omnibus survey who agreed that a deprivation item was a 'necessity of life that everybody should be able to afford'. Twenty-five adult and household items and 24 children's items in the PSE-UK 2012 Omnibus survey passed this test and were used for further analyses (27 items failed this suitability test and were therefore dropped). These deprivation items are considered to represent 'the living conditions and amenities which are customary, or at least widely encouraged or approved, in the societies to which they belong' (Townsend, 1979, p 31). Here, 'suitability' is understood as a measure of face validity among the UK population.

- The *validity* of individual items. We ensure that each item exhibits statistically significant relative risk ratios with independent variables known a priori to be correlated with poverty – specifically, two measures of ill health after controlling for age and gender (health in last 12 months was 'very bad' or 'bad' and long term illness was 'yes') and three subjective poverty measures (genuinely poor now 'all the time', income 'a lot below' the poverty line, standard of living rating 'well below' or 'below' average).

- The *reliability* of the deprivation scale. The reliability of the scale as a whole was assessed using Classical Test Theory (CTT).[18] These analyses were complemented by Item Response Theory (IRT) models[19] that provided additional information on the reliability of *each* individual item in the scale.

- The *additivity* of items. We test that someone with a deprivation indicator score of '2' is suffering from more severe deprivation than someone with a score of '1', that is, that the deprivation index components add up. Additivity is measured for the deprivation items that successfully passed the suitability, validity and reliability tests.

Forty-four household, adult and child deprivation items successfully passed these four tests and were thus considered to be suitable, valid, reliable and additive candidates for being aggregated into a multidimensional deprivation index (see http://www.poverty.ac.uk/ pse-research/attitudes-adult-necessities-uk-2012 and http://www. poverty.ac.uk/pse-research/attitudes-child-necessities-uk-2012 – 32 items failed one or more of the tests). Previous studies have produced flawed measures of deprivation and poverty, that is, they treated children and adults as properties of their households and assumed, if the household is 'poor/deprived', then all household members are also 'poor/deprived'. They have also produced separate deprivation/poverty measures for adults and children with limited intellectual justification for doing this.

The PSE-UK 2012 survey has allowed the construction (for the first time) of a deprivation index for all people (aged 0 to 80+) which includes age appropriate indicators which are also reliable, valid, additive and have broad popular support (50% or more of the UK population). All previous deprivation indices measured difference in living standards between households. The new PSE-UK 2012 deprivation index measures differences both *between* and *within* households. It is thus a better and more accurate measure of deprivation, which can be used to produce a more accurate measure of poverty (when combined with household income).[20] Thus the chapters in this book report results about the nature and distribution of poverty using a 'state-of-the-art' methodologically advanced measure of poverty.

Notes

[1] See: www.bristol.ac.uk/poverty/downloads/background/Tony%20 Blair%20Child%20Poverty%20Speech.doc

[2] See: www.legislation.gov.uk/ukpga/2010/9/contents

[3] Relative poverty – less than 10% of children in families below 60% of median income before housing costs; absolute poverty – less than 5% of children in families below 60% median income in 2010/11, adjusted for RPI inflation; combined low-income and material deprivation – less than 5% of children in families below 70% median income and unable to afford key goods and services; persistent poverty – less than 7% of children in relative poverty for at least three out of the last four years.

[4] See: www.gov.uk/government/organisations/social-mobility-and-child-poverty-commission

[5] "Yes, we've made progress, but let's not kid ourselves.... Our base is too narrow and so, occasionally, are our sympathies. You know what some people call us: the nasty party" (Theresa May, then Chair of the Tory Party, 8 October 2002, speech to the Conservative Party Conference).

[6] See: www.centreforsocialjustice.org.uk/policy/breakthrough-britain

[7] The General Lifestyle Survey (GLF or sometimes referred to as the GLS), formerly known as the General Household Survey (GHS), ran from 1971-2012 in Britain. In Northern Ireland, the Continuous Household Survey (CHS) has collected similar information to the GHS since 1983.

[8] Women in households where the HRP [Household Reference Person] was in a 'large employer and higher managerial' occupation were nearly twice as likely as those in households where the HRP was in an occupation in the 'routine' group to have drunk more than three units of alcohol on any one day (39% compared with 20%). They were also twice as likely to have drunk heavily (more than 6 units of alcohol) on at least one day in the previous week (16% compared with 8%). A similar but less pronounced pattern was seen for men. (ONS, 2013)

[9] See: www.centreforsocialjustice.org.uk/policy/breakthrough-britain

[10] See: www.gov.uk/government/news/commission-publishes-response-to-the-draft-child-poverty-strategy

[11] See: www.gov.uk/government/news/government-to-strengthen-child-poverty-measure

[12] See: http://services.parliament.uk/bills/2015-16/welfarereformandwork/committees/houseofcommonspublicbillcommitteeonthewelfarereformand workbill201516.html

[13] Figure from: www.ons.gov.uk/economy/governmentpublicsectorandtaxes/publicsectorfinance/timeseries/hf6x/pusf

[14] See: www.centreforwelfarereform.org/library/by-date/campaigning-for-a-fair-society.html

[15] The exact number of people using food banks in the UK is difficult to estimate as there are no national statistics collected (Lambie-Mumford et al, 2014).

[16] See: see http://www.poverty.ac.uk/pse-research/pse-uk/methods-development

[17] CONEVAL (El Consejo Nacional de Evaluación de la Política de Desarrollo Social) is the National Council for the Evaluation of Social Development Policy, which is a parastatal with authority to measure multidimensional poverty in Mexico (see http://www.coneval.org.mx/).

[18] Classical Test Theory dates back to the pioneering work of Spearman and others at the turn of the century and distinguishes between the observed score (measurement) on any test or index and the 'true' score. Since all attempts at measurement will inevitably result in the occurrence of some random errors, the observed score is comprised of two components – the true score and random error: $O = T + RE$, where: O = Observed score;

T = True score; RE = Random error. In CTT reliability is defined as the ratio of the 'true' score variance to the observed score variance.

[19] CTT can be used to measure the average reliability of a test/index, by contrast Item Response Theory (IRT) models can be used to measure the reliability of each individual component of a deprivation index. Thus, IRT models can provide important additional information about reliability but they also require more assumptions to be made about the data.

[20] The full technical details of this advanced multidimensional poverty measure will be published elsewhere. The steps required to construct this index are explained briefly in Gordon (2017a, 2017b).

References

Bagguley, P. and Mann, K. (1992) 'Idle thieving bastards: scholarly representations of the "underclass"', *Work, Employment and Society* 6, 113–26.

Baumberg, B., Bell, K. and Gaffney, D. (with Rachel Deacon, Clancy Hood and Daniel Sage) (2012) *Benefits Stigma in Britain*, Turn2us, https://wwwturn2us-2938.cdn.hybridcloudspan.com/T2UWebsite/media/Documents/Benefits-Stigma-in-Britain.pdf

Blacker, C.P. (1937) *A social problem group?* London: Oxford University Press.

Blacker, C.P. (ed.) (1952) *Problem families: Five enquiries*, London: Eugenics Society.

Blyth, M. (2013) *Austerity: The history of a dangerous idea*, Oxford: Oxford University Press.

Boddy, M., Bridge, G., Burton, P. and Gordon, D. (1995) *Socio-demographic change in the inner city*, London: Department of Environment, HMSO.

Booth, C. (1902–03) *Life and labour of the people in London*, 17 vols, London: Macmillan.

Bradshaw, J. (2013) 'Consultation on child poverty measurement', PSE Policy Response Working Paper 8, www.poverty.ac.uk/report-child-poverty-government-policy-editors-pick/pse-team-slam-government-consultation-child

Brewer, M. and O'Dea, C. (2012) 'Measuring living standards with income and consumption: evidence from the UK', IFS Working Paper 12/12, www.ifs.org.uk/wps/wp1212.pdf

Briant, E., Watson, N. and Philo, G. (2011) *Bad news for disabled people: How the newspapers are reporting disability*, Glasgow: Strathclyde Centre for Disability Research and Glasgow Media Unit in association with Inclusion London.

Brown, M. and Madge, N. (1982) *Despite the welfare state: A report on the SSRC/DHSS programme of research into transmitted deprivation*, SSRC/DHSS Studies in Deprivation and Disadvantage, London: Heinemann Educational Books.

Browne, J., Cribb, J., Hood, A., Johnson, P., Joyce, R., O'Dea, C. et al (2013) *Response of IFS researchers to 'Measuring child poverty: A consultation on better measures of child poverty'*, London: IFS.

Caradog Jones, D. (ed.) (1934) *The social survey of Merseyside, vol. III*, London: Hodder & Stoughton.

Cribb, J., Hood, A. and Joyce, R. (2015) 'Living standards: recent trends and future challenges', IFS Election Briefing Note BN165, www.ifs.org.uk/uploads/publications/bns/BN165.pdf

De Agostini, P., Hills, J. and Sutherland, H. (2014) 'Were we really all in it together? The distributional effects of the Coalition's tax-benefit policy changes', Social Policy in a Cold Climate Working Paper 10, London: LSE.

Deeming, C. (2011) 'Unfinished business: Peter Townsend's project for minimum income standards', *International Journal of Sociology and Social Policy* 31: 7/8, 505–16.

Duffy, S. (2014) *A fair society? How the cuts target disabled people*, Sheffield: Centre for Welfare Reform, www.centreforwelfarereform.org/uploads/attachment/354/a-fair-society.pdf

Duncan Smith, I. (2007) *Breakthrough Britain. Ending the costs of social breakdown: Overview, policy recommendations to the Conservative Party*, London, Centre for Social Justice.

DWP (2005) *Opportunity for all: Seventh annual report 2005*, Cm 6673, London: HM Government.

DWP (2012) *Measuring child poverty: A consultation on better measures of child poverty*, Cm 8483, London: HM Government, www.gov.uk/government/uploads/system/uploads/attachment_data/file/228829/8483.pdf

Edwards C. (2012) *The austerity war and the impoverishment of disabled people*, Norwich: University of East Anglia/Norfolk Coalition of Disabled People.

Fahmy, E., Gordon, D., Dorling, D., Rigby, J. and Wheeler, B. (2011) 'Poverty and place in Britain, 1968–99', *Environment and Planning A* 43:3, 594–617.

Field, F. (2010) *The foundation years: Preventing poor children becoming poor adults*, London: Cabinet Office, www.poverty.ac.uk/report-poverty-measurement-life-chances-children-parenting-uk-government-policy/field-review

Gordon, D. (1995) 'Census based deprivation indices: their weighting and validation', *Journal of Epidemiology and Community Health* 49:Suppl. 2, S39–S44.

Gordon, D. (2000) 'The scientific measurement of poverty: Recent theoretical advances', in J. Bradshaw and R. Sainsbury (eds) *Researching Poverty*, Aldershot: Ashgate, 37–58.

Gordon, D. (2004) 'Poverty, death and disease', in P. Hillyard, C. Pantazis, S. Tombs and D. Gordon (eds) *Beyond criminology: Taking harm seriously*, London: Pluto, 251–66.

Gordon, D. (2012) 'Consultation response, Tackling Child Poverty and Improving Life Chances: Consulting on a New Approach', PSE Policy Response Working Paper 1, www.poverty.ac.uk/pse-research/pse-uk/policy-response

Gordon, D. (2017a) *Producing an 'objective' poverty line in eight easy steps: PSE 2012 Survey – Adults and Children*, PSE UK Report, www.poverty.ac.uk/sites/default/files/attachments/Steps-to-producing-the-PSEpoverty-line_Gordon.pdf

Gordon, D. (2017b) *Note on PSE 2012 poverty and deprivation measures*, PSE UK Report, www.poverty.ac.uk/sites/default/files/attachments/Note-on-PSE2012-Poverty-and-Deprivation-measures_Gordon.pdf

Gordon, D. and Nandy, S. (2016) 'The extent, nature and distribution of child poverty in India', *Indian Journal of Human Development* 10:1, 1–21.

Gordon, D. and Pantazis, C. (1997) *Breadline Britain in the 1990s*, Aldershot: Ashgate.

Gordon, D., Adelman, A., Ashworth, K., Bradshaw, J., Levitas, R., Middleton, S. et al (2000) *Poverty and social exclusion in Britain*, York: Joseph Rowntree Foundation.

Guio, A.-C., Gordon, D. and Marlier, E. (2012) *Measuring material deprivation in the EU: Indicators for the whole population and child-specific indicators*, Luxembourg: Publications Office of the European Union.

Guio, A.-C., Gordon, D., Marlier, E., Fahmy, E., Nandy, S. and Pomati, M. (2016) 'Improving the measurement of material deprivation at EU level', *Journal of European Social Policy* 26:3, 219–333.

Hastings, A., Bailey, N., Bramley, G., Gannon, M. and Watkins, D. (2015) *The cost of the cuts: The impact on local government and poorer communities*, York: Joseph Rowntree Foundation.

Hillyard, P., Kelly, G.P., McLaughlin, E., Patsios, D. and M. Tomlinson (2003) *Bare necessities: Poverty and social exclusion in Northern Ireland*, Belfast: Democratic Dialogue.

Innes, D. and Tetlow, G. (2015) 'Central cuts, local decision-making: Changes in local government spending and revenues in England, 2009–10 to 2014–15', IFS Election Briefing Note BN166, www.ifs.org.uk/uploads/publications/bns/BN166.pdf

Jensen, T. (2014) 'Welfare commonsense, poverty porn and doxosophy', *Sociological Research Online* 19:3.

Jones, O. (2011) *Chavs: The demonization of the working class*, London, Verso.

Joseph, K. and Sumption, J. (1979) *Equality*, London: John Murray.

Kennedy, S., McGuinness, F. and Wilson, W. (2016) 'Welfare Reform and Work Bill 2015–16: Lords amendments', House of Commons Library Briefing Paper Number 07508.

Lambie-Mumford, H. and Dowler, E. (2014) 'Rising use of "food aid" in the United Kingdom', *British Food Journal* 116:9, 1418-1425.

Lambie-Mumford, H., Crossley, D., Jensen, E., Verbeke, M. and Dowler, E. (2014) *Household food security in the UK: A review of food aid*, University of Warwick, Food Ethics Council for Defra.

Levitas, R. (2005) *The inclusive society? Social exclusion and New Labour*, Palgrave Macmillan Ltd.

Lewis, O. (1964) *The children of Sanchez*, Harmondsworth: Penguin.

Lewis, O. (1968) *La vida*, London: Panther.

Lidbetter, E.J. (1933) *Heredity and the social problem group*, vol. 1, London: Edward Arnold.

Lupton, R. (2003) *Poverty street: The dynamics of neighbourhood decline and renewal*, Bristol: Policy Press.

Mack, J. and Lansley, S. (1985) *Poor Britain*, London: Allen and Unwin.

MacGregor, S. (2013) 'Barriers to the influence of evidence on policy: are politicians the problem?', *Drugs: Education, Prevention and Policy* 20:3, 225–33.

Macnicol, J. (1987) 'In pursuit of the underclass', *Journal of Social Policy* 16:3, 293–318. Re-published in Byrne, D. (ed.) (2009) *Social exclusion: Critical concepts in sociology*, London: Routledge.

Mann, K. (1994) 'Watching the defectives; The underclass debate in Britain, Australia and the USA', *Critical Social Policy* 14:41, 79–99.

Mooney, G. (2011) *Stigmatising poverty? The 'Broken Society' and reflections on anti-welfarism in the UK today*, Oxford: Oxfam.

Moore, J. (1989) 'The end of the line for poverty', text of a CPC lecture delivered by John Moore at the St Stephens Club, 11 May 1989, Conservative Political Centre, Issue 802.

Mazumdar, P.M.H. (1992) *Eugenics, human genetics and human failings*, London: Routledge.

ONS (2013) *General lifestyle survey: 2011*, London: ONS, www.ons.gov.
uk/peoplepopulationandcommunity/personalandhouseholdfinances/
incomeandwealth/compendium/generallifestylesurvey/2013-03-07

Pantazis, C., Gordon, D. and Levitas, R. (eds) (2006) *Poverty and social
exclusion in Britain*, Bristol: Policy Press.

Perry, J., Williams, M., Sefton, T. and Haddad, M. (2014) *Emergency
use only: Understanding and reducing the use of food banks in the UK*,
London: Child Poverty Action Group (CPAG), Church of England,
Oxfam GB and Trussell Trust.

Reed, H. and Portes, J. (2014) *Cumulative impact assessment: A research
report by Landman Economics and the National Institute of Economic and
Social Research for the Equality and Human Rights Commission*, Research
report 94, London: EHRC.

Rowntree, S. (1901) *Poverty, A study of town life*, London: Macmillan
and Co.

Schoon, I., Barnes, M., Brown, V., Parsons, S., Ross, A. and Vignoles,
A. (2012) *Intergenerational transmission of worklessness: Evidence from the
Millennium Cohort and the Longitudinal Study of Young People in England*,
Department of Education Research Report DFE-RR234, London:
Institute of Education and National Centre for Social Research.

Shildrick, T., MacDonald, R., Furlong, A., Roden, J. and Crow, R.
(2012) *Are 'cultures of worklessness' passed down the generations?* York:
Joseph Rowntree Foundation.

Taylor Gooby, P. (2013) 'Why do people stigmatise the poor at a time
of rapidly increasing inequality, and what can be done about it?',
Political Quarterly 84:1, 31–42.

Townsend, P. (1954) 'Measuring poverty', *The British Journal of Sociology*,
5:2, 130–37.

Townsend, P. (1962) 'The meaning of poverty', *The British Journal of
Sociology*, 13:3, 210-19.

Townsend, P. (1974) 'The cycle of deprivation: the history of a
confused thesis', in British Association of Social Workers, *The Cycle
of Deprivation: Papers Presented to a National Study Conference, Manchester
University, March 1974*, Birmingham: BASW.

Townsend, P. (1979) *Poverty in the United Kingdom*, London: Allen
Lane and Penguin Books.

Townsend, P. (1987) 'Deprivation', *Journal of Social Policy*, 16:2, 125–46.

Townsend, P. and Gordon, D. (eds) (2002) *World poverty: New policies
to defeat an old enemy*, Bristol: Policy Press.

Walker, R. (2014) *The shame of poverty*, Oxford, Oxford University
Press.

Webb, S. and Webb, B. (eds) (1909a) *The Minority Report of the Poor Law Commission, Part I: The break-up of the Poor Law*, London: Longmans, Green & Co.

Webb, S. and Webb, B. (eds) (1909b) *The Minority Report of the Poor Law Commission, Part II: The public organisation of the labour market*, London: Longmans, Green & Co.

Welshman, J. (2013) *Underclass: A history of the excluded since 1880*, London: Bloomsbury.

TWO

The impoverishment of youth: poverty, deprivation and social exclusion among young adults in the UK

Eldin Fahmy

Introduction

Drawing on data from the Economic and Social Research Council-funded 2012 UK Poverty and Social Exclusion survey (PSE-UK 2012), this chapter examines the nature, extent and social distribution of vulnerability to poverty and social exclusion among 18–29-year-olds living in private households in the UK. As discussed elsewhere in this volume, the PSE-UK 2012 is largest and most comprehensive survey on poverty ever conducted in the UK and updates earlier comparable studies conducted in 1990 and 1999. These data can therefore advance our understanding of youth disadvantage in important ways. First, it is now well established that indirect, income-based poverty measures can provide a misleading impression of command over resources and are uninformative about actual living conditions and living standards. As I will argue here, this is especially important in understanding the situation of youth and emphasises the importance of supplementing income data with direct measures of deprivation of basic necessities among young adults. Based upon analysis of the PSE-UK 2012 dataset this chapter therefore examines the extent of social and material deprivation among young adults and how the profile of vulnerability to deprivation compares with income-based estimates.

Second, the PSE methodology allows for meaningful comparisons over time and specifically with the PSE-GB 1999. By comparing data for 1999 and 2012, this chapter therefore also examines how the nature, extent and distribution of youth poverty have changed over the 1999 to 2012 period. In doing so I seek to examine how the profile of vulnerability to youth disadvantage changes across time and the extent to which any variations may be 'explained' by wider changes in the context of youth transitions – most notably as a result of the 2008 economic crises and subsequent austerity policies that have been pursued in the UK and elsewhere. This chapter reveals the shocking growth in social and material deprivation among UK youth over this period and should be a stimulus to more concerted policy action to tackle youth poverty and exclusion. The chapter therefore concludes with some observations on the social policy implications of these findings and how analyses like these can inform the more effective development of policies to tackle youth disadvantage. Before reviewing the empirical evidence, I first contextualise these findings in relation to wider evidence on the situation of youth in the UK and how this has changed as a result of recession and austerity policies.

Recession, austerity and the situation of youth

The impacts for youth of the recession and public spending cuts have been well documented within UK youth studies since the 1980s along with the return of levels of youth unemployment not seen since the Great Depression (for example Roberts, 1995; Bates and Riseborough, 1993). The long-term scarring effects of youth unemployment and persistent disadvantage are now well established (for example Macdonald, 1997; Gregg and Tominey, 2004). Given this context, this chapter seeks to illuminate the potential effects of recession and austerity for young adults (aged 18+) entering the labour market in the post-2008 period. The economic marginalisation of youth since the 1980s has also been a key factor in prolonging transitions to adult independence for many young people, for example, in relation to home leaving, intimate partnership formation and child rearing (Berrington et al, 2010). While recession and austerity may simply reinforce existing class-based inequalities in youth transitions (Edwards and Weller, 2010), the wider theoretical significance of these trends remains hotly disputed among youth studies scholars (see for example Woodman, 2010 and Roberts, 2010 for a lively debate). Nevertheless, most scholars would certainly agree that this period of 'semi-dependency' now typically extends throughout the twenties (and for some young adults, well into their thirties). For this reason, we focus here on the material situation of young adults aged 18 to 29.

However, although tackling poverty has been a key policy objective in the UK since the election of the Labour government in 1997, for the most part youth and young adulthood has featured much more prominently in policy action to address social exclusion rather than poverty. For the previous Labour administration, youth interventions in this area focused primarily upon labour market activation, increased welfare conditionality, and targeted casework interventions with 'excluded' youth (Colley and Hodkinson, 2001; Fahmy, 2008; France, 2008). Subsequent policy interventions under the Coalition and Conservative governments continue to be premised upon individualised, deficit-based explanations of youth disadvantage, and have considerably reinforced a tendency to respond in ways which neglect the structural causes of disadvantage associated, for example, with poor work, limited opportunities and inadequate incomes (Melrose, 2012). Strategies for addressing youth disadvantage therefore continue to reflect faith in supply-side, labour market activation programmes, and a belief that income and wealth redistribution are inappropriate responses to poverty.

Nevertheless, the effects of global recession have focused new attention on young people's circumstances and prospects, and the extent of youth poverty and unemployment feature prominently in the European Union (EU) Youth Strategy for 2010–18 (EC, 2012). European economies have been among those most severely affected by the economic downturn, and young Europeans have suffered disproportionately as a result of rising unemployment, job insecurity and in-work poverty. The remainder of this section documents the effects of recession and subsequent austerity policies for the situation of youth in the UK, and specifically in relation to unemployment and low pay, low income, deprivation and economic strain, and subsequent impacts for youth-specific services and wider welfare reform.

Unemployment

Although unemployment rates for young adults in the UK have fallen quite quickly since their peak in late 2011, they remain substantially higher than for older workers. Even during the early/mid-2000s, following the most prolonged period of economic growth since 1945, unemployment for young adults was almost three times higher than for older adults (MacInnes et al, 2014). Of the 1 million jobs created in the UK economy in the last April 2012–April 2014 period, just 40,000 went to the under 25s (Gregg et al, 2014). Almost 1.5 million young adults were not in education, employment or training in 2012, with around 250,000 young people unemployed for over a year. Aside from the obvious human costs (including the scarring effects of youth unemployment), ACEVO (2012) estimates the current costs of youth unemployment at 2012 levels in direct costs and lost factory output to be over £15 billion, with the long-term costs over a 10-year period exceeding £28 billion. As has been the case across much of the EU, interventions to address the problem of youth unemployment have been mostly supply-side driven, with European youth largely 'left to fend for itself with little appropriate state support' (Chung et al, 2012: 301). Despite the proliferation of activation programmes, recent evaluation suggests that, to date, policy responses to youth unemployment 'lack sufficient scale, intensity and local co-ordination' (Gregg, 2014: 1).

Low pay

While the problem of low pay remains widespread in Britain with over 5 million workers (22% of employees) on low pay in 2013, young people are especially and increasingly vulnerable to low pay. The proportion of 16–30-year-olds on low pay has risen from 30% in 1996 to 39% in 2013, and has also risen steadily since the late 1970s, doubling between 1977 and 2013 (Corlett and Whittaker, 2014). Indeed, recent analysis by Gregg et al (2014) suggests that the fall in real wages for workers aged 18–25 since 2008 has been so extreme that, in real terms, wages are back to levels not seen since the late 1980s. These analyses reflect downward pressure on youth wages in most global regions (despite a declining youth share of the population, falling youth employment rates and rising educational attainment), and the disproportionately large, adverse impact of economic crisis for young adults' labour market prospects across the world (see for example Grimshaw, 2014).

Low income

Given the above trends in youth unemployment and low pay, it is unsurprising that young adults in the UK are also increasingly vulnerable to income poverty. Between 2007 and 2008 and 2012 to 2013, real median household incomes fell by nearly twice the rate for 22–30-year-olds (13%) compared with older working-age adults aged 31–59 (Bellfield et al, 2014). Over the last ten years, the proportion of people living in low-income households has increased most for young adults and fallen most for pensioners, and longer term changes in intergenerational vulnerability to low income have been even more stark (MacInnes et al, 2014). As a result, by 2012/13 nearly one third (29%) of 19–25-year-olds were income poor in the UK (NPI, 2015). Drawing on a Minimum Income Standards methodology, Padley and

Hirsch (2014: 22) show that, since the 2008 recession, 'the risk of having a low income is greater and growing most quickly for younger households'. The proportion of younger households (aged 16–34) with an income insufficient to meet minimum needs rose by seven percentage points over the 2008–12 period (from 29% to 36%).

These trends reflect a wider shift in the profile of poverty vulnerability in the advanced economies, with income poverty increasing for young adults along with a general widening of income inequalities (for example, ILO, 2010; Bell and Blanchflower, 2011; OECD, 2013). Young people in Europe are now generally more vulnerable to income poverty than older working-age adults (see for example Iacovou and Berthoud, 2001; Iacovou and Aassve, 2007; Mendola et al, 2008).

Poverty and deprivation

While evidence is much more limited here, earlier analyses of the PSE-GB 1999 study using a comparable methodology to the present survey reveals that household incomes provide an unreliable guide to actual living conditions and living standards. In 1999, young people (aged 16–29) in Britain were around 50% more likely than adults aged 30+ to be PSE poor, and were also somewhat more likely to report incomes insufficient to avoid poverty. Nevertheless, no significant differences in overall deprivation were evident (Fahmy, 2006). Across Europe as a whole, EU-SILC (EU Survey of Income and Living Conditions) data for 2009 also suggested that young people are not always more vulnerable to social and material deprivation than older working-age adults, though considerable between-country variability exists (Fahmy, 2014).

However, these data largely reflected the situation before the full effects of recession and austerity were manifest and may thus underestimate the impacts of falling incomes for young adults. Similarly, while the PSE-GB 1999 revealed that many young British adults at that time experienced largely the same symptoms of wider exclusion from labour markets, and from community and civic participation, we might expect that the impact of a substantial, sustained reduction in youth wages and incomes post-2008 will result in significantly greater vulnerability to deprivation for UK youth in future. Analysis of European Quality of Life Surveys (EQLS) data for 2007 and 2011 thus suggests that young Europeans are now more likely to face moderate deprivation than older people (but are less likely to face more severe deprivation), and by 2011 nearly half of all young people in the EU lived in households experiencing some form of deprivation (European

Youth Forum, 2014). Moreover, it seems that youth deprivation has increased since 2007 in nearly all EU countries (Eurofound, 2014).

Economic strain

Although evidence on material deprivation is mixed, young Europeans consistently report higher levels of subjective poverty, and greater difficulty in making ends meet, than older working-age adults (see for example Fahmy, 2014). This may reflect age-related differences in respondents' subjective responses to their circumstances (that is, that young people are less accepting of inadequate income). Alternatively, it may be that existing deprivation measures poorly reflect the experience of deprivation during youth and especially its dynamic nature. At any rate, recent evidence suggests significant improvement in UK youth's evaluation of their financial circumstances (ONS, 2016).

Youth work and youth services

Despite the vital role that youth services and professional youth work can play in mitigating the above impacts of recession – and in supporting successful transitions to adulthood for vulnerable youth – public spending in this area amounted to just £350 million in England in 2014, or £77 per young person aged 13–19 (House of Commons, 2011: 32). Recent spending settlements for local authorities have resulted in drastic cuts to youth services, including the complete withdrawal of provision in some areas (Hillier, 2011), leading Davies (2013) to refer to the funding of youth work as at best 'radically reshaped and, at worst, wholly erased'. The House of Commons Education Committee similarly emphasise the 'grossly disproportionate' impact of public spending cuts for local youth work and youth services, which throw into stark relief the 'Government's lack of urgency in articulating a youth policy or strategic vision' (House of Commons, 2011: 3).

Welfare reform

The wider effects of welfare reform have also weighed heavily on the shoulders of young adults in the UK since the election of the Coalition government in 2010. Melrose (2012: 1) thus refers to the disciplinary effects of increased welfare conditionality and sanctioning in driving young people 'to accept low-paid, insecure work and unemployment and thereby entrench their poverty and disadvantage'.

46

The disproportionate impact of sanctions on vulnerable groups has increasingly been recognised (for example Oakley, 2014), and young people are [now] more severely affected by the rapid growth in benefit sanctions than other age groups (Watts et al, 2014: 6).

In summary, in the UK as elsewhere in Europe recession and subsequent austerity policies have seriously undermined both young people's current economic security, and their future prospects and routes to adult independence. Indeed, there is mounting anecdotal evidence that young people may be postponing key life transitions, such as leaving the parental home and starting families, as a result of the financial impacts of recession (for example, unemployment, low pay) and longer term pressures (for example, financing education, declining housing affordability). Of course, these risks are not equally borne and youth poverty vulnerability continues to reflect enduring socio-demographic inequalities of class, ethnicity and gender, as well as life course factors associated with the timing of home leaving and childbirth decisions (for example Vogel, 2002; Aassve et al, 2006; Iacovou and Aassve, 2007; Buchmann and Kriesi, 2011).

Nevertheless, it would be astounding if the effects of economic crisis were not reflected in the increased impoverishment of young adults in the UK. In the remainder of this chapter I go on to assess these effects using different measures of poverty contained within the PSE-UK 2012. In doing so, the chapter seeks to address some critical questions in understanding the contemporary picture of youth poverty vulnerability including: (1) What constitutes minimally acceptable living standards for youth in the UK today, and how many young people experience poverty according to these standards? (2) How does the situation compare with that of older working-age adults, and how have rates of youth poverty changed over time? (3) How does youth poverty vulnerability vary using different measures? The chapter concludes by considering the implications of these findings for policies to tackle youth disadvantage in the UK and internationally.

Youth poverty, deprivation and social exclusion in 2012

What are minimally acceptable living standards for youth in the UK today?

Drawing on Townsend's (for example 1979, 1987) relative deprivation theory, the consensual approach to poverty measurement adopted here understands poverty as an enforced inability to enjoy lifestyles and activities widely approved in contemporary society arising as a result of insufficient resources (principally income). Since its first application in the 1983 *Poor Britain* study (Mack and Lansley, 1985), surveys on public perceptions of the 'necessities of life' in the UK have consistently recorded widespread agreement across social groups (by gender, age, occupation, income level and geography) (Pantazis et al, 2006). Table 2.1 shows older and younger respondents' evaluations of necessities items included in the 2012 Office of National Statistics (ONS) Lifestyles and Opinions Survey Necessities module (undertaken as part of the PSE-UK 2012). The last column of Table 2.1 displays the relative risk ratios associated with these items, that is, the probability of one group classifying an item as a necessity compared with the other group (for example, in this case comparing young adults aged 16–24 with older adults aged 65+).

In most cases, few significant differences are evident and we can therefore conclude that, by and large, there is widespread agreement between younger and older people on the items and activities that *all* people need to avoid poverty in the UK today. Nevertheless, some differences remain. While mindful of the risk that ad hoc explanations may reinforce popular stereotypes, it is perhaps unsurprising that younger respondents appear to value appropriate clothes for job interviews, participating in sport and exercise, and celebrating special occasions more highly than older respondents – and that household facilities and items (phone, TV, decent decoration, all-weather shoes, insurance) appear to be more highly valued by older respondents. Moreover, while we might reasonably infer that a broad consensus exists on the 'core' necessities of life in the UK today, age-appropriate measures of youth disadvantage may nonetheless provide a truer (that is more valid) picture of young adults' experience of poverty and deprivation – though at the cost of undermining strict comparability of measures.

How many young adults are poor according to contemporary standards, and how does this compare with older working-age adults?

Informed by results from the 2012 ONS Necessities module (and equivalent data in Northern Ireland), the PSE-UK 2012 Mainstage Survey then estimated the extent of deprivation of necessities, and the relationship between deprivation and command of resources (income) in private households. Table 2.2 shows the prevalence of overall deprivation of social and material necessities for working-age adults under 30 and aged 30+ in 2012. On the whole, these data suggest that young adults are more likely to experience deprivation of

Table 2.1: Perceptions of the necessities of life in 2012: comparing young and old (%)

	All	18–29	65+	RR
Appropriate clothes to wear for job interviews	69	82	52	1.6*
Taking part in sport/exercise activities or classes	56	61	45	1.3*
Celebrations on special occasions such as Christmas	80	90	77	1.2*
Two meals a day	91	95	90	1.1
Visiting friends or family in hospital or other institutions	90	93	86	1.1
All recommended dental work/treatment	82	85	79	1.1
Attending weddings, funerals and other such occasions	79	86	76	1.1
Regular savings (of at least £20 a month) for rainy days	52	55	54	1.1
Replace or repair broken electrical goods	86	89	85	1.1
Washing machine	82	85	81	1.1
Regular payments into an occupational or private pension	51	50	51	1.0
Heating to keep home adequately warm	96	94	97	1.0
Meat, fish or vegetarian equivalent every other day	76	73	75	1.0
Curtains or window blinds	71	73	76	1.0
Damp-free home	94	96	97	1.0
A hobby or leisure activity	70	70	76	1.0
Fresh fruit and vegetables every day	83	80	83	0.9
A warm waterproof coat	79	72	89	0.9
Telephone at home (landline or mobile)	77	70	89	0.8*
Money to keep your home in a decent state of decoration	69	61	79	0.8*
To be able to pay an unexpected expense of £500	55	49	68	0.8*
A table, with chairs, at which all the family can eat	64	53	77	0.7*
Two pairs of all-weather shoes	54	46	71	0.7*
Household contents insurance	70	55	86	0.7*
Television	51	36	70	0.5*

Note: [] = p>0.01 (Pearson Chi Sq., two-tail). RR – relative risk ratio.

socially perceived necessities than older working-age people (indicated by mostly positive and significant relative risk ratios in Table 2.2).

However, since respondents may plausibly lack items because they do not want them rather than as a result of constrained resources, the PSE-UK 2012 also establishes whether respondents lack items because they cannot afford them or by choice. Although questions of affordability also raise concerns about adaptive preferences in shaping 'choices' (Hallerod, 2006), the overall profile of response in Table 2.2 is in any case consistent with overall deprivation. Young adults are consistently more likely to report lacking socially perceived necessities because they cannot afford them than the older working-age population.

Table 2.2: Deprivation of social and material necessities in the UK among working-age adults by age group, 2012

	% lacks			% cannot afford		
	18–29	30–64	RR	18–29	30–64	RR
Curtains or window blinds	3	2	1.6	2	1	2.2
A table, with chairs, at which all the family can eat	14	11	1.3	8	4	1.7
Household contents insurance	33	19	1.8	20	12	1.7
Damp-free home	28	19	1.5	20	12	1.6
Money to replace/repair broken electrical goods	57	32	1.8	43	27	1.6
Attending weddings, funerals, etc.	17	10	1.6	4	3	1.6
Appropriate clothes for job interviews	16	18	[0.9]	12	8	1.5
Sport/exercise activities or classes	45	55	0.8	16	11	1.4
Two pairs of all-weather shoes	19	11	1.7	12	8	1.4
All recommended dental work/treatment	35	25	1.4	25	18	1.4
Regular occupational or private pension payments	79	55	1.4	38	29	1.3
Fresh fruit and vegetables every day	18	12	1.5	9	7	[1.3]
A warm, waterproof coat	12	7	1.8	6	4	[1.2]
Money to keep home in decent decoration	38	25	1.5	26	22	1.2
Regular savings (£20 a month) for rainy days	46	40	1.1	38	33	1.1
A hobby or leisure activity	26	29	0.9	10	9	[1.1]
Two meals a day	3	5	0.7	2	2	[1.0]
Meat, fish or veggie equivalent every other day	8	8	[1.1]	4	5	[0.9]
Heating to keep home adequately warm	12	9	1.3	7	8	[0.9]
Visiting friends or family in hospital, etc.	34	37	[0.9]	3	3	[0.9]
Celebrations on special occasions (eg Christmas)	7	7	[0.9]	3	4	[0.7]

Note: [] = p>0.01 (Pearson Chi Sq., two-tail).

How have rates of youth poverty changed over time?

While young adults in the UK today are generally more vulnerable to deprivation of socially perceived necessities in 2012, what is most striking is the growth in youth deprivation since the PSE-GB 1999. The PSE-GB 1999 adopts an identical approach to the operational measurement of consensual poverty as the PSE-UK 2012, including sharing many of the same indicators of deprivation. It is therefore possible to compare the prevalence of deprivation among young adults on a consistent basis (at least for the GB sample), as shown in Table 2.3. For all 16 indicators for which comparable data is available, the prevalence of deprivation of socially perceived necessities has either remained constant or increased (sometimes substantially) over the 1999 to 2012 period. Despite the limitations of the PSE-GB 1999 sample,

Table 2.3: Deprivation of socially perceived necessities among young adults aged 18–29 in Britain, 1999 and 2012

	% cannot afford		Diff
	1999	2012	(b-a)
Enough money to replace or repair broken electrical goods	16.9	43.1	26.2
Damp-free home	7.4	20.0	12.6
Regular savings (of at least £20 a month) for rainy days*	25.8	37.7	11.9
Enough money to keep home in decent state of decoration	15.1	26.3	11.2
Household contents insurance*	9.9	19.8	9.9
Appropriate clothes to wear for job interviews	5.3	11.8	6.5
Heating to keep home adequately warm*	3.1	7.5	4.4
Two pairs of all-weather shoes	7.7	11.6	3.8
Meat, fish or vegetarian equivalent every other day	1.1	4.4	[3.4]
Fresh fruit and vegetables every day	5.9	8.6	2.6
A hobby or leisure activity	7.7	10.1	2.4
Two meals a day	0.1	2.4	[2.3]
A warm, waterproof coat	4.7	5.6	[0.9]
Visiting friends or family in hospital or other institutions	2.2	2.9	0.8
Celebrations on special occasions such as Christmas	1.9	2.6	[0.8]
Attending weddings, funerals and other such occasions	4.3	4.3	[0.0]
PSE deprivation (lacks 3+ socially perceived necessities [SPN])	26.7	50.7	1.9
PSE poor (low income and lacks 3+ SPN items)	32.7	30.2	[0.9]
PSE subjective poverty	18.2	28.6	1.6

Note: [] = p>0.01 (Pearson Chi Sq., two-tail). * = minor differences in question wording in 1999 and 2012.

most of these changes are significant at the 0.01 confidence level, indicating that we can be confident that these estimates reflect wider trends in the GB youth population over this period.[1] The growth in financial vulnerability is especially striking with a substantial increase in the proportion of young adults reporting being unable to afford home contents insurance (up 10 percentage points), to replace/repair broken electrical goods (up 26 percentage points), to maintain the home in decent decoration (up 11 percentage points) and to make regular savings (up 12 percentage points).

How does youth poverty vulnerability vary using different measures?

It is now generally accepted that the empirical overlaps between indirect, income-based measures and other operational measures are not substantial (for example Hagenaars and de Vos, 1988; Whelan et al, 2001; Bradshaw and Finch, 2003). Better understanding is therefore needed of the relationship between social and material deprivation and command over resources. As I will argue below, indirect, income-based poverty estimates on their own provide an especially unreliable estimate of young adults' command over resources and need to be supplemented with direct measures of social and material deprivation and subjective data (felt needs) on perceptions of economic strain, as well as by triangulating findings with other established measurement approaches and policy relevant indicators. Using the PSE methodology, Table 2.4 first compares the extent of overall PSE poverty for young adults and for older working-age adults. Individuals are classified as PSE poor if as a result of insufficient resources (low PSE-equivalised household income) they are unable to achieve minimally acceptable living standards (lack 3+ socially perceived necessities). Nearly one third (30%) of young adults in the UK are PSE poor (that is both income and deprivation poor), compared with 22% of older working-age adults. Based upon this optimal deprivation threshold (3+ items), more than half (51%) of young adults in the UK were unable to achieve minimally adequate living standards in 2012, compared with a little over one third (36%) of older working-age adults (though, importantly, not all were living in income-poor households).

Determining the income needed to meet consensually defined minimum needs using budget standards methods is an alternative and highly regarded approach to operationalising a relative deprivation approach to poverty. Based upon Minimum Income Standards (MIS) for 2012 (Davis et al, 2012), Table 2.4 compares the proportion of younger and older working-age adults classified as MIS poor, showing that a substantial majority (57%) of young adults were MIS

Table 2.4: Comparing income, deprivation and subjective measures of poverty in the UK by age group, 2012 (%)

	18–29	30–64	RR	Diff (a-b)
PSE poverty (low income *and* lacks 3+ SPN items)	30.2	22.0	1.4	8.2
PSE deprivation (lacks 3+ SPN items)	50.7	35.8	1.4	14.9
PSE subjective poverty	28.6	23.5	1.2	5.1
UK MIS poverty	57.1	47.2	1.2	9.9
EU2020 targets				
Poverty	31.9	24.5	1.3	7.4
Severe material deprivation (4+ items)	9.6	5.9	1.6	3.7
Material deprivation (3+ items)	26.2	17.1	1.5	9.1
At-risk-of-poverty (less than median household income)	19.5	17.0	[1.1]	[2.5]

Note: [] = p>0.01 (Pearson Chi Sq., two-tail).

poor in 2012 (compared with 47% of older working-age adults). In summary (and as indicated by the relative risk ratios in Table 2.4), whether we focus on deprivation, minimum income, combined PSE measures, or respondents' own subjective evaluations, young adults are approximately 20–40% more likely to experience poverty in the PSE-UK 2012 and these differences are likely to be generalisable to the UK household population.

The EU 2020 strategy (EC, 2010), also commits EU Member States to achieving progress in reducing monetary poverty and (severe) material deprivation. While these indicators imply different thresholds and/or indicators to the PSE measurement approach, they provide useful, policy relevant comparisons. However, for the most part, initiatives to combat poverty and social exclusion in the UK and Europe have been informed by *income*-based estimates, which, as Table 2.4 shows, provide an especially misleading picture of young adults' actual living standards (as well as young adults' own perceptions of economic strain). While young adults are at slightly greater risk of living in low-income households, this effect is not significant at the 0.01 level. In summary, young adults are more likely than older working-age adults to experience *every* indicator of poverty reported in Table 2.4 with the exception of low household income. These data suggest that an exclusive focus on income measures at the expense of direct observation of young adults' living standards and conditions is likely to seriously underestimate the real extent of youth disadvantage. I expand on this issue in the Discussion later in this chapter.

How many young people are experiencing wider forms of social exclusion?

Youth social exclusion has received considerable policy attention in recent years, most notably within the work of New Labour's Social Exclusion Unit (see France, 2008 for a critique). Although an explicit focus on social exclusion has been less visible in subsequent policy development since 2010, a wider concern with related concepts, such as quality of life, well-being and life satisfaction continues to inform UK research, analysis and policy development. The PSE-UK 2012 adopts the Bristol Social Exclusion Matrix (B-SEM) (Levitas et al, 2007) as an operational framework based upon an understanding of social exclusion as describing both a lack of access to economic resources and entitlements, and an inability to participate in social relationships and activities, resulting in diminished well-being. Table 2.5 presents estimates of the prevalence of multidimensional

Table 2.5: Multidimensional exclusion in the UK by age group in 2012, selected indicators (%)

		18–29	30–64		
		Col. %	Col. %	Diff.	RR
RESOURCES	In arrears on any bills in last year	36	21	15	1.7
	Had to borrow money from friends, family or other source	41	23	18	1.8
	Cannot afford unanticipated, necessary expense of £500	48	34	14	1.4
	Not a home owner	48	30	17	1.6
	Has (well) below average living standards	13	15	[–2]	[0.9]
	Lacks adequate access to 3+ local services	21	21	[0]	[1.0]
PARTICIPATION	Speaks to less than 3 relatives monthly	19	26	–8	0.7
	Speaks to less than 3 friends monthly	25	32	–7	0.8
	Not satisfied with personal relationships	23	18	5	1.3
	Low social support (scores <15)	16	16	[–1]	[1.0]
	No working age adults in household in paid work	21	18	3	1.2
	Unemployed more than 12 months in last 5 years	14	8	6	1.7
	Not satisfied with current job (in employment only)	17	14	3	1.2
	Does not participate in 9+ common social activities	47	57	[–10]	[0.8]
	Not member of any listed organisations	46	43	[3]	[1.1]
	Took no action about local or national issue (inc voting)	49	29	19	1.7
WELL-BEING	Poor mental health (GHQ >24)	46	41	6	1.1
	Low life satisfaction (ONS <6)	21	21	[1]	[1.0]
	Multiple problems with accommodation	29	20	9	1.5
	Dissatisfied with accommodation	17	9	8	1.9
	Neighbourhood dissatisfaction	19	13	6	1.4
	Experiencing 3+ neighbourhood problems	27	24	3	1.1
	Experienced harassment or discrimination for any reason	28	15	13	1.8

Note: [] = p>0.01 (Pearson Chi Sq., two-tail).

disadvantage for a selection of indicators of across the B-SEM domains separately for young adults and for older working-age adults.

The nature and manifestations of social exclusion clearly differ across the life course as people's social needs, responsibilities, roles and expectations change. Making reliable comparisons on a consistent basis across the life course therefore provides us with only a partial picture of the nature and extent of youth social exclusion. Nevertheless, in comparison with older working-age adults, exclusion from participation, well-being and especially resources, continues to be a serious problem for too many young adults in the UK in 2012.

Although, interestingly, there are no significant age differences here in subjective evaluations of living standards (or in access to local services), young adults are more likely to report financial difficulties, and tend to lack the physical assets associated with home ownership.

With regard to participation in society, and in line with earlier findings in the PSE-GB 1999 (Fahmy, 2006), while young adults typically report more extensive friendship and familial contact, they do not necessarily benefit from stronger social support, and are around 30% more likely to report dissatisfaction with personal relationships in comparison with older working-age adults. Young adults are also significantly more vulnerable than older working-age adults to employment exclusion, including unemployment, living in workless households and reporting job dissatisfaction, and less likely to engage in political action on local and national issues. Diminished well-being and quality of life is one inevitable consequence of exclusion from resources, and these data suggest that young adults in the UK are substantially more vulnerable to harassment and discrimination, and poor housing conditions and neighbourhood dissatisfaction. Overall, young adults are certainly at heightened risk of multidimensional exclusion across the range of B-SEM indicators reviewed here. Indeed, with the exception of social contact there are *no* indicators where young adults are at significantly lower risk than older working-age adults.

Tackling youth disadvantage: directions for policy

These findings add in several ways to the growing body of evidence reviewed above documenting the contemporary challenges facing young adults in the UK and elsewhere in making successful transitions to economic independence. First, these results shed further light on non-monetary indicators of youth disadvantage, including socially perceived necessities, economic strain and social exclusion. In comparison with widely quoted, semi-official low-income estimates, young adults are substantially more likely to experience deprivation of necessities, economic strain (including subjective poverty) and wider exclusion from economic resources, norms of participation and living conditions. Second, by adopting a methodologically consistent approach to poverty measurement which reflects public perceptions of minimally adequate living standards, the chapter documents an alarming growth in youth deprivation of necessities over the 1999–2012 period. In comparison with the PSE-GB 1999, the PSE-UK 2012 reveals that the proportion of young adults in the UK experiencing unacceptable hardship in living standards (3+ deprivations) has virtually doubled over this period, almost certainly as a result of the precipitous decline in median wages and incomes for young adults in the UK post-2008 (see for example Bellfield et al, 2014; MacInnes et al, 2014; Padley and Hirsch, 2014).

These findings almost certainly reflect the impacts of the 2008 economic crisis and the effects of subsequent austerity policies on young adults' access to economic and social rights, including in relation to jobs, decent pay and housing, and income protection. These are clearly complex processes and a reliable estimate of the 'net effects' of recession and public spending would also need to take account of the indirect impacts of recession in shaping young people's coping and adaptation strategies (for example, living with parents, delayed parenting and so on). Nevertheless, the growth of youth deprivation since 2008 appears to be a consistent trend across Europe (Eurofound, 2014), and these findings should therefore have important implications in refocusing research and policy attention on the problems of youth poverty and exclusion. Existing commentary on government action in this area has long noted the striking absence of a focus on economic inequalities and the structural roots of youth disadvantage in preference for individualised explanations and solutions (Colley and Hodkinson, 2001; Fahmy, 2008; France, 2008; Melrose, 2012). While sustained economic growth in the pre-2008 period may have disguised deeper changes in social vulnerability to poverty, the demonstrable growth in youth deprivation of minimally adequate living standards over the 1999–2012 period means that sustained policy action to tackle the structural roots of youth disadvantage is more urgent than ever.

In the UK context, the policy response since 2010 could not have been more different. Scandalous cuts to youth services, together with the increasingly widespread use of conditionality, sanctioning and private sector contracting as part of a (re)emerging regime of 'disciplinary welfare' for young adults, means that persistent and entrenched youth disadvantage is likely to remain unaddressed. While the UK continues to lack a comprehensive and coherent youth strategy addressing problems of poverty and social exclusion (or indeed *any* wider prioritisation of youth issues), the need to develop new, more effective responses to the problem of youth disadvantage is nevertheless also a pressing global challenge. Delivering decent jobs, educational opportunities and adequate living conditions for youth in the context of widening within-country economic inequalities is a critical global challenge. Growing income and wealth inequalities in the UK and internationally also have important implications for the distribution of assets, opportunities and risk across the life course, which are likely to exert a long-term downward pressure on young adults' living standards in addition to any scarring effects of the 2008 recession and subsequent austerity policies. As part of the Europe 2020 agenda, the EU is committed to achieving a 25% reduction in the share of the EU population at risk of poverty and social exclusion by 2020. On the basis of the evidence reviewed here, young adults in the UK are likely to miss out on this commitment.

Note

[1] Standard errors for the PSE-UK 2012 sample can be calculated taking into account the study's complex design using *SPSS Complex Samples*. Due to data limitations, this information is unavailable for the PSE-GB 1999. Given the study's stratified random cluster sampling methodology this is likely resulting in biased standard errors and to (partially) compensate for this, a higher significance threshold ($p<0.01$) is used here.

References

Aassve, A., Iacovou, M. and Mencarini, L. (2006) 'Youth poverty and transition to adulthood in Europe', *Demographic Research* 15, 21–50.

ACEVO (2012) *Youth unemployment: The crisis we cannot afford*, London: ACEVO Commission on Youth Unemployment.

Bates, I. and Riseborough, G. (eds) (1993) *Youth and inequality*, Buckingham: Open University Press.

Bell, D. and Blanchflower, D. (2011) 'Young people and the Great Recession', IZA Discussion Paper 5674, Bonn: Institute for the Study of Labour.

Bellfield, J., Cribb, C., Hood, A. and Joyce, R. (2014) *Living standards, poverty and inequality in the UK: 2014*, London: IFS.

Berrington, A., Stone, J. and Falkingham, J. (2010) 'The changing living arrangements of young adults in the UK', *Population Trends* 138:1, 27–37.

Bradshaw, J. and Finch, N. (2003) 'Overlaps in dimensions of poverty', *Journal of Social Policy* 32:4, 513–25.

Buchmann, M. and Kriesi, I. (2011) 'Transition to adulthood in Europe', *Annual Review of Sociology* 37, 481–503.

Chung, H., Bekker, S. and Houwing, H. (2012) 'Young people and the post-recession labour market in the context of Europe 2020', *Transfer: European Review of Labour and Research* 18, 301–17.

Colley, K. and Hodkinson, P. (2001) 'Problems with bridging the gap: The reversal of structure and agency in addressing social exclusion', *Critical Social Policy* 21:3, 335–59.

Corlett, A. and Whittaker, M. (2014) *Low pay Britain*, London: Resolution Foundation.

Davies, B. (2013) 'Youth work in a changing policy landscape', *Youth and Policy* 110, 6–32.

Davis, A., Hirsch, D., Smith, N., Beckhelling, J. and Padley, M. (2012) *A minimum income standard for the UK in 2012: Keeping up in hard times*, York: Joseph Rowntree Foundation.

EC (European Commission) (2010) *Europe 2020: A European strategy for smart, sustainable and inclusive growth*, Brussels: EC.

EC (European Commission) (2012) *EU youth strategy, 2010–18: Implementation of the renewed framework for European cooperation in the youth field*, Brussels: EC.

Edwards, R. and Weller, S. (2010) 'Trajectories from youth to adulthood: choice and structure for young people before and during recession', *Twenty-First Century Society* 5:2, 125–36.

Eurofound (2014) *Social situation of young people in Europe*, Luxembourg: Publications Office of the European Union.

European Youth Forum (2014) *Youth in the Crisis: What went wrong?*, www.youthforum.org/assets/2014/11/YFJ-Publication-What-went-wrong.pdf

Fahmy, E. (2006) 'Youth, poverty and social exclusion', in C. Pantazis, D. Gordon and R. Levitas (eds) *Poverty and social exclusion in Britain: The Millennium Survey*, Bristol: Policy Press.

Fahmy, E. (2008) 'Tackling youth exclusion in the UK: challenges for current policy and practice', *Social Work and Society* 6:2, 280–87.

Fahmy, E. (2014) 'The complex nature of youth poverty and deprivation in Europe', in L. Antonucci, M. Hamilton and S. Roberts (eds) *Young people and social policy in Europe*, London: Palgrave Macmillan.

France, A. (2008) 'From being to becoming: the importance of tackling youth poverty in transitions to adulthood', *Social Policy & Society* 7:4, 495–505.

Gregg, P. (2014) 'Youth employment – still waiting for the upturn', Bath Institute Policy Briefing, University of Bath.

Gregg, P., Machin, S. and Fernández-Salgado, M. (2014) 'The squeeze on real wages – and what it might take to end it', *National Institute Economic Review* 228:1, R3–16.

Grimshaw, D. (2014) *At work but earning less: Trends in decent pay and minimum wages for young people*, Geneva: ILO.

Hagenaars, A. and de Vos, K. (1988) 'The definition and measurement of poverty', *Journal of Human Resources* 23:2, 211–21.

Hallerod, B. (2006) 'Sour grapes: relative deprivation, adaptive preferences and the measurement of poverty', *Journal of Social Policy* 35:3, 371–90.

Hillier, A. (2011) 'True scale of council youth service cuts revealed', *Children and Young People Now*, 7 February.

House of Commons (2011) *Services for young people*, Third Report of the House of Commons Education Committee Session 2010–12, London: The Stationery Office.

Iacovou, M. and Aassve, A. (2007) *Youth poverty in Europe*, York: Joseph Rowntree Foundation.

Iacovou, M. and Berthoud, R. (2001) *Young people's lives: A map of Europe*, Colchester: Institute for Social and Economic Research, University of Essex.

ILO (International Labour Organization) (2010) *Global employment trends for youth*, Geneva: ILO.

Levitas, R., Pantazis, C., Fahmy, E., Gordon, D., Lloyd, E. and Patsios, D. (2007) *The multi-dimensional analysis of social exclusion*, Bristol: University of Bristol.

MacDonald, R. (ed.) (1997) *Youth, the 'underclass' and social exclusion*, London: Routledge.

MacInnes, T., Aldridge, H., Bushe, S., Tinson, A. and Born, T. (2014) *Monitoring poverty and social exclusion, 2014*, York: Joseph Rowntree Foundation.

Mack, J. and Lansley, S. (1985) *Poor Britain*, London: George Allen Unwin.

Melrose, M. (2012) 'Young people, welfare reform and social insecurity', *Youth and Policy* 108, 1–19.

Mendola, D., Busetta, A. and Aassve, A. (2008) 'Poverty permanence among European youth', Institute for Social and Economic Research (ISER) Working Paper 2008-04, Colchester: ISER.

NPI (New Policy Institute) (2015) 'Why has poverty risen so much for young adults?', 26 February, http://npi.org.uk/publications/children-and-young-adults/why-has-poverty-risen-so-much-young-adults/

Oakley, M. (2014) *Independent review of the operation of Jobseeker's Allowance sanctions validated by the Jobseekers Act 2013*, London: DWP.

OECD (Organisation for Economic Co-operation and Development) (2013) *Crisis squeezes income and puts pressure on inequality and poverty*, Paris: OECD.

ONS (Office for National Statistics) (2016) 'Young people's well-being and personal finance: UK, 2013 to 2014', *Statistical Bulletin*, 11 May.

Padley, M. and Hirsch, D. (2014) *Households below a minimum income standard: 2008/9 to 2011/12*, York: Joseph Rowntree Foundation.

Pantazis, C., Gordon, D. and Townsend, P. (2006) 'The necessities of life', in C. Pantazis, D. Gordon and R. Levitas (eds) *Poverty and social exclusion in Britain: The Millennium Survey*, Bristol: Policy Press.

Roberts, K. (1995) *Youth and employment in modern Britain*, Milton Keynes: Open University Press.

Roberts, S. (2010) 'Misrepresenting "choice biographies"? A reply to Woodman', *Journal of Youth Studies* 13:1, 137–49.

Townsend, P. (1979) *Poverty in the UK*, London: Penguin Books.

Townsend, P. (1987) 'Deprivation', *Journal of Social Policy* 16:2, 125–46.

Vogel, J. (2002) 'European welfare regimes and the transition to adulthood: a comparative and longitudinal perspective', *Social Indicators Research* 59:3, 275–99.

Watts, B., Fitzpatrick, S., Bramley, G. and Watkins, D. (2014) *Welfare sanctions and conditionality in the UK*. York: Joseph Rowntree Foundation.

Whelan, C., Layte, R., Maître, B. and Nolan, B. (2001) 'Income, deprivation and economic strain: an analysis of the European Community Household Panel', *European Sociological Review* 17:4, 357–72.

Woodman, D. (2010) 'Class, individualisation and tracing processes of inequality in a changing world: A reply to Steven Roberts', *Journal of Youth Studies* 13:6, 737–46.

THREE

Improvement for some: poverty and social exclusion among older people and pensioners

Demi Patsios

Broader policy and research context

Research into older people and pensioners[1] has garnered a lot of academic and policy attention during the past decade. There are of course good reasons for this. From a demographic or population ageing perspective the sheer number of older people in the UK is at the highest level it has ever been in both absolute and relative terms. Estimates place the proportion of people aged 65 years or older at approximately 22% of the population which equates to roughly 13 million persons (ILC-UK, 2013). The number of pensioners has also increased dramatically last 20 years, with an estimated 26 million having reached state pension age (SPA).[2] While longevity is a cause for celebration, it is also important to recognise that the UK's rapidly ageing society offers a number of short- and long-term policy challenges (McKee, 2010). Although the main policy focus to date has been on care and pensions, great strides have been made in improving the financial situation of older people and pensioners, particularly those on lower incomes who are reliant on state pensions and other age- or disability-related benefits (for example, housing benefit, pension credit guarantee, council tax benefit, disability living allowance, carer's allowance) to make ends meet. A lot has been written over the past decade or so regarding the generally improved economic, material and social position of pensioners and older people in the UK. At the time of the UK Poverty and Social Exclusion Survey 2012 (PSE-UK 2012), the proportion of pensioners living in low-income poverty was at the lowest level it had been for almost thirty years (MacInnes et al, 2013). Pensioners are now less likely to be in financial poverty than the majority of non-pensioners after housing costs (McKee, 2010). McKee goes on to suggest that although this progress should be welcomed, 'much less progress has been made in helping those pensioners in more severe and persistent poverty' (2010, p 20). In short, the poorest pensioners have fallen further behind middle-income pensioners, although inequality within most of the top half of the pensioner income distribution has changed little (Cribb et al, 2013). In addition, the measurement of social exclusion is a relatively recent endeavour, with little attention paid to older people (Price, 2008). Past studies of social exclusion have tended to focus on children, young people and families. However, research has emerged which suggests that older people might be more susceptible to social exclusion due to diminishing material and social resources, lower economic and social participation, and poorer outcomes in quality of life measured in terms of health and well-being, and deteriorating conditions in their living environment (Scharf et al, 2005; Barnes et al, 2006; Patsios, 2006; Becker and Boreham, 2009; Kneale, 2012). For example, Becker and Boreham's (2009) study showed that 50% of all those aged 60 and older experienced multiple risk markers of social exclusion as found in Bristol Social Exclusion Matrix (B-SEM) (such as, poor access to services and to transport, were physically inactive, had a fear of their local area after dark, had low social support, and had poor general and emotional health). The older old (aged 80 years and over)[3] are more likely to experience multiple risk markers than their younger counterparts. Taken together, much is known separately about how poverty and social exclusion affects – and is experienced by – older people, but very few studies exist which are able to look simultaneously at both as well as key differences between and within pensioner households using a large nationally representative sample of older people.

Overview of the chapter

This chapter adds to the rapidly evolving evidence base of poverty and social exclusion among older people and pensioners by analysing data from the PSE-UK 2012 using the B-SEM conceptual model (Levitas et al, 2007). The sample size and B-SEM sub-themes available in the PSE-UK 2012 provide a unique opportunity to look more closely at the relationship between poverty and social exclusion and how it affects the situation of a broad group of older people living in different pensioner household types. Each section begins with an overview of key literature/themes, followed by findings from the PSE-UK

2012. The chapter concludes with a discussion of key findings and implications for further policy.

Resources

Having adequate material, economic and social resources is central to personal well-being and these resources are important elements in understanding poverty and social exclusion among older people. According to Zaidi, 'while social exclusion for older people can take many forms, being excluded from material resources is the key initial catalyst, which either starts the process of involuntary detachment from participation in society *or* serves as the identifier for other forms of social exclusion' (2011, p 2). Lack of income and an inability to afford the types of goods and services that most people in a society have access to or to participate in common social activities figure centrally in exclusion from material and economic resources in B-SEM. Access to affordable and adequate public and private services, and community-based health and social services is a key resource older adults can draw on in order to live independently and well in their own homes. Social networks and social support are also key components of older people's social resources, and when these informal networks are lacking (or weak) this can result in isolation, loneliness, poor health and well-being, less satisfaction with relationships and lower overall satisfaction with life.

Material and economic resources

Low income (at-risk-of-poverty)

Low-income poverty is defined as people living in households with income below 60% of the median for that year. The UK government's preferred measure of low income for pensioners is based on equivalised incomes measured after housing costs (AHC), as around three quarters of pensioners own their own home (DWP, 2013a). Considering pensioners' incomes compared to others after deducting housing costs allows for more meaningful comparisons of income between working-age people and pensioners, and for pensioners over time (DWP, 2013a). The PSE-UK 2012 findings show that relative low-income poverty varies according to older adults living in various pensioner household types, as well as the poverty measure used (see 'Low-income poverty' in Table 3.1). Across the various low-income measures, younger pensioner couples are least likely to be at-risk-of-poverty (AROP), whereas single pensioners (younger and older, as well as pensioners living in other households) are relatively more likely to be AROP according to PSE and Department of Work and Pensions (DWP) AHC measures. Before housing costs (BHC) measures fall only slightly below AHC measures across households.

Material deprivation

McKay (2010) argues that low-income (households below average income – HBAI) figures are good for measuring changes over time, but do not necessarily reflect the multidimensional nature of poverty. As such, it is better to look at more 'indirect' measures of poverty. The DWP measures material deprivation among people aged 65 using the Family Resources Survey (FRS)[4] and estimates have been included in the HBAI report since 2011 (DWP, 2013b). However, material deprivation is not officially used in government pensioner poverty reduction targets (such as those found in the Child Poverty Act 2010) or as an official means test for allocation of benefits. HBAI figures leading up the PSE-UK 2012 showed that the percentage of those in material deprivation fell from 9% in 2010/11 to 8% in 2011/12 (DWP, 2013b). In contrast, the PSE-UK 2012 uses a final validated set of 22 items and activities in the PSE adult deprivation index (see chapter one for an overview). Overall, one out of four older adults report material deprivation on two or more items and activities, one out of six report three or more deprivations, and approximately one in ten report four or more deprivations (see 'Deprivation groupings' in Table 3.1). Findings also reveal differences in deprivation grouping by pensioner household type. Older adults in other household types and younger single pensioners are twice as likely to report all three deprivation groupings. Older adults in couple households are least likely to report three or more or four or more deprivations, however, older pensioner couples are more likely than younger pensioner couples to report two or more deprivations.

Low income and material deprivation

Past research suggests that low income does not automatically result in a pensioner living in material deprivation (Bartlett et al, 2013), with some pensioners managing well on a low income (Kotecha et al, 2013). Analyses of FRS data show that only 2% of older people are in both relative poverty and material deprivation (Bartlett et al,

Table 3.1: B-SEM domain – Resources; theme – Material and economic resources

	Younger pensioner couple (N = 1,148)	Older pensioner couple (N = 156)	Younger single pensioner (N = 494)	Older single pensioner (N = 282)	Pensioner in other household (N = 215)	Total (N = 2,296)
	%	%	%	%	%	%
Low-income poverty						
PSE AROP 60% AHC	15	21	23	22	21	19
DWP AROP 60% AHC	15	26	19	18	20	17
EU/DWP AROP 60% BHC	14	28	14	25	23	17
DWP AROP 50% BHC	8	12	9	13	12	9
Deprivation groupings						
Two or more	17	23	35	21	40	24
Three or more	11	9	25	12	30	16
Four or more	8	6	18	8	22	11
PSE poverty group						
Poor	7	7	17	10	15	11
Rising	0	0	0	0	0	0
Vulnerable	12	18	15	19	10	13
Not poor	81	74	68	71	75	76

2013). PSE–UK 2012 analysis confirms that there is little overlap (3%) between low income and three or more material deprivations.

PSE poverty measure: combined low income and material deprivation

In the PSE–UK 2012, two main poverty measures, which combined equivalised household income and number of deprivations, were created: poverty group (poor, rising, vulnerable, not poor) and poor group (poor vs. not poor) (see chapter one for an overview of how the poverty measures were constructed). Older adults in pensioner households are less than half as likely to be poor as adults in non-pensioner households according to the main PSE measure. Findings also show that PSE poverty group varies both between and within pensioner household types, particularly when gender is considered. Younger single pensioners (17%) and older adults in other households (15%) are most likely to be poor, whereas younger and older pensioner couples are more likely to be vulnerable to poverty (that is, to have an equivalised household income just above that used to allocate adults into different poverty groups) rather than poor (see 'PSE poverty group' in Table 3.1). Further analyses by gender reveal that younger single female pensioners are more likely to be poor than their male counterparts (20% compared with 13%) and that older single female pensioners are more likely to be poor compared with older single male pensioners (11% versus 8%), whereas the opposite is true for older women living in other households (14% of female pensioners compared with 17% of male pensioners).

Access to public and private services

Services for older people

The main focus of community-based health and social care services for older people is on promoting their independence and intervening early to prevent them from requiring long-term care and support or hospital admissions. Older people are the main users of health and social care services but sometimes services do not meet their needs, either because they are unaffordable, or unavailable or inadequate. In the PSE-UK 2012, persons 65 years of age and older (n = 1,806) were asked about a number of services for older persons[5] and the extent to which they thought that the services were adequate or not (if they were used), and reasons for not using them. Over these five services the largest category is that older adults do not want to use the service or it is not relevant to them. Older single pensioners are relatively more likely to report using a chiropodist (51%), home help/home care (25%) and day centre/lunch clubs (20%) and that these services were adequate. Affordability and lack of availability also appear to be barriers to service use, particularly for younger single pensioners and for those living in other households. Single pensioners (younger and older) are relatively more likely to report that they use a chiropodist but that it is inadequate.

Social resources

Social support (affective and instrumental)

There are various types of informal social support, including emotional, informational and practical support. The amount of practical and emotional support available in times of need is a key indicator of an older adult's social resources. Greater anticipated support (that is, the belief that others will provide assistance in the future if needed) is also associated with a deeper sense of meaning and personal well-being over time (Krause, 2007). The PSE-UK 2012 asked respondents how much support they would get in seven situations.[6] Findings show that single pensioners (younger and older) are most likely to report that they would not receive any support for the practical and emotional items and pensioner couples (younger and older) are most likely to report at least some potential help (see 'Potential support' in Table 3.2).

Social networks: frequency and quality of contact with family members/friends

The frequency and quality of older people's contact with their social networks is a key indicator of a person's social resources. Social networks and relationships are central to maintaining good physical, mental health and overall well-being (Windle et al, 2011; Nicholson, 2012; Steptoe et al, 2013). Even weak social relationships, as long as they exist in some numbers, have been shown to influence older people's well-being (Haines and Henderson, 2002). However, as people age their social networks or social 'convoys' contract due to retirement, separation, divorce or death (Antonucci and Akiyama, 1987). In short, as people get older they are more likely to live alone. Changes in the nature of the social network and social relationships can lead to loneliness, which in turn increases the need for social care services and residential care (Age UK, 2014a). Although the PSE-UK 2012 did not collect information on loneliness per se, respondents were asked to report the frequency and number of family members and friends or neighbours (other than those they lived with, such as spouse/partner) they saw or spoke with, or contacted socially in other ways (letters, texts, email and so on).[7] A derived variable was computed that combined frequency and level of contact with family and friends. Findings reveal that social contact varies between older adults living in different household types (see 'Social network contact' in Table 3.2). Younger single pensioners are relatively more likely to report that they see or speak with relatives 'less than weekly' (19%), but also relatively less likely to report seeing or speaking with friends 'less than weekly' (12%). Older pensioners (couples and singles) are relatively least likely to contact family and friends via text, emails, social networking and so on. Pensioners in other households and older pensioner couples are most likely to report lack of social contact with at least three family members and friends at least once a month (15% and 14% respectively). Approximately six out of ten older adults report seeing family and friends as often as they want to, but many also reported that they live too far away (see 'Reasons preventing meeting up with family and friends more often' in Table 3.2).

Table 3.2: B-SEM domain – Resources; theme – Social resources

	Younger pensioner couple (N = 1,148) %	Older pensioner couple (N = 156) %	Younger single pensioner (N = 494) %	Older single pensioner (N = 282) %	Pensioner in other household (N = 215) %	Total (N = 2,296) %
Potential support						
Practical – None all 4	3	3	10	12	5	6
Emotional – None all 3	2	4	8	6	3	4
Combined – None all 7	4	5	13	13	7	8
Social network contact						
Sees/speaks to relatives 'Less than weekly'	14	15	19	13	19	16
Sees/speaks to 'Fewer than 3 relatives at least once a month'	22	36	36	28	33	28
Sees/speaks to friends 'Less than weekly'	18	29	12	15	28	18
Sees/speaks to 'Fewer than 3 friends at least once a month'	20	32	23	24	33	23
Contacts friends and family 'Less than weekly'	55	81	62	80	68	63
No social contact with at least 3+ family members and friends at least once per month	7	14	12	11	15	10

(continued)

Table 3.2: B-SEM domain – Resources; theme – Social resources (continued)

	Younger pensioner couple (N = 1,148)	Older pensioner couple (N = 156)	Younger single pensioner (N = 494)	Older single pensioner (N = 282)	Pensioner in other household (N = 215)	Total (N = 2,296)
	%	%	%	%	%	%
Reasons preventing meeting up with family and friends more often						
I see them as often as I want to	60	51	56	50	53	57
Too far away	29	29	24	28	36	28
Prevented by poor health	7	16	11	18	15	11
Difficulties with transport	3	7	6	16	8	6
Other reason	4	6	6	11	1	5
Can't afford to	3	1	6	1	8	4
Prevented by other caring responsibilities	5	2	1	1	6	3
My lack of time due to paid work	1	0	2	0	3	1
Not interested in meeting up with family and friends	0	0	3	0	1	1
Fear of crime	0	0	2	0	0	1
My lack of time due to childcare responsibilities	0	0	0	0	0	0

Participation

Economic participation, social participation, and civic and political engagement are key components of active, productive and successful ageing (Johnson and Mutchler, 2013). However, when people enter old age, economic and social participation changes because of life course transitions (such as retirement, empty nest), and in later life changes again due to declining physical and mental health (Bukov et al, 2002). Participation in social and political activities is an important component of well-being in later life. Being socially connected with other people and with social institutions, such as clubs and organisations, fosters social interaction, improves older people's sense of belonging and overall life satisfaction.

Economic participation

Paid work

The labour market provides an important arena for social contact for an increasing number of older adults of SPA. Employment is a major driver of an adequate income and a means of escaping relative income poverty for older adults still in paid work (POST, 2011). In the PSE–UK 2012, employment status is only available for those of working age through 79 years of age and as such excludes workers 80 years of age or older in older pensioner households (single and couple). Findings reveal minor differences between younger pensioners who report being employed full-time or part-time (approximately 14% combined). In contrast, 17% of older adults living in other household types report being employed (12% of whom are employed full-time). Additional analyses did not reveal any significant differences between older adults of SPA who are employed versus unemployed or economically inactive, gender differences in full-time versus part-time employment, and in terms of low levels of social contact with family and friends.

Unpaid work

Many retired people take on unpaid work in older age, which might include volunteering for charities, providing care to family members and friends, and taking care of grandchildren. This unpaid work has many social and economic benefits (Hammond et al, 2015). However, carers often report becoming isolated because of their caring responsibilities (Carers UK, 2015), while the opposite appears to be true for those who volunteer (Nazroo and Matthews, 2012).

Those with poorer health are less likely to participate in unpaid work (Carers UK, 2015) and providing care has been shown to have negative health consequences (The Princess Royal Trust for Carers, 2011). Past research also suggests that some caregivers might suffer from stress due to their caring role and have lower levels of life satisfaction (The Princess Royal Trust for Carers, 2011). However, being involved in a charitable or voluntary activity has also been linked with better mental health and life satisfaction (Nazroo and Matthews, 2012). PSE-UK 2012 respondents were asked about voluntary work, caring for family members and friends, and providing care for children (including grandchildren).[8] Findings show that approximately one in five older adults are involved in all three activities and that younger pensioners (singles and couples) and older adults in other household types report the highest levels of involvement. Further analyses did not reveal significant differences in unpaid work between women and men, however, younger single female pensioners are more likely than their male peers to provide unpaid care to a family member or friend (79% versus 65%) and child care (80% versus 66%). There was some evidence that older adults active in unpaid work are more likely to have poor mental health using the General Health Questionnaire 12-item version (GHQ12) (Goldberg and Williams, 1988). Examination of the relationship between unpaid work and subjective well-being[9] showed that the proportion of older adults reporting very low personal well-being is lower for those volunteering compared with those who did not volunteer. Similar results are found in terms of provision of unpaid care to family members and friends or children.

Social participation

Past research has shown that maintaining social participation in later life has a positive influence on quality of life, better self-rated health and mental and physical well-being (Bowling and Dieppe, 2005). The level of social participation is positively associated with the availability of social resources (such as social contact and social support) (Pollak and Von Dem Knesebeck, 2004) and negatively associated with affordability (Patsios, 2014).

Participation in common social activities

Findings show that one in four older adults participate in fewer than five[10] common social activities (see 'Common social activities' in Table 3.3). Older pensioners (singles and couples) and older adults in other household types are more likely to report low social participation. In contrast, younger pensioner couples are less likely to report low levels of social participation. In terms of physical and mental health, findings show that older adults with low social participation are more likely to report a longstanding illness. Low levels of social participation due to longstanding illness particularly affected younger and older single pensioners and those in living in other household types. Moreover, older adults with low rates of social participation are twice as likely to have poor mental health, with single pensioners (younger and older) and younger pensioner couples most likely to be affected. In terms of subjective well-being, findings reveal that older adults with lower levels of social participation are several times more likely to report 'very low' satisfaction[11] with day-to-day activities and 'very low' life satisfaction. Younger pensioners (single and couples) are much more likely to report low levels of satisfaction. There also appears to be a strong link between social participation and social contact. Older adults with low rates of social participation are over three times as likely to report not seeing three or more family members and friends at least once per month, with younger pensioners (singles and couples) in particular significantly less likely to report regular social contact. Low social participation also appears to be strongly related to lack of anticipated practical and emotional support, however this only appears to affect younger single pensioners. Finally, PSE poor older adults are twice as likely to report lower levels of social participation, with younger pensioners most affected.

Enforced lack

The issue of 'enforced lack' (that is, older adults reporting not being able to afford participation in common social activities) is covered more thoroughly in earlier analyses of PSE-UK 2012 data (Patsios, 2014). The focus here is to examine how enforced lack varies between older adults in different household types. Approximately one in seven older adults report that they are not able to afford participation in three or more[12] common social activities (see 'Important factors preventing' in Table 3.3). Older adults in other household types and younger single pensioners are most likely to report affordability as the reason for not participating in common social activities. Follow-up analyses of younger single pensioner households showed that females are twice as likely as males to report exclusion from common social activities due to affordability. No other gender-related differences between households were found.

Table 3.3: B-SEM domain – Participation; theme – Social participation

	Younger pensioner couple (N = 1,148) %	Older pensioner couple (N = 156) %	Younger single pensioner (N = 494) %	Older single pensioner (N = 282) %	Pensioner in other household (N = 215) %	Total (N = 2,296) %
Common social activities – summary 'Do' less than five	19	33	24	32	33	24
Common social activities – summary 'Don't do' – 'Can't afford' three or more	11	9	22	8	29	15
Important factors preventing participation in common social activities						
None of these	68	42	58	38	47	59
Poor health/disability	19	34	25	46	38	26
No vehicle/poor public transport	3	5	9	22	9	7
No one to go out with (social)	2	14	9	14	7	6
Lack of time due to other caring responsibilities	7	9	1	3	6	5
Problems with physical access	2	7	5	9	6	4
Lack of time due to paid work	4	0	4	0	0	3
Fear of personal attack	0	4	6	4	5	3
Fear of burglary or vandalism	2	3	3	2	5	3
Lack of time due to childcare responsibilities	0	0	1	2	8	1
Feel unwelcome (eg due to disability, ethnicity, gender, age etc)	0	0	1	1	2	1

Political and civic participation

Political and civic participation can take a variety of forms, from voting in a local or general election to being a member of a political party or community-based organisations, taking an active role within a range of cultural or leisure interactions, contacting a politician to voice ecological or environmental concerns, signing a petition and so on (Lamprianou, 2012).

Political participation

PSE-UK 2012 respondents were asked if they had taken any of nine actions in an attempt to solve a problem affecting people in their local area or to show their concern over a national issue (see 'Political participation' in Table 3.4). Findings show that seven out of ten older adults voted in the 2010 general election and just over one quarter report signing a petition (in person or online). Younger pensioner couples are most likely and older single pensioners least likely to have done both in the three-year period leading up to the PSE-UK 2012. Findings also show that one quarter of older adults did not carry out any form of political participation (voting in a general election or alternative political action) in the last three years. Approximately one third of older single pensioners and older adults in other households report taking any political action.

Civic participation

Over four out of ten older adults report that they are not members of any of the 13 organisations listed (see 'Community organisations' in Table 3.4). Only half of older pensioner couples and those in other households report membership compared to two thirds of younger pensioner couples. Beyond this, there are no discernible patterns in terms of membership of specific organisations between pensioner households. There are, however, differences according to PSE poor group and satisfaction with feeling part of the community. Taken together, older adults who are PSE poor are twice as likely to report not being a member of any community organisation. Furthermore, older adults who are not a member of any organisation are more than twice as likely to report very low satisfaction with feeling part of the community. These differences are most evident for younger and older single pensioners as well as younger pensioner couples.

Table 3.4: B-SEM domain – Participation; theme – Political and civic participation

	Younger pensioner couple (N = 1,148)	Older pensioner couple (N = 156)	Younger single pensioner (N = 494)	Older single pensioner (N = 282)	Pensioner in other household (N = 215)	Total (N = 2,296)
	%	%	%	%	%	%
Political participation						
Voted in the last General Election	76	66	65	56	61	69
Signed a petition (in person or online)	32	14	27	10	25	26
None of the above	19	24	26	36	31	24
Contacted a local councillor or MP	19	12	20	14	15	18
Attended a public meeting	17	14	13	10	14	15
Taken part in an online campaign	10	1	7	3	10	8
Boycotted certain products for political or ethical reasons	10	1	7	4	2	7
Taken part in a demonstration or protest	2	4	4	1	2	2
Been an officer of a campaigning organisation or pressure group	1	0	1	2	1	1
Taken part in a strike or picket	1	0	1	0	0	0
						(continued)

Table 3.4: B-SEM domain – Participation; theme – Political and civic participation (continued)

	Younger pensioner couple (N = 1,148)	Older pensioner couple (N = 156)	Younger single pensioner (N = 494)	Older single pensioner (N = 282)	Pensioner in other household (N = 215)	Total (N = 2,296)
	%	%	%	%	%	%
Community organisations						
None of these	36	50	45	46	50	42
Sports, leisure or social club	31	20	24	16	22	26
Conservation or animal welfare group (eg The National Trust, RSPB)	22	9	16	8	18	18
Religious organisation	14	14	18	15	14	15
Other group	13	6	11	13	13	12
Neighbourhood or civic group	12	6	7	8	7	9
Health, disability or welfare group	6	7	6	7	11	7
Women s group (eg Women s Institute)	6	4	6	8	7	6
Trade union or staff association	5	3	5	2	2	4
Political party	2	4	3	7	1	3
Environmental pressure group (eg Greenpeace)	2	1	3	1	0	2
Humanitarian or peace group	1	0	2	3	2	1
Youth group (eg Scouts, youth club)	1	0	0	0	0	1
Minority ethnic organisation	0	0	1	1	0	1

Quality of life

The concept of quality of life has received increased academic and policy attention in the past decade. There is a clear push towards measuring the more intangible but critical elements of the living condition such as personal well-being and life satisfaction (for example, the physical and mental of health of older people is a crucial determinant of social exclusion in its various forms), living in good neighbourhood, and feeling safe. The strong links between health and well-being (a key sub-theme/dimension in B-SEM) and pensioner poverty and social exclusion has been covered at various points in this contribution. This section focuses on the living environment, including housing and local area conditions.

Living environment

For older people, home is a place to which people have considerable psychological attachment and they may be unwilling to move out of a neighbourhood that they have lived in for most of their adult lives. The 'pull' factors that compel older people to remain living in their current home for as long as possible are strong even where there are clear problems with the accommodation (Hughes, 2012). However, not all housing is suitable for people with frailties or disabilities (Price, 2008; Age UK, 2014b). Poor health can be brought on or exacerbated by housing conditions and poor housing conditions can result in poor health (Housing LIN, 2012). For example, cold, damp, mouldy housing affects people's health and well-being (Howden-Chapman et al, 2011, p 2). For older people more prone to certain health conditions, their housing conditions may be both a contributory factor as well as a solution to such problems (IPC, 2012: 13).

Housing and accommodation

One out of three older adults report at least one problem with their accommodation, including four out of ten older pensioner couples and older adults in other households, one in three younger pensioners (singles and couples alike), and one in five older single pensioners (see 'Problems with accommodation' in Table 3.5). Older pensioner couples are several times more likely to report that their heating system or radiators are not sufficient and twice as likely to report that they have damp or mould. Pensioners in other households are twice as likely both to report shortage of space and to report damp or mould.

Table 3.5: B-SEM domain – Quality of life; theme – Living environment, sub-theme – Housing quality

	Younger pensioner couple (N = 1,148)	Older pensioner couple (N = 156)	Younger single pensioner (N = 494)	Older single pensioner (N = 282)	Pensioner in other household (N = 215)	Total (N = 2,296)
	%	%	%	%	%	%
Problems with accommodation						
At least one problem with accommodation	35	39	35	24	40	34
Shortage of space	11	7	10	5	19	10
Damp or mould on walls, ceilings, floors, foundations, etc	8	14	8	4	14	9
Draughts	7	2	10	7	12	8
Condensation	6	6	5	3	9	6
Heating system or radiators not sufficient	2	13	5	3	9	4
Rot in window frames or floors	5	6	4	3	3	4
Heating faulty or difficult to control or regulate	4	1	5	2	2	4
Leaky roof	3	2	4		5	3
Too dark, not enough light	2	2	5	3	4	3
No place to sit outside, eg no terrace, balcony or garden	2	1	4	3	2	2
Other	3	2	2	1	2	2
Problems with plumbing or drains	1	0	4	2	3	2

(continued)

Table 3.5: B-SEM domain – Quality of life; theme – Living environment, sub-theme – Housing quality (continued)

	Younger pensioner couple (N = 1,148) %	Older pensioner couple (N = 156) %	Younger single pensioner (N = 494) %	Older single pensioner (N = 282) %	Pensioner in other household (N = 215) %	Total (N = 2,296) %
Ways cut back on fuel use last winter						
Cut back in at least one way	31	32	43	34	48	36
Cut the number of hours the heating was on to reduce fuel costs	18	18	24	21	24	20
Turned heating down or off, even though it was too cold in the house/flat	13	4	19	8	24	14
Turned out more lights in my home than I/we wanted to, to try to reduce the electricity bill	10	14	17	14	18	13
Only heated and used part of the house	10	13	15	13	10	12
Used less hot water than I/we needed to reduce fuel costs	5	7	7	7	5	6
Other cut back on fuel use to reduce fuel costs	5	6	5	4	6	5
Had fewer hot meals or hot drinks that I/we needed to reduce fuel costs	0	1	2	0	0	1
Satisfaction with accommodation						
Very satisfied	76	72	74	73	62	74
Fairly satisfied	19	27	20	22	30	21
Neither satisfied nor dissatisfied	3	0	2	2	4	3
Slightly dissatisfied	2	0	2	2	2	2
Very dissatisfied		1	2	1	1	1

In contrast, older single pensioners are much less likely to report shortage of space. The PSE-UK 2012 also sought to determine the ways in which accommodation problems affected members of the households, including, among other things, making an existing health condition worse or bringing on a new health problem. Of those older adults reporting problems with their accommodation (n = 300), six out of ten also report that these problems had not affected any members of the household. Older adults in other household types and younger single pensioners are most likely to report that accommodation problems affected them, the most common effects being that: housing problems made me/us feel miserable, anxious or depressed; made an existing health problem (or problems) worse, I/we stayed in bed longer than we wanted to stay warm.

Fuel poverty – cutting back on fuel use

Poverty and inadequate housing are a particularly dangerous combination to older people in the winter. Keeping warm in the colder weather can be a challenge for many older people (McKee, 2010, p 24). Cold homes and fuel poverty are also associated with excess winter deaths (PHE, 2014, p 12). The PSE-UK 2012 asked whether their household had cut back on fuel use at home in any of seven ways in the winter prior to the survey because they could not afford the costs. Findings show that more than one third of older adults are living in households which cut back on fuel use the previous winter in at least one way (see 'Ways cut back on fuel use last winter' in Table 3.5), ranging from just under one half those in other household types and three out of ten pensioner couples (younger and older). For those cutting back on fuel use, cutting the number of hours the heating was on to reduce fuel costs, turned heating down or off (even though it was too cold in the house/flat), particularly by those pensioners in other household types and younger single pensioners.

Satisfaction with accommodation

The PSE-UK 2012 asked about satisfaction with accommodation. Three quarters of older adults living in pensioner households are 'very satisfied' with their accommodation (see 'Satisfaction with accommodation' in Table 3.5), ranging from a low of six out of ten older adults in other household types to a high of three quarters of younger pensioner couples. Not surprisingly those without accommodation problems are relatively more likely to report being very satisfied with their accommodation.

Neighbourhood

Problems with accommodation may be a determining factor of health, but problems in the wider neighbourhood also play an important role in the quality of life of older people who 'stay put' or 'age in place' (Scharf et al, 2005). The PSE-UK 2012 asked respondents which among a series of 16 items they considered problems in the area (such as poor street lighting, rubbish or litter lying around, vandalism and so on). Two thirds of older adults report one or more of these problems in their local area (see 'Problems in local area' in Table 3.6). Across all pensioner households, younger pensioner couples are more likely to report the range of various problems and older single pensioners least likely. Poor street lighting, potholed roads and broken pavements is the problem most frequently cited by older adults (34%), followed by dogs and dog or cat mess in their area (24%). One in five older adults also report rubbish or litter lying around as a problem in their area.

Satisfaction with area

The PSE-UK 2012 also asked respondents how satisfied they are with this area as a place to live. Results show that older single pensioners are most likely and pensioners in other households least likely to be 'very satisfied' with their local area as a place to live (see 'satisfaction with local area' in Table 3.6). Again, older adults reporting at least one problem in their local area are less likely to report being satisfied with their local area compared with those older adults not reporting any problems in their local area.

Discussion of key findings and their implications for policy

Resources

Differences are found in terms of older adults' access to material, economic and social resources. The degree to which older adults living in different pensioner households are prone to be AROP and their capacity to afford key items and activities of expenditure varies between and within pensioner households. However, the importance of using AHC versus BHC AROP when analysing pensioner households is not confirmed (McGuinness, 2015). This is likely due

Table 3.6: B-SEM domain – Quality of life; theme – Living environment

	Younger pensioner couple (N = 1,148)	Older pensioner couple (N = 156)	Younger single pensioner (N = 494)	Older single pensioner (N = 282)	Pensioner in other household (N = 215)	Total (N = 2,296)
	%	%	%	%	%	%
Problems in local area						
At least one problem in local area	69	66	64	57	66	66
Poor street lighting, potholed roads or broken pavements	38	39	25	29	34	34
Dogs and dog or cat mess in this area	27	16	24	18	20	24
Rubbish or litter lying around	21	15	23	13	21	20
Illegal parking (eg on pavements)	15	16	12	14	9	14
Risk from traffic for pedestrians and cyclists	13	12	9	7	12	11
Noise (eg traffic, businesses, aircraft)	10	11	10	10	14	11
People using or dealing drugs	5	2	8	1	11	6
People being drunk or rowdy in the street/park	4	4	8	3	9	5
Homes and gardens in bad condition	5	0	4	4	2	4
Vandalism and deliberate damage to property	3	5	7	3	6	4
Noisy neighbours or loud parties	4	1	5	3	6	4
Joy riding	4	0	4	1	6	4
Air pollution	2	0	2	3	5	3
Lack of open public spaces	2	0	2	3	5	2

(continued)

Table 3.6: B-SEM domain – Quality of life; theme – Living environment (continued)

	Younger pensioner couple (N = 1,148)	Older pensioner couple (N = 156)	Younger single pensioner (N = 494)	Older single pensioner (N = 282)	Pensioner in other household (N = 215)	Total (N = 2,296)
	%	%	%	%	%	%
Problems in local area (continued)						
Graffiti on walls and buildings	2	2	3	2	6	2
Insults or harassment	1	1	2	0	2	1
Satisfaction with local area						
Very satisfied	61	59	60	66	50	60
Fairly satisfied	31	33	29	25	39	31
Neither satisfied nor dissatisfied	3	7	3	3	1	3
Slightly dissatisfied	5	1	6	5	9	5
Very dissatisfied	1	0	3	1	1	1

to the number of households created for use in the analyses as well as including older adults in 'other households'. The higher poverty rates for single female pensioners are associated with lower earnings compared with men and lower individual incomes, particularly in terms of that from occupational or personal schemes (DWP, 2013c). Enforced lack appears to particularly affect younger single pensioners, with females much more likely than males to report affordability as an issue. In contrast, the relative advantage of pensioner couples can explained both by the economies of scale of living in a multi-person household and the likelihood that one (increasingly both) of the older persons living as a couple is likely to be in receipt of an occupational or personal pension rather than reliant solely on the basic state pension plus supplemental, means-tested benefits (such as pension credit guarantee, housing/council tax benefits). The general debate around the extent to which adaptive preferences (that is, the unconscious altering of preferences in light of the options available) played an influential role in older adults reporting an 'enforced lack' of necessities has been addressed critically by other authors (McKay, 2004, 2008, 2010; Halleröd, 2006; Legard et al, 2008; Hick, 2013), but is difficult to establish in the present analyses due to very low sample sizes of older adults in some pensioner household types.

Although the government has taken several steps to help those on lower incomes (such as the 'triple lock guarantee', pension credit, winter fuel/cold weather payments, free eye tests, free prescriptions, bus passes and TV licences for the over-75s, and additional support for those with disabilities or caring responsibilities), pensioner poverty persists. The receipt of benefits provides a vital source of income for many lower income older people and pensioners, however, non-take-up of the benefits remains high, with take-up being higher with non-pensioners, compared with pensioners (Finn and Goodship, 2014). As such, there needs to be a renewed campaign to ensure that those older adults, particularly those on lower incomes, who are entitled to means-tested benefits actually know about these and receive them. Moreover, the lack of a strong overlap between low income and material deprivation confirms the need for a broader measure of pensioner poverty which goes beyond low income (Kotecha et al, 2013). The reliance on low income as the key measure of poverty fails to capture a large number of older people and pensioners who fall just above this threshold, or those who are not income poor but report high levels of material and social deprivation. A new bespoke measure of pensioner poverty should combine low income and material and social deprivation following the approach found in the Child Poverty

Act 2010. Official (government) targets for reducing low income and material deprivation should be produced and reviewed annually.

Findings also reveal that a large number of older adults do not access services for older people because they are either unavailable or unaffordable. In recent years, there has been an extraordinary rationing of health and social care services due to budget cuts and this has had a profound impact on community-based care for older people. Several issues regarding the availability, adequacy and affordability of community-based preventative services are found in the Care Act 2014 (which came into effect April 2015) but as this legislation came into effect post the PSE-UK 2012 it is difficult to comment on the extent to which it will impact on barriers to service use. Moreover, the care cap and means test, which were due to come into effect from April 2016, have been delayed until April 2020, making it difficult to assess affordability under this legislation. Despite these delays, any policy reforms should include incentives for funding low-level services which prevent the need for more costly intermediate and re-ablement care for older people at a later date.

Furthermore, study findings show that single pensioners (younger and older) report lower levels of potential social support and have less frequent contact with family and friends. In terms of policy, there is increasing appreciation 'that changes in circumstances of the life course in relation to social exclusion can begin to occur in middle age, and that policies to prevent or address social exclusion should be based around the concept of ageing rather than being targeted specifically at older people' (Age UK, 2014b, p 13). It has been suggested elsewhere that loneliness and social isolation should be taken up by the newly established Health and Well-being Boards, as loneliness increases the need for social care services and residential care (Age UK, 2014a).

Participation

PSE-UK 2012 findings show that paid work continues to play an important role in the lives of older adults of SPA. However, the exclusion of workers 80 years of age and older in the PSE-UK 2012, changes to women's SPA from April 2010, and the abolition of the Default Retirement Age (DRA) from October 2011, make it quite difficult to provide any definitive commentary on how the present findings can be interpreted in light of the quickly changing work and pension policy environments. Following the PSE-UK 2012, there are some signs of a change in employment rates in the 'SPA and over' group, with quarter-on-quarter falls in employment rates of this group in four (out of six) quarters since April 2010 (ONS, 2013). According to Institute for Fiscal Studies (IFS) research, SPA equalisation for women aged 60 and 61 has caused a statistically significant boost to employment; however, the increased female SPA is not wholly responsible for increased labour force participation of women over 50, as the average age of exit from the labour market has been rising for both women and men since before the changes to SPA (Cribb, Emmerson and Tetlow, 2013, 2014). Close monitoring of employment trends of older workers and the influence of changes to SPA and DRA are needed in order to assess any systemic changes in future employment patterns by gender.

PSE-UK 2012 findings also provide some – but minimal – support for differences in unpaid work according to age and living arrangement, gender and poor mental health. Moreover, there is evidence to support the positive link between unpaid work and isolation, as well as volunteering and overall life satisfaction (Nazroo and Matthews, 2012). The extent to which people working longer could affect the numbers of people willing or able to carry out these jobs should be considered, as the burden may fall on the state (for example, in the form of childcare vouchers or increased costs of long-term care) if there are fewer people doing them. In short, the amount of care needed by people could be exacerbated by older people working longer (Hammond et al, 2015). It is also important for government to adopt policies which support those providing unpaid care for a partner, family or others as only one in ten of an estimated 1 million carers aged 65 years of older receive carer-specific support services (Age UK, 2013). Although the Carers Act 2014 guarantees entitlement for assessment of the carer's needs, it does not provide a similar guarantee for the provision of care-specific support services for carers falling below the national minimum eligibility threshold (Carers UK, 2015).

PSE-UK 2012 findings show that approximately one in four older adults report low social participation and that this is linked to poorer physical and mental health, older age, living alone, less contact with one's social network, lower potential social support, being poor and lower ratings of subjective well-being. However, findings also reveal that although contracting social networks are a natural part of growing older, many older adults maintain their social convoys through doing voluntary work, remaining active within civic and religious organisations and maintaining strong social networks (Wright, 1989). There is some evidence, however, that the oldest old and those living alone suffer from exclusion from political and civic participation. As such, government should consider initiatives aimed at promoting affordable (that is, subsidised) opportunities for social participation and civic engagement for older adults, particularly the oldest old (80 years of age or older) and those living alone. Such debates have not taken place to date due to a focus on care, pensions and benefit reforms.

Quality of life

The PSE-UK 2012 findings on the link between several dimensions of quality of life (such as health and well-being) confirm something we have known for quite some time: that economic participation, access to services for older people and health, social contact, anticipated social support, and levels of social and political (and civic) participation affect – and are affected by – personal health and well-being. In other words, they are at the same time both drivers and outcomes of personal well-being and quality of life. Housing quality and the wider neighbourhood continue to play a vital role in the quality of life and well-being of older people living in the community. Government policy needs to take a holistic approach to ageing and the life course which recognises these vital linkages. Shortly after completion of the PSE-UK 2012, the ONS Measuring National Well-being programme began producing a series of headline indicators in areas such as health, relationships, education and skills, what we do, where we live, our finances, the economy, governance, the environment and measures of 'personal well-being' (individuals' assessment of their own well-being) (ONS, 2011). Although these measures represent a positive development in our ability to measure well-being of the nation and certain measures of individual subjective well-being, the B-SEM framework applied in the PSE-UK 2012 offers greater scope for assessing the extent to which the older people and pensioners suffer from poverty and social exclusion and how this changes over time.

Conclusion

There are of course several other important domains from B-SEM which have not been covered in this contribution (that is, subjective poverty, debts and arrears, financial stress), which would have provided an even fuller picture of pensioner poverty and social exclusion. There is also much scope to look further into the linkages and associations between and within B-SEM domains and dimensions. However, this snapshot has provided some compelling evidence that although a great many older adults living in pensioner households have high levels of resources, participation and quality of life, there are still many older adults who are poor and deprived and suffer from multiple social exclusion.

Notes

[1] Older people are defined as women and men who are 65 years of age or older. Pensioners are defined as all adults above state pension age (SPA). For the purposes of the PSE-UK 2012 we assume that the pensionable age for women is 61 years and for men that it is 65 years.

[2] Under the Pensions Act 2011, women's SPA will increase more quickly to 65 between April 2016 and November 2018. From December 2018 the SPA for both men and women will start to increase to reach 66 by October 2020. The Pensions Act 2014 brought the increase in the SPA from 66 to 67 forward by eight years. The SPA for men and women will now increase to 67 between 2026 and 2028. Under the Pensions Act 2007 the SPA for men and women will increase from 67 to 68 between 2044 and 2046. See: https://www.gov.uk/government/uploads/system/uploads/attachment_data/file/310231/spa-timetable.pdf

[3] Aged 80 years and older is used as the selection criterion for assigning older adults into older pensioner household types (that is, singles and couples) in the analyses found in this contribution.

[4] The measure uses questions to find out if older people have access to 15 basic items or services that research has shown to be good indicators of quality of life (McKay, 2010). People are considered to be in material deprivation if they reach a certain threshold which links to lacking 3 or 4 items or more.

[5] Services included: Home help/home care; Meals on Wheels; Day Centres/lunch clubs/social clubs; Chiropodist; and Special transport for those with mobility problems. For the services used, respondents were asked whether they think they are adequate or inadequate. For the services they did not do not use, they were asked to state whether they do not use them because they 'don't want to' or because they are 'unavailable or inadequate' or because they 'can't afford to' use them.

[6] Four items related to instrumental/practical support: Ill in bed and needed help at home; Practical help around the home such as moving heavy furniture, DIY jobs; Someone to look after your home or possessions when away; and A lift somewhere in an emergency. Three items related to affective/emotional support: Advice about an important change in your life, such as changing jobs, moving to another area; Upset because of relationship problems or were feeling a bit depressed and needed someone

to talk to; and, Serious personal crisis and needed someone to turn to for comfort and support.

[7] Response categories for seeing, speaking and contacting friends and relatives: Less than once a month, Once a month, A few times a month, Once a week, A few times a week, and Every day. Response categories for number of family members and friends: None, One, Two, Three or four, Five to eight, and Nine or more.

[8] Response categories for the three questions on unpaid work: (1) Yes, 1–4 hours per week, (2) Yes, 5–9 hours per week, (3) Yes, 10–19 hours per week, (4) Yes, 20–34 hours per week, (5) Yes, 35–49 hours per week, (6) Yes, 50 hours or more a week, (7) No.

[9] Measured as a score of 0 to 4 (out of 10) on the 'life satisfaction' scale (ONS, 2012).

[10] Defined as participation in 0 to 4 common social activities. This threshold equates to the lowest quintile of pensioner participation in 14 common social activities covered in the PSE survey.

[11] Measured as a score of 0 to 4 (out of 10) on the 'satisfaction with day-to-day activities' scale.

[12] Calculated using the lowest quintile of pensioners' reporting lack of affordability in 14 common social activities covered in the PSE survey.

References

Age UK (2013) *Later life in the United Kingdom*, London: Age UK.

Age UK (2014a) *Evidence review: Loneliness in later life*, London: Age UK.

Age UK (2014b) *Housing in later life*, London: Age UK.

Antonucci, T.C. and Akiyama, H. (1987) 'Social networks in adult life and a preliminary examination of the convoy model', *Journal of Gerontology* 42:5, 519–27.

Barnes, M., Blom, A., Cox, K., Lessof, C. and Walker, A. (2006) *The social exclusion of older people: Evidence from the first wave of the English Longitudinal Study of Ageing (ELSA)*, London: Office of the Deputy Prime Minister, Social Exclusion Unit.

Bartlett, A., Frew, C. and Gilroy, J. (2013) *Understanding material deprivation among older people*, In-House Research 14, London: DWP.

Becker, E. and Boreham, R. (2009) *Understanding the risks of social exclusion across the life course: Older age*, London: Cabinet Office.

Bowling, A. and Dieppe, P. (2005) 'What is successful ageing and who should define it?', *British Medical Journal* 331:7531, 1548–51.

Bukov, A., Maas, I. and Lampert, T. (2002) 'Social participation in very old age: cross-sectional and longitudinal findings from BASE', *Journals of Gerontology* Series B 57:6, 510–17.

Carers UK (2015) *Caring into later life The growing pressure on older carers*, London: Carers UK.

Cribb, J., Emmerson, C. and Tetlow, G. (2013) 'Incentives, shocks or signals: labour supply effects of increasing the female state pension age in the UK', IFS Working Paper W13/03, London: Institute for Fiscal Studies.

Cribb, J., Emmerson, C. and Tetlow, G. (2014) 'Labour supply effects of increasing the female state pension age in the UK from age 60 to 62', IFS Working Paper W14/19, London: Institute for Fiscal Studies.

Cribb, J., Hood, A., Joyce, R. and Phillips, D. (2013) *Living standards, poverty and inequality in the UK: 2013*, IFS Report R81, London: Institute for Fiscal Studies.

DWP (Department for Work and Pensions) (2013a) *Households below average income: An analysis of the income distribution 1994/95– 2011/12 June 2013 (United Kingdom)*, London: DWP.

DWP (2013b) *Low income and material deprivation in the UK, 2011/12*, London: DWP, https://www.gov.uk/government/uploads/system/ uploads/attachment_data/file/206850/first_release_1112.pdf

DWP (2013c) *The pensioners' incomes series, United Kingdom, 2011/12*, London: DWP.

Finn, D. and Goodship, J. (2014) *Take-up of benefits and poverty: An evidence and policy review*, London: Centre for Economic and Social Inclusion.

Goldberg, D. and Williams, P. (1988) *A user's guide to the General Health Questionnaire*. Windsor: NFER-Nelson.

Haines, V.A. and Henderson, L.J. (2002) 'Targeting social support: a network assessment of the convoy model of social support', *Canadian Journal on Aging* 21:2, 243–56.

Halleröd, B. (2006) 'Sour grapes: relative deprivation, adaptive preferences and the measurement of poverty', *Journal of Social Policy* 35:3, 371–90.

Hammond, R., Baxter, S., Bramley, R., Kakkad, A., Mehta, S. and Sadler, M. (2015) 'Considerations on state pension age in the UK', A Sessional Paper presented to the Institute and Faculty of Actuaries, Edinburgh, 16 March 2015.

Hick, R. (2013) 'Poverty, preference or pensioners? Measuring material deprivation in the UK', *Fiscal Studies* 34:1, 31–54.

Housing LIN (Housing Learning and Improvement Network) (2012) 'Health, wellbeing, and the older people housing agenda', Briefing Paper 2, London: Housing LIN.

Howden-Chapman, P.L., Chandola, T., Stafford, M. and Marmot, M. (2011) 'The effect of housing on the mental health of older people: the impact of lifetime housing history in Whitehall II', *BMC Public Health* 11:682, 1–8.

Hughes, N. (2012) *A better fit? Creating housing choices for an ageing population*, London: Shelter.

ILC-UK (2013) *Ageing, longevity and demographic change: A factpack of statistics from the International Longevity Centre-UK*, London: ILC-UK.

IPC (Institute for Public Care) (2012) *Identifying the health gain from retirement housing*, Oxford: Oxford Brookes University.

Johnson, K.J. and Mutchler, J.E. (2013) 'The emergence of a positive gerontology: from disengagement to social involvement', *The Gerontologist* 54:1, 93–100.

Kneale, D. (2012) *Is social exclusion still important for older people?* London: ILC-UK.

Kotecha, M., Arthur, S. and Coutinho, S. (2013) *Understanding the relationship between pensioner poverty and material deprivation*, Research Report 827, London: DWP.

Krause, N. (2007) 'Longitudinal study of social support and meaning in life', *Psychology and Aging* 22:3, 456–69.

Lamprianou, I. (2012) 'Contemporary political participation research: a critical assessment', in K.N. Demetriou (ed.) *Democracy in transition: Political participation in the European Union*, Berlin: Springer-Verlag, 21–42.

Legard, R., Gray, M. and Blake, M. (2008) 'Cognitive testing: older people and the FRS material deprivation questions', Working Paper 55, London: DWP.

Levitas, R., Pantazis, C., Fahmy, E., Gordon, D., Lloyd, E. and Patsios, D. (2007) *The multidimensional analysis of social exclusion*, London: Social Exclusion Task Force.

MacInnes, T., Aldridge, H., Bushe, S., Kenway, P. and Tinson, A. (2013) *Monitoring poverty and social exclusion 2013*, York: Joseph Rowntree Foundation.

McGuinness, F. (2015) 'Poverty in the UK: statistics', Briefing paper 7096, 11 September, London: House of Commons.

McKay, S. (2004) 'Poverty or preference: what do "consensual deprivation indicators" really measure?', *Fiscal Studies* 25, 201–23.

McKay, S. (2008) 'Measuring material deprivation among older people: methodological study to revise the Family Resources Survey questions', Working Paper 54, London: DWP.

McKay, S. (2010) 'Using the new Family Resources Survey question block to measure material deprivation among pensioners', Working Paper 89, London: DWP.

McKee, S. (2010) *The forgotten age: Understanding poverty and social exclusion in later life*, Interim Report by the Older Age Working Group, London: Centre for Social Justice.

Nazroo, J. and Matthews, K. (2012) *The impact of volunteering on wellbeing in later life*, Cardiff: WRVS.

Nicholson, N.R. (2012) 'A review of social isolation: an important but underassessed condition in older adults', *Journal of Primary Prevention* 33:2-3, 137–52.

ONS (Office for National Statistics) (2011) *Measuring what matters: National statistician's reflections on the national debate on measuring well-being*, London: ONS.

ONS (2012) *First annual ONS experimental subjective well-being results*, London: ONS.

ONS (2013) 'The labour market and retirement', in *Pension Trends, 2013 Edition*, London: ONS.

Patsios, D. (2006) 'Pensioners, poverty and social exclusion', in D. Gordon, R. Levitas and C. Pantazis (eds) *Poverty and social exclusion in Britain: The Millennium Survey*, Bristol: Policy Press, 431–58.

Patsios, D. (2014) 'Trends in older people's perceptions of necessities and deprivation in Great Britain and Northern Ireland: what difference did a decade (or so) make?', *Journal of Poverty and Social Justice* 22:3, 227–51.

PHE (Public Health England) (2014) *Local action on health inequalities: Fuel poverty and cold home-related health problems*, Health Equity Evidence Review 7, London: PHE.

Pollak, C.E. and Von Dem Knesebeck, O. (2004) 'Social capital and health among the aged: comparisons between the United States and Germany', *Health and Place* 10, 383–91.

POST (Parliamentary Office of Science and Technology) (2011) 'An ageing workforce', POSTNOTE 391, London: POST.

Price, D. (2008) *Measuring the poverty of older people: A critical review*, London: Institute of Gerontology, King's College London.

Princess Royal Trust for Carers, The (2011) *Always on call, always concerned: A survey of the experiences of older carers*, London: The Princess Royal Trust for Carers.

Scharf, T., Phillipson, C. and Smith, A.E. (2005) *Multiple exclusion and quality of life amongst excluded older people in disadvantaged neighbourhoods*, London: Office of the Deputy Prime Minister.

Steptoe, A., Shankar, A., Demakakos, P. and Wardle, J. (2013) 'Social isolation, loneliness, and all-cause mortality in older men and women', *Proceedings of the National Academy of Sciences of the United States of America* 110:15, 5797–801.

Windle, K., Francis, J. and Coomber, C. (2011) 'Preventing loneliness and social isolation: interventions and outcomes', Social Care Institute for Excellence (SCIE) briefing 39, London: SCIE.

Wright, P.H. (1989) 'Gender differences in adults' same- and cross-gender friendships', in R.G. Adams and R. Blieszner (eds) *Older adult friendship: Structure and process*, Newbury Park, CA: Sage, 197–221.

Zaidi, A. (2011) *Exclusion from material resources among older people in EU countries: New evidence on poverty and capability deprivation*, Vienna: European Centre for Social Welfare Policy and Research.

FOUR

Which men and women are poor? Gender, poverty and social exclusion

Esther Dermott and Christina Pantazis

Introduction

In this chapter we make the case for reasserting the importance of gender to poverty and social exclusion. Within mainstream policy and political debates in the UK today, gendered poverty is barely on the agenda. In the face of ongoing concerns about how to reduce childhood poverty, a focus on the role of employment, and measures based on the household which disguise gendered inequalities, gender has taken a much lower profile. However, given the continued relevance of gender to involvement in paid and unpaid work, and caring responsibilities, across the life course, we argue that gender matters for understanding poverty. Gender is also key for considering the extent and nature of social exclusion. Social exclusion in political debates tends to narrowly concentrate on levels of participation in paid employment (Pantazis and Ruspini, 2006). Instead we focus here on social relations in order to highlight how gender makes a difference to this important but neglected aspect of social exclusion.

We also argue that academics and policy makers need to reconfigure gendered poverty as more than simply studying 'poor women'. While on a global scale women remain substantially more disadvantaged than men (Gornick and Boeri, 2016), within the most developed countries, including the UK, it is not uniformly the case that *all* women are worse off (Dermott and Pantazis, 2015a). Therefore, as noted by Bennett and Daly (2014) researching gender should not only mean studying the lives of women; a gendered perspective needs to explore the experiences of different groups of men as well. Moreover, in advancing thinking about the relationship between gender and living standards, we adopt a life course perspective, which focuses on integrating different aspects of individuals' gendered experience of poverty, and avoids the problem of simply 'adding gender on' to other significant variables. Our analysis therefore explores the circumstances of both women *and* men, and how gender intersects in significant ways with age and household type. This is consistent with evidence highlighting that age and household living arrangements do make a substantial difference to levels of poverty (Bennett and Daly, 2014).

Gender, poverty and social exclusion: what we know

Academic, political and policy discussions of gendered poverty in the UK over the last thirty plus years has taken inspiration from the 'feminisation of poverty' thesis (Goldberg, 2010). In drawing attention to the 'female face' of poverty, interest has largely been on the disadvantaged situation of older solo-living women and lone mothers.

In the Poverty and Social Exclusion Survey 1999 (PSE-GB 1999) (Pantazis et al, 2006), the greatest gender poverty gap was between men and women aged over 65. Older women's situation has substantially improved since then, to the extent that this group no longer stands out as having high levels of poverty (Dermott and Pantazis, 2014; see also Patsios, chapter three, this volume). Policy changes first initiated under New Labour and subsequently continued by Conservative-led governments have prioritised reducing pensioner poverty. These changes have notably reduced the impact of significant periods of caring on women's state pensions (Ginn and MacIntyre, 2013). The growth in the extent of women's involvement in the labour market, with greater numbers working longer hours and throughout the life course, is also likely to have contributed to their improved financial circumstances in later life. However, despite the policy changes noted above, a 'masculine' model of full-time employment over 40 years is still required to build up substantial private pension contributions (Ginn and MacIntyre, 2013). Changes to household composition, with couples surviving longer into old age and increased rates of re-partnership, mean that fewer older women are living alone (ONS, 2013); and this is associated with greater financial prosperity.

While the employment situation of lone mothers has changed markedly in response to policy measures (Whitworth, 2013) their experience of poverty has not: 'not having a second earner [in the household] is increasingly associated with a high risk of poverty' (Harkness, 2013, p 2; see also Dermott and Pomati, chapter seven, in this volume). Lone mothers continue to have the highest levels of poverty with two thirds being deprived and income poor in 2012; a very similar figure to that found in the PSE-GB 1999 survey (Dermott and Pantazis, 2014). The presence of children increases household poverty rates (Main and Bradshaw, chapter six, in this volume) but this is severely exacerbated when there is only one adult present (Misra et al, 2012) and the impact seems to be greater for women (although small numbers of lone fathers make reliable comparisons difficult) (Dermott and Pantazis, 2014).

Feminist analyses of poverty in the UK have recognised the importance of multidimensional disadvantage and that income-focused measures may be especially limited in capturing the experiences of women (Millar, 2003). Millar suggested that engaging with the concept of social exclusion would allow relational aspects of disadvantage to be considered. Yet, when social exclusion is discussed the focus is largely on inclusion or exclusion from paid work (Levitas, 2005; Bailey, 2016). Relational issues include social participation, social integration and lack of power, thereby drawing attention to the link between paid and unpaid work and the effect of this on living standards. Moreover, social exclusion can capture dynamic processes (Room, 1999), with critical life events, such as unemployment or divorce, playing an important role for social inclusion and exclusion (Levitas et al, 2007). In addition, critical life events and their impact are in themselves gendered, for example, work and health problems have a greater impact in men's lives (Pantazis and Ruspini, 2006).

Intra-household poverty

Both traditionally and contemporaneously poverty studies tend to rely on the household as the unit of analysis and focus on comparing poverty rates between different types of household. This requires researchers to make a series of assumptions about resources and living standards; namely, that resources coming into the household are pooled so that everyone has an equal standard of living. The focus on comparisons between households has meant that more complicated arrangements which arise within couple households have been largely ignored. In highlighting the potential gendered implications of this assumption, feminist researchers have referred to the household as a 'black box' which needs to be opened up. However, to date, few quantitative studies have been designed to explore intra-household inequalities (Daly et al, 2012; Bennett, 2013). The limited research which does exist has found some evidence of gendered inequalities in relation to deprivation, economising and money management. Studies in Ireland (Cantillon and Nolan, 1998, 2011) found differences between couples regarding the consumption of household items, individual items and social activities. Women were less likely to have access to heating, cars, food, personal spending money and leisure activities. Studies have also found evidence of 'parental sacrifice', that is, the willingness of parents, especially mothers, to sacrifice their own needs in favour of their children. The classic study by Middleton et al (1997) has been reconfirmed by more recent work on black and minority ethnic (BME) families (Warburton Brown, 2011) and analysis of the Poverty and Social Exclusion Survey 2012 (PSE-UK 2012) undertaken by Main and Bradshaw (2016) and Dermott and Pomati (2016, in relation to lone parents). Recent work on poverty across the European Union found that using the standard household-based measure of income poverty underestimates gender inequalities that exist *within* households (Corsi et al, 2016).

Economic and political context

The gendered impacts of the recession of 2008–9 and subsequent austerity programme which has been pursued since 2010 have been noted (for example, Harkness, 2013). The economic consequences of the downturn in terms of patterns of employment suggest that women may be less affected than men. Initially more men lost their jobs as the first areas to be affected were male-dominated cyclically sensitive industries such as manufacturing and construction: between 2008 and 2010, 90% of the fall in employment was experienced by men – leading to the identification of a British 'mancession' (McKay et al, 2013). Data since the height of the recession show that men were, and still are, slightly more likely to be classed as officially unemployed than women (ONS, 2017). Research has also suggested that women's greater ability to maintain employment throughout the recession and post-recessionary period, along with the previous and ongoing reduction in the gender pay gap, has meant that women's earnings are of greater significance to household incomes than in past downturns (Harkness, 2013). The political response to the recession, involving a broad and deep programme of cuts, is likely to continue to impact on women disproportionately. Analysis by the House of Commons Library shows that the vast majority (86%) of current and planned budgetary savings between 2010 and 2020 will fall on women (Women's Budget Group, 2016). Moreover, female-headed households will see the greatest reduction in living standards, taking into account women's reliance on public services and tax and benefit changes introduced since 2010 (Women's Budget Group, 2016).

Methods

The main poverty measure used for our analysis is PSE poverty and is based on a combination of deprivation and low income. Following the consensual approach, respondents were classified as poor if (due to a lack of money) they were deprived of three or more items or activities categorised by the majority of the population as necessities, and had a low income (Gordon, chapter one, this volume). As a household-level measure, it can distinguish poverty rates between male- and female-headed households, and can therefore identify particular groups of interest such as lone mothers, although it is important to acknowledge its limitations for capturing the extent of different levels of poverty within couple households (see Dermott and Pantazis, 2015b). Alongside this objective measure of poverty we also include other objective and subjective assessments of poverty: income poverty measured as 60% below national median income after housing costs; lacking three or more necessities; self-perception of current and past poverty; and self-assessment of living standards (see Table 4.2 for results).

In assessing economising behaviours we rely on a set of eight questions asked on cutting back in order to keep living costs down in the last 12 months, with overall economising defined as cutting back on four or more items.[1] The inclusion of questions around practices as a response to constrained circumstances is important as previous studies have shown that this is an additional dimension of gender inequality within households (Scullion and Hillyard, 2005). In capturing the extent and quality of social relations we use questions which asked individuals about the frequency of their contact with families and friends and perceived access to social support in a range of circumstances. We are therefore able to provide an assessment of both the extent of men's and women's social networks, and the degree to which individuals can rely on them.

The PSE-UK 2012 survey takes into account important conceptual developments for understanding the relationship between gender and poverty that have occurred since the PSE-GB 1999 survey. Notably, it addresses the key limitation of the household as the unit of analysis which underplays or fails to capture the extent of distribution of resources within households, and assumes that households are entirely independent from each other (Daly et al, 2012; Daly and Kelly, 2015; Dermott, 2016). All adult household members completed individual questions, as opposed to adopting the practice of the majority of poverty studies in which one individual responds on behalf of the entire household. This means that for this chapter we can examine the circumstances of individual men and women. Some analysis also specifically discusses men and women who are living as couples in the same household.[2] The questionnaire included a self-completion section for a range of questions deemed sensitive (including those on economising behaviour) so that other household members could not see the responses. The large sample of 9,010 adults allowed for a more robust subgroup analysis than is often feasible (Table 4.1). This is especially relevant for a meaningful analysis of living standards, given what is already known about the significance of age and household living arrangements in revealing gender differences (Bennett and Daly, 2014; Dermott and Pantazis, 2014).

Gender and poverty

Across all six measures of current and historic poverty, women were marginally poorer than men but these differences were not statistically significant (Table 4.2). This pattern was repeated among those living at the margins of poverty; slightly higher percentages of women were in both the 'rising' category of people who were deprived of necessities but did not have low incomes and the 'vulnerable' group who had low incomes but who were not deprived (see Gordon, this volume for details).

Rowntree's (1901) observations from his classic study noted that poverty varied over the life course, with the periods of bringing

Table 4.1: Distribution of respondents by age and household type

	Men (%)	Women (%)
Age (grouped)		
16–24	7.9	7.1
25–34	11.6	13.9
35–44	17.5	17.6
45–54	19.1	18.4
55–64	17.5	17.4
65–74	16.4	14.6
75+	10.1	10.9
Total	100 (N = 4,114)	100 (N = 4,896)
Household type		
Single adults	15.3	20.0
2+ adults	51.1	42.7
Adult(s) and children	33.6	37.4
Total	100 (N = 4,114)	100 (N = 4,896)

Table 4.2: Percentages of men and women experiencing poverty

Measures of poverty	Male % (no.)	Female % (no.)
PSE poverty (deprived and low income)	20.0 (870)	22.2 (1,034)
Income poverty (<60% median household income after household costs)	23.2 (1,011)	23.6 (1,103)
Lacking three or more necessities	25.7 (1,122)	29.6 (1,381)
Self-perception of current poverty ('all the time' or 'sometimes')	33.0 (1,282)	35.7 (1,577)
Self-perception of past poverty ('often' or 'most of the time')	8.8 (345)	11.4 (502)
Self-rated standard of living ('below' or 'well below' average)	12.3 (480)	13.0 (574)

up children and post-employment old age most associated with deprivation, in between periods of relative affluence. Our analysis points to the importance of taking gender into account alongside life course transitions. There were more poor women than men in every age category, with the exception of the very youngest (16–24) and the very oldest (75+) groups (Figure 4.1). The largest discrepancies were among those aged 25–34 years: 32% of women were categorised as poor compared to 25% of men. We interpret this as evidence of the difference in overall employment rates between men and women of working age due to time out of the labour market to care for children and, to a lesser extent, the impact of the gendered wage gap which

Figure 4.1: Percentage of poor men and women (PSE poverty) by age

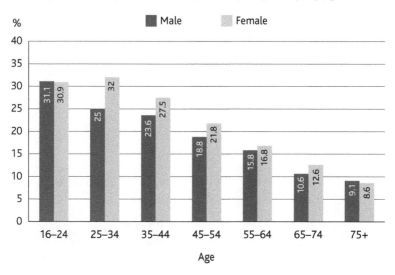

has most effect when women return to employment after periods of maternity leave and childcare (ONS, 2016). More equal labour market participation rates for young adults and the 'feminisation' of higher education are likely to be responsible for equalising the position of men and women in this age group. For the oldest age groups, the improved position of female pensioners, as discussed earlier, has closed the gap between men and women. Looking at household type reinforces the importance of child rearing for adults' experience of poverty, and that the presence of children has a greater impact on women's experience (Figure 4.2). The poverty risk was highest among women living either alone with their children or as part of a couple with children. Lone mothers had a poverty rate which was double that of lone fathers (64.0% compared to 30.6%),[3] while women living in two-adult households with children were 4% more likely to experience poverty than men. Meanwhile, among single people, men were more likely to be poor than women.

Our analysis of the relationship between poor status and certain critical life events also highlights the significance of children for women's living standards. Women living in poverty were 2.5 times as likely to have had a child in the last year compared to those who were not; there was a smaller gap between poor and non-poor men's likelihood of having a child in the last year (1.5 times). Gendered differences also emerged in relation to losing/leaving a job in the last year; but this affected men much more than women. Poor men were 2.3 times more likely than non-poor men to mention they had lost or

Figure 4.2: Percentage of poor men and women (PSE poverty) by household type

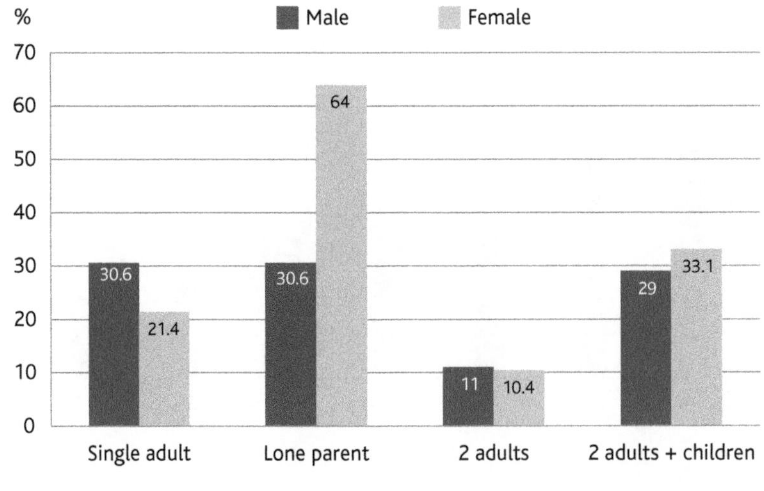

102

left their job in the last year; poor women were 1.7 times as likely to mention this event. This illustrates how the ongoing gendered division of labour potentially has broad implications for the living standards of men and women.

Deprivation

In relation to individual items and activities viewed as necessities, statistically significant differences were found between men and women on nine out of the nineteen listed, although most of the gaps were small in percentage terms (Table 4.3). Of the nine, women were more likely to report deprivation due to affordability on six items; the largest differences were in relation to personal finance items and social activities. It should be noted that it is not the case that this is due to different views over what counts as necessities since there was close consensus between men and women across the items and activities (Dermott and Pantazis, 2015).

It is plausible to make the association between women's access to lower levels of *individual* income and their reduced financial security and consumption. In planning their immediate and longer term finances, women are less likely report being able to make small regular savings and private pension contributions. Women are also much less likely than men to report being able to spend money on themselves to engage in leisure and sport.

When we look at differences in types of deprivation between men and women *living together* in couple households the data initially suggests that there is a pooling of resources, with individuals reporting

Table 4.3: Percentages of men and women lacking items and activities because 'cannot afford' (only necessities with significant differences)

Item/activity	Male (%)	Female (%)	Difference + women higher − men higher
Replace or repair broken electrics	24.5	27.3	+2.8
Two pairs of all-weather shoes	8.1	6.5	−1.6
Regular savings (£20 a month)	28.5	33.2	+4.7
Meat, fish or vegetarian equivalent every other day	4.8	3.5	−1.3
Fresh fruit and vegetables every day	6.8	5.4	−1.4
Appropriate clothes for job interviews	6.8	8.5	+1.7
Regular pension payments	25.1	27.9	+2.8
A hobby or leisure activity	6.5	9.2	+2.7
Taking part in sport/exercise or classes	8.8	11.8	+3.0

similar levels of going without. However, significant gender differences do emerge when children are present. The discrepancy between men and women's levels of deprivation is particularly marked in relation to personal spending money (a 6% gap) and across all social activities (women are more likely to say that they lack them due to affordability with the largest gap – 6% – in relation to going to the cinema, theatre or music events). We speculate that the gender gap in personal spending and social activities found in the PSE-UK 2012 survey reflects how access to individual income plays a significant part in expenditure decisions for *non-essential* items and activities: women are less likely to use shared financial resources in these ways.[4] This highlights that the resources of households *and* individuals need to be taken in account to get a fuller picture of deprivation and poverty (Bennett and Daly, 2014; Corsi et al, 2016). Evidence has shown that for husbands and wives, women's independent income is important for reducing inequalities in living standards (Cantillon, 2013).

Economising behaviours

When faced with constrained financial circumstances a common strategy is to cut back on spending (see Pemberton et al, 2013). Previous research has indicated that women are more likely to economise than men (Scullion and Hillyard, 2005) because of the tendency for women to have responsibility for managing budgets in poorer households (Goode et al, 1998). We anticipated that the PSE-UK 2012 survey questions on economising practices on eight items and activities over the last 12 months would reproduce this finding. Using an 'economising threshold' of four or more, women were significantly more likely to say they had cut back; 49.1% of women compared to 39.3% of men had done so. However, the patterns of gender difference were not the same across all households. In poor households, substantial gender gaps emerged in relation to skimping on food, buying second-hand clothes and cutting back on haircuts (Figure 4.3). Counter to expectations from previous research, gender differences were most marked among those who were *not* classified as poor. Economising practices are pervasive among all members of poor households. Among non-poor households there are also relatively high levels of economising, perhaps as a consequence of austerity and the financial downturn. More than one in ten respondents had economised on each of the measures, with over half cutting back on social visits. The new finding from this research is that in non-poor households the gender gap in economising behaviour is three times greater than

Figure 4.3: Gender gap in economising behaviours in poor and non-poor households

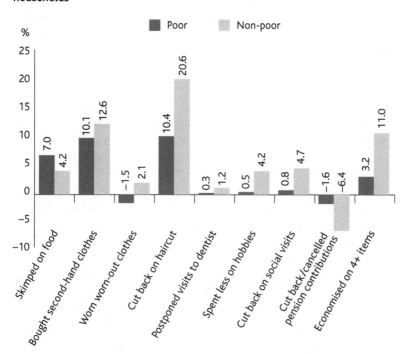

in poor households (11% versus 3.2%). Thirty-nine per cent of non-poor women economised in relation to four or more items in the previous year in contrast to 28% men. So while in poor households both men and women cut back, in non-poor households women take the responsibility for economising. This may be a pre-emptive measure to maintain living standards over the longer term, suggesting that women have a greater role in everyday financial planning and cost cutting. Methodologically, this finding also underscores the importance of looking at expenditure and consumption patterns across the population as a whole, as gendered differences do not only emerge within poor households.

Reviewing existing evidence about gender differences across household types, indicates that it is mothers more than fathers who cut back in order to protect the living standards of their children (Middleton et al, 1997). This would lead us to expect that in households with two adults and children women economise more than men, and indeed 64.7% of women in this group did cut back in the last year across four or more items compared to 55.7% of men. Single-adult households provide an interesting contrast in that men were more likely to have cut back; 41.8% of men said they had economised on four or more items compared to 37.4% of women. This can partly be explained by our earlier finding that men in single-adult households are more likely to be poor than women in similar circumstances. However, we have identified that non-poor women in the PSE-UK 2012 are highly likely to engage in economising practices. The difference between these single-person household women and their peers with other living arrangements is that they have an independent income and are not sharing household resources. In other words, this result further supports the argument that non-poor women engage in economising in order to support or improve the living standards of people with whom they live.

To further explore whether gender differences are maintained for men and women living as a couple within the same household, we examine whether they adopt economising behaviours together. It is important to note that living in a couple does, as we know from previous work (Himmelweit et al, 2013), provide some degree of protection from lower living standards: the overall level of economising for men and women in couples is 5–7% less than for men and women in the general population. However, almost a quarter of couples (23.9%) are *not* adopting the same economising behaviour and this is because women are more likely than men to cut back on any item or activity; 42.9% compared to 34.7%. Twice as many women as men are also cutting back according to the broader measure of four or more items or activities (15.3% versus 8.6%).

These women could be cutting back to support the living standards of their partner or to protect their children's well-being. In order to assess whether gendered economising within couples reflects responses to economic hardship and/or the presence of dependent children, we examined the relationship across different households; poor and non-poor, and households with children and those without. There is a gender gap in couple households both with and without children, although the difference is larger when children are present. In households with no children 13.5% of women and 8.0% of men say that they have economised in the last year on four or more items or activities, while in households with children the figures are 18.0% for women and 9.5% for men. This reflects two processes. First, the financial demands of children means that household resources are stretched so that men and women are more likely to have to cut back. Second, the discrepancy between men and women in the same households is illustrative of women's greater responsibility for children, which extends beyond meeting day-to-day needs to planning for the future (Smeby, 2016).

Whether couples are living in poor or non-poor couple households affects the gender economising gap. In poor households there is minimal gender difference (10.9% of women said they economised compared to 9.2% of men). This is perhaps unsurprising since, as for the general population, those already living in poverty have limited choices in spending decisions and this applies to both women and men. The gender gap here is even smaller than for poor households as a whole which suggests that poor couples equally engage in cutting back as a response to low incomes. It is possible, in the context of recession and austerity, we are seeing a new loss of the protection previously afforded to men by their female partners since all adults in poor households are cutting back. In non-poor households, where we might anticipate greater discretion around spending, we find that almost twice as many women as men say that they have cut back recently (16.3% versus 8.4%). In households where there is a degree of choice over how resources are used, it seems that women take on the role of reducing their personal consumption, perhaps as a precaution against future adversity. Again, this is strong confirmation of the value in looking at the internal dynamics of household behaviours rather than assuming couples always act as a single unit with respect to consumption and expenditure practices.

Social relationships and support

Sociological work on families has long suggested that women take primary responsibility for maintaining relationships with family members outside of their immediate household (for example, Doucet, 1993; Mitchell and Green, 2002). In line with this, the frequency of contact with relatives within the PSE-UK 2012 survey is strongly differentiated by gender. While 22.5% of men spoke to a relative every day, this figure rose to 39.4% among women. At the other end of the spectrum 25.2% of men compared to 14.3% of women had contact with family members less than once a week. The pattern of women's higher levels of daily contact with family members is maintained across all age groups and household types. Women's level of daily contact with family members is consistent whatever their age, whereas for men this drops off markedly in middle age (35–54) and is in any case lower in every age group. Similarly, irrespective of their household living arrangements, women have higher levels of family contact than men. Gender differences are most marked though when children are present.

The gendered pattern of contact with friends is less distinct. A slightly higher percentage of women say they speak to friends on a daily basis, although the difference was not large enough to be of statistical significance. The only really notable gendered difference in relation to daily contact with friends is among 16–24-year-olds: in this group men were much more likely to have said that they had frequent contact (69.3%) than women (49.9%). This may be a genuine disparity but could also reflect different definitions of friendship in which men use a more generous interpretation of who counts as a friend. This would be consistent with other research suggesting that gender does have an influence on the perception of friendship networks (Spencer and Pahl, 2006).

The reasons that men and women gave for *not* meeting up with friends and family reflect the relative involvement of men and women in paid and unpaid work. While men were more likely to report that paid work prevented them seeing friends and family (20.9% compared to 17% of women), women were more likely to cite childcare and caring responsibilities (11.4% of women mentioned childcare responsibilities compared to 8.1% of men, and 4.3% of women mentioned caring responsibilities compared to 2.5% of men). Linking this up with the earlier discussion on the frequency of women's contact with family members, we suggest that the degree of social inclusion women experience through regular social interaction also involves obligations that, in turn, restrict personal relationships beyond immediate family members. Meanwhile, men cite paid work as the most important factor in limiting their involvement with friends and family; this may be most acute for middle-aged men who are working the longest hours and who tend to report lower levels of contact with family outside of their household.

Levels of contact are related to the practical and emotional support people can access; those reporting more frequent contact also said they felt they had more practical and emotional support. Exploring the extent to which individuals can draw on social networks in times of need therefore gives some sense of the quality of their personal relationships and potential gender differences in this regard. Respondents in the PSE-UK 2012 survey were asked a hypothetical set of questions about how much support they would get from people they live with, family and friends, or other support in a range of circumstances. Forms of practical support were: help at home if you were ill in bed; practical help around the home such as moving heavy furniture or DIY; someone to look after your possessions or home when you were away; a lift somewhere in an emergency. Emotional support consisted of: needing advice about an important change in your life; if you were upset because of relationship problems or feeling a bit depressed; you had a serious personal crisis and needed someone to turn to.

In terms of practical support, the composite measure produced no significant difference between men and women (Table 4.4). There was however a significant difference with respect to emotional support; 19.7% of men had low emotional support compared to 15.6% of women. This pattern of men saying that they have less access to emotional support than women was largely consistent across age categories. In contrast to the PSE-GB 1999 survey results (Levitas et al, 2006), household type did not make a difference to women's ability to access emotional support, that is, women living in single-person households did not suffer from a lack of emotional support. This finding is in line with in-depth studies on solo living which have critiqued the idea that living alone can be equated to a lack of social engagement and networks (Jamieson and Simpson, 2013). The situation of men is markedly different; a third of men living alone said that they did not have someone they could talk to about significant life events and choices. This suggests that men are more reliant on the support they receive from their co-resident partners; Jamieson and Simpson (2010) similarly found that socially isolated solo livers were more likely to be men.

Table 4.4: Percentage of men and women lacking practical or emotional support by household type

	Male % (no.)	Female % (no.)
One or more response 'not much'/'none at all' for practical support		
Single adults	37.6 (270)	30.8 (257)
2 adults	16.0 (244)	15.4 (227)
2 adults + child(ren)	21.5 (195)	28.4 (268)
One or more response 'not much'/'none at all' for emotional support		
Single adults	34.9 (250)	19.7 (165)
2 adults	13.3 (197)	10.7 (135)
2 adults + child(ren)	20.3 (184)	19.3 (183)

Conclusion

The empirical analysis and discussion in this chapter contributes to developing a more fully explored and substantiated understanding of the ways in which gender interacts with other significant social characteristics.

Our analysis has significant implications for the study of gendered living standards. First, that poverty studies need to look at intersections over the life course and take into account critical life events, rather than restrict their focus only to those groups that have traditionally been the subject of attention. Using age and household type, this chapter has illustrated the way in which gendered differences play out across the life course and depend on living arrangements.

Second, our analysis shows that that limiting research to concentrate on poor households underplays the significance of the role that gender plays in determining individual and household living standards. The results of the PSE survey indicate that viewing gendered inequalities as a problem only for poor households is mistaken. In fact, poor men and women engage in economising behaviours in largely equal measure (although we should be aware that the measure of economising used in the PSE-UK 2012 focuses on the extent but not the depth or duration of cutting back). Gender inequality affects the non-poor to a greater degree, with more women taking the lead in economising. Our findings therefore draw attention to gendered practices in non-poor households, albeit at a moment in time when many in the UK are feeling financially insecure. Our work highlights the necessity of looking at poverty, deprivation and economising across the whole population in order to get a better picture of living standards, rather than only looking at those who are most deprived.

Finally, this research points to the need to reflect on and update measures of gendered poverty and inequality. Building on the PSE-UK 2012 methodological advancements with respect to capturing intra-household inequalities, we have illustrated the need for poverty researchers to incorporate both household and individual measures in their analysis. Moreover, our work has indicated women's responsibility for thinking ahead and planning for the future as a major element in protecting living standards for household members, thus there is a requirement for research to develop measures that are sensitive to various elements of gender inequality.

Notes

[1]   See PSE questionnaire at poverty.ac.uk. Further information is listed in the Technical Appendix.

[2]   Further analysis of men and women living as couples within a joint household is forthcoming.

[3]   Although the numbers of lone fathers in the survey are small.

[4] See Patsios and Nandy (2013) for PSE items and activities perceived as necessities or desirable.

References

Bailey, N. (2016) 'Exclusionary employment in Britain's broken labour market', *Critical Social Policy* 36:1, 82–103.

Bennett, F. (2013) 'Researching within-household distribution: overview, developments, debates and methodological challenges', *Journal of Marriage and Family* 75:3, 593–610.

Bennett, F. and Daly, M. (2014) *Poverty through a gender lens: Evidence and policy review on gender and poverty*, York: Joseph Rowntree Foundation.

Cantillon, S. (2013) 'Measuring differences in living standards within households', *Journal of Marriage and Family* 75:3, 598–610.

Cantillon, S. and Nolan, B. (1998) 'Are married women more deprived than their husbands?', *Journal of Social Policy* 27:2, 151–71.

Cantillon, S. and Nolan, B. (2011) 'Poverty within households: measuring gender differences using nonmonetary indicators', *Feminist Economics* 7:1, 5–23.

Corsi, M., Botti, F. and D'Ippoliti, C. (2016) 'The gendered nature of poverty in the EU: individualized versus collective poverty measures', *Feminist Economics* 22:4, 82–100.

Daly, M. and Kelly, G. (2015) *Families and poverty: Everyday life on a low income*, Bristol: Policy Press.

Daly, M., Kelly, M., Dermott, E. and Pantazis, C. (2012) 'Intrahousehold poverty', PSE Conceptual Note 5, www.poverty.ac.uk/pse-research/pse-uk/conceptual-notes

Dermott, E. (2016) 'Non-resident fathers in the UK: living standards and social support', *Journal of Poverty and Social Justice* 24:2, 113–25.

Dermott, E. and Pantazis, C. (2014) 'Gender and poverty in Britain: changes and continuities between 1999 and 2012', *Poverty and Social Justice* 22:3, 253–69.

Dermott, E. and Pantazis, C. (2015a) 'Gender, poverty and social exclusion: final report of the 2012 PSE study', PSE Working Paper, December, University of Bristol.

Dermott, E. and Pantazis, C. (2015b) 'Money management, deprivation and economising within UK households', SPA Symposium on Women, Work and Welfare Reform: Changing Faces of Inequality in an Era of Austerity, Social Policy Association Conference, Belfast.

Dermott, E. and Pomati, M. (2016) 'The parenting and economising practices of lone parents: policy and evidence', *Critical Social Policy* 36:1, 62–81.

Doucet, A. (1993) 'Who remembers birthdays? Who cleans the loo? Issues of methods and methodology in data collection on gender and household labour', Research Paper 13, Essex: Institute for Economic Research.

Ginn, J. and MacIntyre, K. (2013) 'UK pension reforms: is gender still an issue?', *Social Policy & Society* 13:1, 91–103.

Goldberg, G.S. (ed.) (2010) *Poor women in rich countries: The feminization of poverty over the life course*, New York: Oxford University Press.

Goode, J., Callender, C. and Lister, R. (1998) *Purse or wallet? Gender inequalities and income distribution within families on benefits*, London: Policy Studies Institute.

Gornick, N. and Boeri, N. (2016) 'Gender and poverty', in D. Bray and L.M. Burton (eds) *The Oxford Handbook of the Social Science of Poverty*, Oxford: Oxford University Press.

Harkness, S. (2013) 'Women, families and the "great recession" in the UK', in *Social Policy Review 25*, Bristol: Policy Press.

Himmelweit, S., Santos, S., Sevilla, A. and Sofer, C. (2013) 'Sharing of resources within the family and the economics of household decision making', *Journal of Marriage and Family* 75:3, 625–39.

Jamieson, L. and Simpson, R. (2010) 'Living on your own: social integration, quality of life and aspirations for the future', Centre for Research on Families and Relationships Briefing 47 (Jan.). Edinburgh: CRFR.

Jamieson, L. and Simpson, R. (2013) *Living alone: Globalization, identity and belonging*, Basingstoke: Palgrave Macmillan.

Levitas, R. (2005) *The inclusive society? Social exclusion and New Labour*, Basingstoke: Palgrave Macmillan.

Levitas, R., Head, E. and Finch, N. (2006) 'Lone mothers, poverty and social exclusion', in C. Pantazis, D. Gordon and R. Levitas (eds) *Poverty and social exclusion in Britain: The Millennium Survey*, Bristol: Policy Press.

Levitas, R., Pantazis, C., Fahmy, E., Gordon, D., Lloyd, E. and Patsios, D. (2007) *The multi-dimensional analysis of social exclusion*, London: Department for Communities and Local Government.

McKay, A., Campbell, J., Thomson, E. and Ross, S. (2013) 'Economic recession and recovery in the UK: what's gender got to do with it', *Feminist Economics* 19:3, 108–23.

Middleton, S., Ashworth, K. and Braithwaite, I. (1997) *Small fortunes: Spending on children, childhood poverty and parental sacrifice*, York: Joseph Rowntree Foundation.

Millar, J. (2003) 'Gender, poverty and social exclusion', *Social Policy and Society* 2:3, 181–8.

Misra, J., Moller, S., Strader, E. and Wemlinger, E. (2012) 'Family policies, employment and poverty among partnered and single mothers', *Research in Social Stratification and Mobility* 30:1, 113–28.

Mitchell, W. and Green, E. (2002) '"I don't know what I'd do without our Mam": motherhood, identity and support networks', *Sociological Review* 50:1, 1–22.

ONS (Office for National Statistics) (2013) 'What does the 2011 census tell us about older people?', www.ons.gov.uk/ons/dcp171776_325486.pdf

ONS (2016) 'The gender pay gap: what is it and what affects it?', http://visual.ons.gov.uk/the-gender-pay-gap-what-is-it-and-what-affects-it/

ONS (2017) 'Unemployment', www.ons.gov.uk/employment andlabourmarket/peoplenotinwork/unemployment

Pantazis, C. and Ruspini, E. (2006) 'Gender, poverty and social exclusion', in Pantazis, C., Gordon, D. and Levitas, R. (eds) *Poverty and social exclusion in Britain*, Bristol: Policy Press.

Pantazis, C., Gordon, D. and Levitas, R. (eds) (2006) *Poverty and social exclusion in Britain*, Bristol: Policy Press.

Patsios, D. and Nandy, S. (2013) 'Attitudes to necessities 2012: Great Britain versus Northern Ireland in the UK Omnibus data set', PSE Statistical Briefing Note 4, http://poverty.ac.uk/pse-research/pse-uk/statistical-notes

Pemberton, S., Sutton, E. and Fahmy, E. (2013) 'A review of the qualitative evidence relating to the experience of poverty and exclusion', PSE Working Paper Methods Series 22, University of Bristol.

Room, G. (1999) 'Social exclusion, solidarity and the challenge of globalisation', *International Journal of Social Welfare* 8:3, 166–74.

Rowntree, B.S. (1901) *Poverty: A study of town life*, London: Macmillan.

Scullion, F. and Hillyard, P. (2005) 'Gender and poverty in Northern Ireland', *Northern Ireland Statistics and Research Agency Bulletin* 6, www.poverty.ac.uk/sites/default/files/PSENI%20bulletin_6_0.pdf

Simpson, R. (2006) 'The intimate relationships of contemporary spinsters', *Sociological Research Online*, 11:3, www.socresonline.org.uk/11/3/simpson.html

Smeby, K.W. (2016) 'When work meets childcare: competing logics of motherhood and gender equality', European Sociological Association RN13 Interim Meeting, 6–8 July, Bristol.

Spencer, L. and Pahl, R. (2006) *Rethinking friendship: Hidden solidarities today*, Princeton, NJ: Princeton University Press.

Warburton Brown, C. (2011) *Exploring BME maternal poverty: The financial lives of 30 ethnic minority mothers in Tyne and Wear*, Oxford: Oxfam UK.

Whitworth, A. (2013) 'Lone parents and welfare-to-work in England: a spatial analysis of outcomes and drivers', *Social Policy and Administration* 47:7, 826–45.

Women's Budget Group (2016) *The impact on women of the 2016 budget*, http://wbg.org.uk/wp-content/uploads/2016/03/WBG_2016Budget_FINAL_Apr16.pdf

FIVE

Better understandings of ethnic variations: ethnicity, poverty and social exclusion

Saffron Karlsen and Christina Pantazis

Introduction

A review of the evidence from 350 studies carried out in the UK between 1991 and 2006 revealed that minority ethnic groups are more likely to be living in poverty, regardless of the measure of poverty or deprivation used, with the highest rates among Bangladeshi, Pakistani and Black African groups (Platt, 2007). On most measures, the poverty experienced by Bangladeshi people was found to be more severe and longer lasting than that for any other group examined. But this picture of ethnic disadvantage varies according to the measure used. For example, Pakistanis have been found to be severely disadvantaged on many, but not all, measures. Similarly, around two fifths of Black Caribbean (and Bangladeshi) people – traditionally not among those ethnic groups considered in research as particularly disadvantaged – said that they were either worried about money 'all the time' or did not manage 'very well' on their incomes, compared with just under a third of Pakistani people and a fifth of people in white and Indian groups (Berthoud, 1997). Black Caribbean people also experienced more debt and debt-related anxiety than might be expected from their income level.

According to the 2011 England and Wales Census, over a third of Bangladeshi and Pakistani people lived in a deprived area, but there were some subtle differences in aspects of that disadvantage (Jivraj and Khan, 2015). Almost half of Bangladeshis lived in areas with a high concentration of low incomes and a third lived in areas experiencing barriers to housing and other services. Meanwhile, those in Pakistani groups were most likely to live in areas with a poor environment, poor education and high unemployment. Black African people, by contrast, were most likely to live in areas affected by high levels of crime (Jivraj and Khan, 2015).

There are also ethnic groups which have traditionally been ignored in poverty studies but have since been identified as experiencing significant disadvantage. For example, the addition of further minority ethnic categories in 2011 England and Wales Census revealed that while those of white ethnicities were in a more advantaged position generally in the labour market than those of other ethnicities, there were considerable differences between white British, white Irish, and white Gypsies and Irish Travellers in this group (Kapadia et al, 2015).

There is also a concern regarding the value of standard measures of socio-economic status for examining ethnic variations in socio-economic position (Kaufmann et al, 1997, 1998; Nazroo, 2001). These typically relate to the more limited applicability of measures of socio-economic status designed with reference to a white majority experience to the lives of those with very different experiences and circumstances. For example, the use of educational qualifications or occupational class as markers for particular socio-economic positions are less useful where processes of social exclusion affect the extent to which educational qualifications map onto labour market success, and also where higher occupational class does not always result in relative improvements in income.

Ethnic minority groups have been found to be significantly disadvantaged compared with others in the same socio-economic categories, commanding lower wages for similar work and compared with those with comparable levels of qualification (Longhi and Platt, 2008). Strikingly, the incomes of Pakistani and Bangladeshi people with occupations classified in the highest groups (I and II) of the Registrar General's Classification of Occupations (the 'go to' measure of socio-economic status until the introduction of the National Statistics Socio-Economic Classification [NSSEC] in the mid-1990s) have been found to be *less* than those of white people in occupations classified in the lowest (IV and V) (Nazroo, 2001). Further, the 2011 England and Wales Census indicated that while people with ethnic minority backgrounds were more likely to live in deprived areas than the white British majority (Jivraj and Khan, 2015), they were also more likely to experience deprivation than white British people living in similar areas. Adjusting only for qualification, occupational class or area deprivation therefore cannot fully account for these socio-economic differences between groups.

Similarly, traditional markers of housing tenure assume that owner occupation indicates a position of financial security and affluence.

But research has identified a relative lack of amenities available in, and generally poorer quality of, accommodation inhabited by owner occupiers with ethnic minority backgrounds compared with that of those in the ethnic majority (Berthoud, 1997; Lakey, 1997). This may be explained by evidence regarding ethnic variations in routes into owner occupation: which, for people with ethnic minority backgrounds has been argued to be a consequence of discrimination which limits their access to the public and private rental sector (Beider and Netto, 2012), rather than a more positive choice. Reflecting on the assumptions underpinning standard markers of social position and employing more nuanced measures in our analyses therefore has the potential to reveal the extent of ethnic variations in socio-economic status much more effectively.

This chapter updates this evidence regarding ethnic inequalities in socio-economic position using the Poverty and Social Exclusion Survey 2012 (PSE-UK 2012); the most recent and comprehensive study of living standards in the UK to date. The PSE-UK 2012 survey offers a unique opportunity to examine in depth ethnic inequalities in poverty and social exclusion using a range of objective and subjective measures covering multiple domains, including employment, housing and living environment. It allows us to also scrutinise the experiences of people living on the margins of poverty and the coping strategies used to avoid falling into poverty. The analysis presented here provides a detailed assessment of the socio-economic position of non-white groups, as well as white minority groups which have thus far received little academic attention. We are able to explore some of the more complex and subtle variations missed by broader proxies to provide a more accurate assessment of the levels of poverty and social exclusion experienced by people with different ethnic backgrounds and the variations between them.

Methods

The PSE-UK 2012 survey sample consists of respondents who participated in the 2010/11 Family Resources Survey (FRS) and gave permission to be re-contacted for further research. The inclusion of a representative sample of people with a range of ethnic backgrounds in the FRS made it possible to select a sample which could be used to compare differences between ethnic groups. This sample was subsequently boosted using Office for National Statistics (ONS) data. The overall response rate for the ethnic boost population was 49%, which was lower than that achieved for the survey population overall

(58%). If the respondent did not speak English, the interview proceeded if there was a friend, relative or carer or someone else in the household aged 18 or over who could assist with the interview by acting as an interpreter. For the purposes of the analysis presented in this chapter, data is weighted to adjust for non-response and sampling error unless otherwise stated. Further details on the methods, sampling and response rates are available at: www.poverty.ac.uk (see also NatCen, 2013).

The ethnic background of respondents was established, in the England and Wales sample, in response to a question very similar to that asked in the 2001 England and Wales Census. This asked respondents to identify which ethnic group they considered they belonged to. The specific ethnic categories examined in these analyses, with unweighted sample sizes, are: White majority (living in Britain and Northern Ireland) (N = 7,182), White Irish migrants (living in Britain) (N = 42), White Polish (N = 93), White Other (N = 241), Black Caribbean (N = 169); Black African (N = 154); Asian Indian (N = 279); Asian Pakistani (N = 182); Asian Bangladeshi (N = 43); Asian Other (N = 194); Other (N = 112). The small number of Bangladeshi people and Irish migrants may make findings for this group unreliable. These analyses group together those who might be considered members of an ethnic majority group: specifically, those in the England and Wales sample describing themselves as white British and those in the Northern Ireland sample describing themselves as white Irish or white British. People assigning themselves to the remaining 'white' categories were considered people with white minority backgrounds, whose heritage linked them with a migrant population. These categories included white Irish people in the England and Wales sample, white Polish people and 'other white' people. White Polish people were identified using detail on their ethnic background and responses to a question on spoken language use. There were too few people with other white ethnicities, including white Irish Travellers and Gypsies, for them to be analysed separately. These were combined into the 'other white' group. For the purposes of these analyses, those with mixed ethnicities were recoded according to their ethnic minority affiliation, with the exception of those who classified themselves as 'white and Asian', who were classified with those with 'any other Asian or Asian British background', due to the lack of sufficient specificity in this category. Those in the 'other mixed' and 'Chinese' category were coded as 'any other ethnic background' due to small numbers in these groups.

The analysis presented in this chapter utilises a range of objective and subjective markers of poverty and social exclusion. The main objective poverty measure (PSE poverty) is based on a combination of deprivation and low income. Respondents were classified as poor if they had a low income and were deprived – due to lack of money – of three or more essential items or activities. This measure was developed using the consensual approach to poverty which takes as its reference point the items and activities identified by 50% or more of the respondents in the 2012 Omnibus survey, as being necessary for a minimum standard of living. The Omnibus survey was based on a representative sample of the adult population (1,447 adults aged 16 or over in Britain and 1,015 in Northern Ireland) and sought to establish whether there is a consensus among the population of the UK as a whole and between different social groups about the necessities of life. Forty-six items and activities relevant to adults, and an additional 30 relevant to children, were included in the GB and NI Omnibus surveys and 25 adult items and 24 child items were considered essential by the majority of the respondents. It should be noted that while there were only small ethnic differences in what was considered 'necessary' (such as holidays abroad, attending a place of worship), it is also important to acknowledge that – due to the nature of the sample – the consensual approach prioritises a white majority perspective (see also chapter one for details of the poverty measures). Deprivation is also analysed separately according to whether the individual lacks three or more of these necessities. In addition, the analysis uses an income poverty measure which identifies people as poor if their equivalised household income is 60% below the median national income after housing costs, based on income data collected from the FRS. The information on income was updated in the PSE-UK 2012 survey interview by asking whether and by how much their household's income had changed since the FRS.

To complement these objective measures, this analysis includes a range of subjective measures which report on the respondent's self-perception of their poverty status or standard of living. Respondents were questioned about their current and past experiences of poverty and asked to rate their standard of living according to whether they believed it was above or below the average for the UK population as a whole. The chapter also presents data on economising behaviours and other coping strategies often employed by people on low incomes. In addition to these various markers of poverty and living standards, we examine social exclusion in relation to employment and living environment, building upon previous analyses to offer a more nuanced appreciation of people's experiences. All the bivariate analyses presented in the chapter show statistically significant variations at the p < 0.01 level or lower, unless otherwise stated. Those associations described as being of marginal significance have a p-value between 0.05 and 0.1.

Findings

Poverty

Ethnic variations in poverty using the key summary measures available in the PSE-UK 2012 survey are shown in Table 5.1. In contrast to earlier studies, the main measure of poverty used in the current study (PSE poverty) identifies Black African people as being most at risk of poverty; one in two Black African people live both on a low income and with higher levels of deprivation. Pakistani, Black Caribbean and Bangladeshi people are also at high risk of poverty, while white Irish and Indian people, and people in the white majority group are at lower than average risk. Looking just at the measure of income poverty provides a somewhat different picture of those at greatest disadvantage, however: Pakistani people are most likely to experience income poverty followed by Black Africans, then Bangladeshi people, all with considerably higher risk of poverty than those in other ethnic groups.

On the other hand, examining deprivation of socially perceived necessities alone, we find that Black African people report exceptionally high levels of deprivation: 71% lack three or more items or activities which are considered as necessary for an adequate standard of living by the majority population. More than half of Polish, Black Caribbean, Pakistani or Bangladeshi people also report going without three or more necessary items or activities. These differences are reflected in the average deprivation scores also shown Table 5.1, with Black African groups on average lacking 5.3 necessities, Black Caribbean people lacking four and Bangladeshi, Polish and Pakistani people lacking just over three necessities, compared with just over two for white majority, Irish migrant and Indian groups.

Turning to the more subjective measures of poverty included in the survey, between 50% and 60% of Polish, Black African, Black Caribbean, Pakistani and Bangladeshi people report themselves currently to be in poverty 'always' or 'sometimes', compared with around a third of Irish, Indian and white majority populations. Black African and Caribbean people are around twice as likely as white majority and Indian groups to say that they have been poor 'often' or 'mostly' throughout their lives.

Table 5.1: Objective and subjective poverty by ethnicity

Ethnic group	'Objective' poverty					'Subjective' poverty		
	PSE poverty (%)	Income poverty (%)	Lacking three or more socially perceived necessities (%)	Average deprivation score of socially perceived necessities	Currently poor 'always' or 'sometimes' (%)	'Often' or 'mostly' poor in the past (%)	Standard of living is a 'little' or 'a lot' below average (%)
White majority (GB/NI)	20	23	32	2.3	33	10	12
White Irish (GB)	16	17	30	2.0	31	6	16
White Polish	28	33	53	3.2	59	7	18
White Other (GB)	24	16	37	2.8	26	7	15
Black Caribbean	35	27	59	4.0	55	17	20
Black African	50	48	71	5.3	55	20	32
Asian Indian	17	28	32	2.2	31	9	9
Asian Pakistani	44	53	53	3.4	49	14	15
Asian Bangladeshi	33	43	53	3.2	48	1	13
Asian Other	18	22	35	2.5	52	10	11
Other	37	34	53	2.5	57	24	20
Total	21	23	34	2.5	34	10	13

One third of Black African and one fifth of Black Caribbean respondents perceive their standard of living to be 'below' or 'well-below' the average. Interestingly, Pakistani and Bangladeshi people report a similar assessment of their standard of living as white majority people – despite presenting higher than average poverty rates on the objective measures analysed. We speculate that these individuals may be conceptualising living standards more broadly than access to material goods and services and include aspects of their lives which they consider more positively, such as familial, friendship or religious networks and amenities. Alternatively, they may not have the same opportunities as others to compare their living standards with others in different social circumstances, due to their concentration in residential areas or occupations with others who are similarly deprived – and this may serve to normalise such experiences of disadvantage.

In summary, Table 5.1 reveals the extreme levels of poverty experienced by some ethnic (minority) groups, particularly the Black African population. Our analysis has also identified some heterogeneity in the socio-economic position of individuals within particular groups, however. For example, Figure 5.1 presents the distribution of incomes within particular ethnic groups. This shows that although there is an even spread of income among the Black Caribbean, Indian and white majority groups – with relatively equal proportions of people in each of the income quintiles – the incomes of between 60% and 70% of Pakistani and Polish people are in the poorest quintiles. But while similar proportions of the Black African population have incomes in these poorest quintiles, almost one fifth of Black Africans have

Figure 5.1: Distribution of income by ethnicity

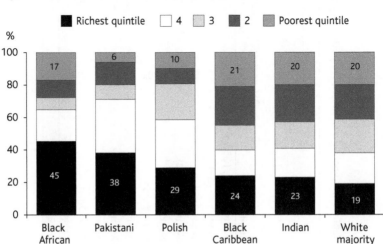

incomes in the highest quintile. While many Black African people clearly live in very difficult economic circumstances, there is also a substantial minority of relatively affluent individuals in this group. This finding suggests that it could be misleading to treat 'Black Africans' as a homogeneous group; Mitton and Aspinall (2011) argue that factors such as country of birth and age at migration are significant sources of diversity among Black Africans living in the UK.

Managing low incomes

A number of different coping strategies are used by individuals and households living on a reduced income. These include engaging in economising behaviour by cutting back on items and services, falling behind with financial commitments and borrowing money to make ends meet. These strategies may prevent people from falling into poverty, but given the stresses that go hand in hand with coping on a low income, 'tightening one's belt' should not be interpreted as a sign of resilience. Significantly too, people in such situations will not be identified in poverty measures. Demonstrating the presence of ethnic differences in the use of these coping strategies therefore provides important additional detail regarding ethnic differences in socio-economic status to evidence available elsewhere and encourages us to reflect on the implications of the boundaries between 'poor' and 'not poor' categories.

Table 5.2 shows that economising behaviour is prevalent across the PSE-UK 2012 survey population, but is much more extensive among certain ethnic groups, such as Black African, Polish and Bangladeshi people, around 70% of whom report that in the last 12 months they cut back on four or more items including food, clothes, socialising, dental visits and contributions to pensions in order to reduce expenditure. Black Africans are the most likely to report failing to keep up with their financial commitments, such as bills. In addition to the 20% of Black Africans who have actually failed to manage these demands, a further 70% (and 63% of Black Caribbeans and Pakistanis) report struggling with these commitments at least from time to time. Respondents were also asked whether during the previous 12 months they had borrowed money (from lenders, friends or family, for example) in order to pay for their day-to-day needs. Borrowing was highest among Black Caribbean and Black African respondents, closely followed by Bangladeshi and Pakistani people.

The impression given by these data, then, is that as well as the large proportion of Black Africans, and others, currently living in poverty,

Table 5.2: Managing on low incomes by ethnicity

Ethnic category	Economising on four or more items/ activities in last 12 months to keep costs down (%)	Struggling from time to time with financial commitments (%)	Behind with financial commitments (%)	Borrowed money last 12 months (%)
White majority (GB/NI)	43	44	6	20
White Irish (GB)	40	42	1	18
White Polish	69	50	1	24
White Other (GB)	48	36	9	18
Black Caribbean	59	63	12	38
Black African	72	69	20	34
Asian Indian	39	41	2	14
Asian Pakistani	50	63	5	31
Asian Bangladeshi	69	52	6	31
Asian Other	52	49	9	19
Other	62	46	12	24
Total	**45**	**44**	**6**	**21**

a significant majority find themselves vulnerable to poverty and living with extreme financial difficulties. These coping strategies may also explain the discrepancy between the findings for measures of subjective and objective poverty for the Black Caribbean group identified in Table 5.1 – their behaviour contributing to a sense of difficulty, but enabling them to avoid crossing the thresholds examined by standard measures of poverty.

Paid and unpaid work

The PSE-UK 2012 survey asked respondents a range of questions about paid and unpaid work. Paid employment has been promoted by UK governments and international organisations like the Organisation for Economic Co-operation and Development (OECD) as the main route out of poverty. Interestingly, the rates of unemployment identified in the study do not map straightforwardly onto those of poverty described earlier: those groups most likely to be living in, or vulnerable to, poverty are also consistently more likely to be in employment than the white majority (with the exception of Pakistani people who have similar rates) (Table 5.3). There are some differences in the ethnic patterning of economic inactivity and unemployment, however. Bangladeshi and white majority people are more likely to be inactive than other groups, while Black African, Pakistani and Black Caribbean people are the most likely to be unemployed. These ethnic variations in economic activity only show marginal statistical significance, however ($p = 0.08$). But there is a statistically significant ethnic variation in the experience of long-term unemployment: Pakistani and Black African people have been unemployed for longer than those in other groups, with long-term unemployment rates of around twice those of the white majority group.

While figures from the 2011 England and Wales Census show that unemployment rates among Pakistani and Bangladeshi men have improved since 1991 (falling by 15 percentage points to around 10%), their rates remain far in excess of those for white men, at 6% (Kapadia et al 2015). Moreover, this fall is explained by (further) increases in part-time work in these groups, which for example saw an 11-fold increase for Bangladeshi men between 1991 and 2011. By contrast, the PSE-UK 2012 survey shows significant ethnic variations in part-time employment which are much starker for Pakistani than for Bangladeshi people; with only half of Pakistani people employed full-time compared with three quarters of all Bangladeshi workers. Looking at gender, across all the ethnic groups examined, men are more likely to work full-time with the exception of the Pakistani population where

Table 5.3: Economic activity, work deprivation and in-work poverty by ethnicity

Ethnic category	Economic activity (%)			Very low work intensity (%)	In-work poverty (%)
	Employed/ self-employed	Inactive	Unemployed/ long-term*		
White majority (GB/NI)	51	44	5/9	17	16
White Irish (GB)	49	44	7/11	23	1
White Polish	78	18	4/3	1	22
White Other (GB)	62	33	5/8	8	25
Black Caribbean	57	36	8/13	22	26
Black African	57	32	11/19	19	44
Asian Indian	60	34	6/10	7	14
Asian Pakistani	50	41	9/18	27	33
Asian Bangladeshi	47	49	4/8	8	32
Asian Other	53	43	3/9	18	15
Other	44	40	16/13	34	24
Total	52	43	5/9	16	17

Note: *Of those unemployed, proportion unemployed for more than one year.

that is reversed: 50% of employed Pakistani men are working full-time compared with 63% Pakistani women. Further, women in the Pakistani group are the least likely to be working full-time (compared to other women), suggesting a particularly high reliance on incomes from part-time working in Pakistani households. Using a more formal marker, around 16% of all PSE-UK 2012 survey respondents live in households characterised by very low work intensity as defined by the European Union. Quasi-joblessness affects more than one in four Pakistani respondents and around one in five Black Caribbean, Black African and Irish, but only 8% of Bangladeshi and 1% of Polish respondents. These high levels of quasi-joblessness and part-time working may explain the significantly higher levels of poverty among these groups despite apparent limited variation in their employment activity. Again, this highlights the need to conduct more nuanced and sophisticated analyses to effectively determine, and understand, ethnic variations in socio-economic position.

Table 5.3 also shows more explicitly the percentages of the people in paid work who live in poverty according to the PSE measure. Despite the political mantra that 'work pays', over two fifths of Black African, a third of Bangladeshi and Pakistani, and over a quarter of Black Caribbean people in work live in poverty. While rates of in-work poverty are lower for the Indian and white majority groups, the findings indicate that around 15% of the working population in these groups is also poor.

Living environment

Dissatisfaction and problems with living environment, both in terms of accommodation and the local area, also show variation by ethnicity (Table 5.4). Black African and Polish respondents report the highest levels of dissatisfaction with their accommodation (with rates among Black African people four times those of the white majority group). They are also, along with Black Caribbean people, more likely to perceive that their home is in a 'poor' state of repair. Black African, Black Caribbean and Polish people report the highest number of problems with their accommodation such as shortage of space; damp or mould on walls, ceilings or floors; draughts; and condensation. Black African and Black Caribbean people report the highest rates of dissatisfaction with their local area: around twice the rate of white majority groups, although the results are only of marginal significance (p = 0.07). Across the entire population, the most frequently reported local problems are poor street lighting, dog and cat mess, and litter.

Table 5.4: Living environment and ethnicity

Ethnic category	'Fairly' or 'very' dissatisfied with accommodation (%)	Home is in 'poor' state of repair (%)	Mean number of accommodation problems	'Fairly' or 'very' dissatisfied with local area (%)
White majority (GB/NI)	4	6	1.0	8
White Irish (GB)	3	4	1.2	7
White Polish	14	11	1.4	2
White Other (GB)	4	8	1.4	6
Black Caribbean	7	10	1.5	14
Black African	17	15	1.5	16
Asian Indian	1	1	0.7	6
Asian Pakistani	9	7	1.0	8
Asian Bangladeshi	–	–	0.9	5
Asian Other	1	0	1.3	3
Other	6	8	1.2	11
Total	4	6	1.1	8

Findings from the 1993–4 FNS (Fourth National Survey of Ethnic Minorities) suggested that people with ethnic minority backgrounds were significantly more likely to live in overcrowded accommodation: only 2% of white households and 10% or fewer of Chinese and Caribbean households were found to be overcrowded, compared with 13% of Indian, 33% of Pakistani and 43% of Bangladeshi households (Lakey, 1997). Bangladeshi and Caribbean people included in the FNS were more likely to report being fairly or very dissatisfied with their housing than other groups (Lakey, 1997). This was associated with levels of overcrowding and housing tenure, and it was hypothesised that this may be related to the large number of people in these groups in local authority accommodation.

Discrimination and the 'ethnic penalty'

Explaining the ethnic variations identified in these analyses is beyond the scope of this chapter. However, previous research suggests that these inequalities cannot be explained by variations in individual or group capacity; with pay penalties persisting even after adjusting for variations in level of educational qualifications, occupational group, age, health, marital and familial status, and place of birth/generation (Heath and Cheung, 2006; Longhi and Platt, 2008). Indeed, those groups identified here as most likely to experience these difficulties are extremely heterogeneous in terms of these characteristics: Black Caribbean people, for example, have a much longer history of residency in the UK than other groups experiencing similar rates of poverty.

A more convincing explanation proposed for this 'ethnic penalty' has been the historical and persistent prejudice experienced by (white and non-white) ethnic minority populations in the UK, and elsewhere (Heath and Smith, 2003; Platt, 2005; Borjas, 2006; Longhi and Platt, 2008). The PSE-UK 2012 survey identified significant ethnic differences in rates of reported interpersonal racism: with 16% of Polish, 13% of Black Caribbean and Black African, 10% of Pakistani, white Irish and Indian people reporting being harassed, abused or made to feel uncomfortable in the 12 months prior to the PSE-UK 2012 interview. There are also significant ethnic differences in people's sense of being treated less favourably by people in a position of authority: 12% of Black Caribbean, 11% of Black African, 9% of Polish and 7% of Pakistani and Indian described exposure to institutional racism in the previous 12 months. It is difficult to apply these figures directly to explain ethnic differences in poverty and social exclusion, however, due to the complex and multifaceted nature of the processes by which such experiences lead to socio-economic disadvantage. For example, among migrants, it is argued that a two-pronged 'immigration penalty' operates to depress their occupational achievement relative to their skills and education (Heath and Ridge, 1983; Platt, 2005). Because qualifications, skills and experience gained outside of the UK are considered by employers to be less relevant in the UK context, this discourages them from offering appropriate positions to migrant applicants.

This (and other) evidence speaks to an ongoing issue affecting the lives of people with a range of ethnic minority backgrounds, including their present and past socio-economic status (as individuals and groups) and the extent to which this may be overcome by investments in education and so on. Indeed, the positivity regarding the economic implications of increasing numbers of people with ethnic minority backgrounds attending higher education (Modood, 2004; Heath and Cheung, 2006; Platt, 2007) has been offset by evidence of persistent (and dramatically increasing) greater over-qualification in employment among, particularly, Black African, Black Caribbean, Chinese and Pakistani/Bangladeshi male and female graduates, compared with the white UK-born population (Rafferty, 2012). The extent to which qualifications – even those awarded in the UK – produces occupational improvements also shows variations by ethnicity which it is difficult to explain away based on individual or group characteristics.

But the operation and implications of discrimination are often difficult to identify (and measure). Discrimination may force people to take less desirable jobs (Commission for Racial Equality, 1996), to become self-employed (Clark and Drinkwater, 1998), or to spend longer periods in unemployment; all outcomes that are difficult to definitively ascribe to discriminatory practices. Institutional and other forms of racism also influence areas of life, such as access to good housing or health, which then directly impact on an individual's ability to function effectively in the education and labour market. As Wrench and Solomos (1993, p 171) reflect:

> the deflating of 'unrealistic' aspirations [and] the protective channelling [by careers advisers], and the anticipatory avoidance of apparently racist employers by young people, all combine to lessen the likelihood that an act of racial discrimination will occur. But the processes of discrimination are still there, ensuring that black young people are not going to have fair access to opportunities for which they are qualified.

While the impact of discriminatory processes may be difficult to identify, the significance of their influence should not be underestimated.

Discussion and conclusions

This chapter presents compelling evidence regarding the presence and persistence of ethnic variations in experiences of poverty and social exclusion. It shows that the disadvantage experienced by Bangladeshi and Pakistani people identified in previous investigations of poverty persists, but there are other groups whose needs should be recognised and addressed. On almost every measure examined here, Black African people appear to experience disadvantage more extreme than that of Bangladeshi and Pakistani people. And there are other groups, Polish and Black Caribbean people, whose disadvantage may be less ubiquitous but remains present, at times disguised by the extreme actions adopted by these individuals to manage on low incomes, which prevents them from being identified as poor. We have also shown, then, how the markers used to examine poverty and social exclusion can produce subtle variations in our impression of individual lives and how more nuanced measures, incorporating multiple domains, can provide a much more comprehensive picture of the extent of ethnic variations in socio-economic position.

A more detailed investigation of ethnic variations in socio-economic position, and possible explanations for these, is beyond the scope of this chapter. Evidence from existing research suggests that there are additional avenues for enquiry which need exploring before a comprehensive picture of ethnic inequalities in socio-economic status (and the drivers of these) can be realised. For example, those with ethnic minority backgrounds have also been shown to be more concentrated in particular industries and employed in less skilled jobs, at lower job levels than white people and to experience less social mobility (Mason, 2013; Virk, 2012). Our analysis of income inequalities also fails to account for ethnic variations in wealth. Figures presented to the National Equality Panel (2010) indicated median total household wealth of £15,000 for Bangladeshi, £75,000 for Black Caribbean, £97,000 for Pakistani and £200,000 or more for Indian and white British households.

There are also important variations in the experiences of individuals within particular ethnic groups which need more detailed examination: for example, by age, gender and religion. Research suggests that religious affiliation can play a significant role in the generation of 'ethnic' inequalities in pay (Longhi and Platt, 2008) and influences performance evaluation (Castilla, 2008) and gaining promotion (Maume, 1999; Battu and Sloane 2002), again as a consequence of the discrimination directed towards particular ethnic/religious groups (Virdee, 2006). Moreover, Muslims (with a range of ethnic backgrounds) and Sikhs have been found to experience particularly high levels of socio-economic disadvantage (Karlsen and Nazroo, 2010) as well as reporting increasing levels of harassment and discrimination (Karlsen and Nazroo, 2014). That Pakistani, Bangladeshi and Black African people are concentrated among those with Islamic backgrounds could suggest this to be a fruitful line of further enquiry.

There are issues related to the study of ethnicity more generally which should be acknowledged. People relate to their ethnicities in different and multifaceted ways, which vary across time and circumstance and in response to particular personal, social and political factors. Reflecting these complexities is extremely difficult, particularly in quantitative surveys. A range of academic and official surveys collect data on ethnicity and many of these employ a measure which approximates to that used in the Census, in part due to the considerable, and ongoing, groundwork put into the development of these questions and also the wish to establish comparability across surveys. But while these generally benefit from the use of self-classification, the definitional markers employed in these surveys, which frame ethnicity using markers of geographical heritage and phenotype, are only one approach to defining ethnicity. Even if people feel able to assign themselves to one of these categories, it should not be assumed that these are labels that have relevant or consistent meanings across individuals or over time or ones that individuals would choose to apply to themselves.

References

Battu, H. and Sloane, P.J. (2002) 'To what extent are ethnic minorities in Britain over-educated?', *International Journal of Manpower* 23(3), 192–208.

Beider, H. and Netto, G. (2012) 'Minority ethnic communities and housing: access, experiences and participation', in G. Craig, K. Atkin, S. Chattoo and R. Flynn (eds) *Understanding 'Race' and Ethnicity*, Bristol: Policy Press.

Berthoud, R. (1997) 'Income and standards of living', in T. Modood, R. Berthoud, J. Lakey, J. Nazroo, J., P. Smith, S. Virdee et al (eds) *Ethnic minorities in Britain: Diversity and disadvantage*, London: PSI.

Borjas, G.J. (2006) *Making it in America: Social mobility in the immigrant population*, National Bureau of Economic Research Working Paper 12088, Cambridge, MA, US: National Bureau of Economic Research.

Castilla, E.J. (2008) 'Gender, race, and meritocracy in organizational careers', *American Journal of Sociology* 113:6, 1479–1526.

Clark, K. and Drinkwater, S. (1998) 'Ethnicity and self-employment in Britain', *Oxford Bulletin of Economics and Statistics* 60:3, 383–407.

Commission for Racial Equality (1996) *We regret to inform you...*, London: CRE.

Gervais, M. and Rehman, H. (2005) *Causes of homelessness amongst ethnic minority population*, London: CLG.

Heath, A. and Cheung, S.Y. (2006) *Ethnic penalties in the labour market: Employers and discrimination*, Research Report 341, London: Dept of Work and Pensions.

Heath, A. and Ridge, J. (1983) 'Social mobility of ethnic minorities', *Journal of Biosocial Science* Suppl 8, 169-84.

Heath, A. and Smith, S. (2003) 'Mobility and ethnic minorities: Levels of employment are greater cause for concern than social immobility', *New Economy*, 199–204.

Jivraj, S. and Khan, O. (2015) 'How likely are ethnic minorities to live in deprived neighbourhoods?', in S. Jivraj and L. Simpson (eds) *Ethnic identities and inequalities in Britain: The dynamics of diversity*, Bristol: Policy Press.

Kapadia, D., Nazroo, J. and Clark, K. (2015) 'Have ethnic inequalities in the labour market persisted?', in S. Jivraj and L. Simpson (eds) *Ethnic identities and inequalities in Britain: The dynamics of diversity*, Bristol: Policy Press.

Karlsen, S. and Nazroo, J.Y. (2010) 'The circumstances and attitudes of different Muslims groups in England and Europe', in J. Stillwell, P. Norman, C. Thomas and P. Surridge (eds) *Spatial and Social Disparities: Understanding Population Trends and Processes – Volume 2*, London: Springer.

Karlsen S. and Nazroo, J.Y. (2014) 'Ethnic and religious variations in the reporting of racist victimization in Britain: 2000 and 2008/2009', *Patterns of Prejudice* 48:4, 370–97.

Kaufman, J.S., Cooper, R.S. and McGee, D.L. (1997) 'Socioeconomic status and health in blacks and white: The problem of residual confounding and the resiliency of race', *Epidemiology* 8, 621–28.

Kaufman, J.S., Long, A.E., Liao, Y., et al. (1998) 'The relation between income and mortality in U.S. blacks and whites', *Epidemiology* 9:2, 147–55.

Lakey, J. (1997) 'Neighourhoods and housing', in T. Modood, R. Berthoud, J. Lakey, J. Nazroo, P. Smith, S. Virdee et al (eds) *Ethnic minorities in Britain: Diversity and disadvantage*, London: PSI.

Longhi, S. and Platt, L. (2008) *Pay gaps across equalities areas*, Research report 9, Manchester: Equality and Human Rights Commission.

Mason, D. (2013) 'Ethnicity', in G. Payne (ed.) *Social divisions*, London: Palgrave Macmillan.

Maume, Jr, D.J. (1999) 'Glass ceilings and glass escalators: Occupational segregation and race and sex differences in managerial promotions', *Work and Occupations* 26:4, 483–509.

Mitton, L. and Aspinall, P. (2011) 'Black Africans in the UK: Integration or segregation? Understanding population trends and processes', www.restore.ac.uk/UPTAP/wordpress/wp-content/uploads/2011/01/uptap-findings-mitton-jan-11.pdf

Modood, T. (2004) 'Capitals, ethnic identity and educational qualifications', *Cultural Trends* 13:2, 87-105.

NatCen (2013) *Poverty and social exclusion survey technical report*, London: NatCen.

National Equality Panel (2010) *Anatomy of economic inequality in the UK*, London: Government Equalities Office/LSE.

Nazroo, J.Y. (2001) *Ethnicity, class and health*, London: PSI.

Platt, L. (2003) 'Ethnicity and inequality: British children's experience of means-tested benefits', *Journal of Comparative Family Studies* 34:3, 357–77.

Platt, L. (2005) *Migration and social mobility: The life chances of Britain's minority ethnic communities*, Bristol: Policy Press.

Platt, L. (2007) *Poverty and ethnicity in the UK*, Bristol: Policy Press.

Rafferty, A. (2012) 'Ethnic penalties in graduate level over-education, unemployment and wages: Evidence from Britain', *Work, Employment and Society* 26:6, 987–1006.

Virdee, S. (2006) '"Race", employment and social change: A critique of current orthodoxies', *Ethnic and Racial Studies* 29, 605-28.

Virk, B. (2012) 'Minority ethnic groups in the labour market', in G. Craig, K. Atkin, S. Chattoo and R. Flynn (eds) *Understanding 'race' and ethnicity*, Bristol: Policy Press.

Wrench, J. and Solomos, J. (1993) 'The politics and processes of racial discrimination in Britain', in J. Solomos and J. Wrench (eds) *Racism and Migration in Western Europe*, London: Berg Publisher, 157–76.

SIX

Improving lives? Child poverty and social exclusion

Gill Main and Jonathan Bradshaw

Introduction

This chapter details findings on child poverty and social exclusion from the 2012 UK Poverty and Social Exclusion Survey (PSE-UK 2012). The 1999 Poverty and Social Exclusion Study of Great Britain (PSE-GB 1999), which at the time offered the most comprehensive data on child poverty and social exclusion gathered in Britain, was completed amidst an atmosphere of hope in relation to the outlook for poor children and families. New Labour's landslide victory in the 1997 general election was followed by then Prime Minister Tony Blair's commitment in 1999 to end child poverty within a generation. This commitment was made in the aftermath of 18 years of Conservative governments, under Prime Ministers Margaret Thatcher (1979–90) and John Major (1990–7), who had overseen drastic increases in the child poverty rate.[1] Lloyd (2006), in her analysis of child poverty in the PSE-GB 1999, details many of the policy changes and interventions designed to combat child poverty. These changes culminated in the Child Poverty Act 2010, which committed the government to monitoring and reporting on progress in relation to four targets to be achieved by 2020:

- fewer than 10% of children in *relative poverty* (equivalised household income <60% national median, before housing costs);
- fewer than 5% of children in *combined low income and material deprivation* (equivalised household income <70% national median before housing costs and having a score of 25 or less on the Households Below Average Income child material deprivation measure; see Carr et al, 2014 for more details);
- fewer than 5% of children in *absolute poverty* (equivalised household income <60% national median of the base year [2010/11], fixed in real terms);

- fewer than 7% children in *persistent poverty* (equivalised household income <60% national median for three out of the previous four years; target set October 2014).

Child poverty declined steadily over the course of the Labour government,[2] and the Child Poverty Act 2010 passed through Parliament with cross-party support. However, long before that milestone, analyses of the progress being made towards policy goals demonstrated that greater efforts would be needed to achieve the targets. Brewer et al's (2002) report highlighted the need for a significant increase in investment if policy targets were to be met; Harker's (2006, p 7) report for the Department for Work and Pensions reaffirmed these concerns, despite policy developments in the second Blair ministry of 2001–5, stating that 'current policies [are] unlikely to meet the 2010 target to halve child poverty'. Concerns were exacerbated by the global financial crisis which hit the UK in 2007/8. Labour's initial response of anti-cyclical spending, including the early uprating of benefits and increasing taxation on higher incomes, offered some protection to poor families, but declining real wages, growing unemployment and the increasing cost of necessities such as food, fuel and private rents resulted in child poverty rates flat-lining post-2010. The 2010 general election delivered no clear winner and the resulting Conservative-led Coalition government, in partnership with the Liberal Democrats, oversaw a reversal of Labour economic policy. An austerity agenda was pursued, with substantial cuts impacting families through direct reductions in social security spending, and indirectly through cuts to funding for services. The 2015 general election returned a slight Conservative majority, cementing austerity as the dominant economic policy.

Elsewhere we make a detailed examination of the emerging impact of the crisis and subsequent policy changes on child poverty (Bradshaw et al, 2017), arguing that while the Coalition and Conservative governments have positioned austerity as economic necessity, a closer examination of their response reveals an ideological basis to their reforms which has disproportionately impacted children and families. Here, we examine findings from the PSE-UK 2012, relating our results to government policy and rhetoric about poor children and families, and developing practice in child poverty measurement. One important advantage of the PSE surveys is the production of data in relation to various resources, which enables the examination of different approaches to assessing poverty and deprivation. While many studies of poverty rely on household-based measures of income, the PSE-UK 2012 can be used to provide measures of deprivation (based on access to resources and activities), income poverty (based on household income) and a combined measure of the two which enables the creation of an individualised poverty measure combining a focus on individually experienced deprivations and household-level resources (that is, income and other material resources which relate to the household rather than the individual, such as those relating to living conditions). Gordon (2017) provides details of the construction of the measure. The combination of income and deprivation into a PSE poverty indicator both acknowledges the impact of shared household income on the living standards of all household members, and simultaneously incorporates a concern with child-specific needs and access to resources. As such it can provide a more nuanced measure than income or deprivation alone, and enables an examination of the living standards of separate household members (due to the inclusion of child- and adult-specific necessities). As a result, the PSE-UK 2012 offers a unique insight not only into poverty rates among children but also into how these compare to the poverty experienced by the adults children live with. This enables assumptions about equitable household sharing, and about parental behaviours, to be tested, as detailed below.

In the remainder of this chapter we go on to examine perceptions of the necessities of life for children in 2012, and some trends over time in these perceptions where data are available from earlier, similar surveys. The consensual approach to poverty measurement as applied to children is discussed, and an argument is made for the inclusion of children as respondents in similar future studies. We then examine child poverty and social exclusion using several of the measures available in the PSE-UK 2012 survey. Finally, we discuss the sharing of resources within children's households.

The necessities of life for children

In the PSE-UK 2012, necessities of life for children were established in the Omnibus survey, using adult (aged 16+) reports on items and activities seen as necessary for children. Table 6.1 shows the proportion of the population viewing a range of items and activities as necessities for children, comparing PSE-UK 2012 and PSE-GB 1999. There is a fairly high level of stability for most items. Based on confidence intervals,[3] there are significant differences for 11 of the 20 comparable items and activities (shaded in grey). For four of these items, a higher proportion saw them as a necessity in 2012; for the remaining seven a higher proportion saw them as a necessity in 1999. Elsewhere (Main

Table 6.1: Proportion of the adult population viewing items and activities as necessities, and comparisons between 2012 and 1999

	Proportion viewing item/activity as a necessity	
	2012	1999
A warm winter coat (coat)	97	95
Fresh fruit or vegetables at least once a day (veg)	96	93
Three meals a day (3 meals)	93	90
New, properly fitting, shoes (shoes)	93	94
A garden or outdoor space nearby where they can play safely (garden)	92	(68)
Books at home suitable for their ages (books)	91	89
Meat, fish or vegetarian equivalent at least once a day (meat)	90	77
A suitable place to study or do homework (study)	89	–
Indoor games suitable for their ages (games)	80	(83)
Enough bedrooms for every child of 10 or over of a different sex to have their own bedroom (bedroom)	74	78
Computer and internet for homework (computer)	66	(41)
Some new, not second hand, clothes (clothes)	65	70
Outdoor leisure equipment (leisure)	58	60
At least four pairs of trousers, leggings, jeans or jogging bottoms (trousers)	56	69
Money to save (save)	54	–
Pocket money (money)	54	–
Construction toys (toys)	53	62
A bicycle (bike)	45	54
Clothes to fit in with friends (style)	31	–
A mobile phone for children aged 11 or over (mobile)	26	–
An MP3 player (mp3)	8	–
Designer/brand name trainers (pumps)	6	–
Celebrations on special occasions (celebrations)	91	92
A hobby or leisure activity (hobby)	88	89
Toddler group or nursery or play group at least once a week for pre-school aged children (nursery)	87	88
Children's clubs or activities such as drama or football training (clubs)	74	–
Day trips with family once a month (family trip)	60	–
Going on a school trip at least once a term (school trip)	55	74
A holiday away from home for at least one week a year (holiday)	52	70
Friends round for tea or a snack once a fortnight (snack)	49	59

Note: 2012 figures based on own analysis of the PSE-UK 2012 data; 1999 figures taken from Lloyd (2006); shaded cells indicate a statistically significant difference; figures in brackets denote a change in question wording between the two surveys.

and Bradshaw, 2014) we detail relative stability in four of the items which can be traced through four surveys conducted since 1983.

Overall, we found no evidence of a systematic increase in expectations around what children should have. As noted above, Main and Bradshaw (2014) provide more detail. For some of the items with an increased proportion seeing them as necessities, this is likely a result of technological developments in the intervening years (such as the increase from 41% to 66% viewing a computer as a necessity for children). Other items saw commensurate declines in the proportions seeing them as necessities; for example, the proportion viewing an annual holiday as a necessity reduced from 70% to 52%, moving it from well within the definition of a necessity much closer to the 50% cut-off. One interpretation of this stability over time is that measures of child deprivation are capturing the same underlying construct that they have been in previous years, challenging claims in the popular press (see Malone, 2014) that greed, rather than poverty, has increased.

Child deprivation and children's perspectives

The enforced lack approach used in PSE-UK 2012 – based on the position that lacking a socially perceived necessity is only considered a deprivation if the reason for lacking it is inability to afford the item/ activity – was instigated by Mack and Lansley (1985) in response to criticisms of Townsend's (1979) approach from Piachaud (1981) that counting all items lacking irrespective of the reason for the lack may miscount as poor those who lack items/activities through personal preference. However, complications arise with this approach when child, rather than adult, poverty is the issue of concern. Such complications (not all of which are relevant to the PSE-UK 2012 survey, but which are relevant to deciding on an approach) comprise:

- Where adults are respondents, how suitable and accurate is it to rely on them as proxies for reporting children's preferences?
- Where children are respondents, can an adequate knowledge of household finances be assumed to enable trust in 'can't afford' responses?
- Further to the above, if child reports are used and indicate the child lacks and wants an item/activity, is the ability of adults to afford this item a relevant factor in whether the child is deprived or not, given that the child's preferences are not being met whether or not adults can afford it?

- Where children's preferences (or adults' reports of children's preferences) indicate that a child does not want items/activities widely believed to be instrumental to survival and healthy development towards successful adulthood (such as nutritional, educational and developmental resources), what does a non-enforced lack indicate?

Such questions are important considerations in deciding on how to conceptualise, define and measure poverty. For example, Gordon et al (2003) base their decisions around cut-off points in the diagnosis of poverty on a consideration of whether factors such as sexism or illness, rather than limited household resources, may be the reason some children lack necessities. They cite the example of girls going without educational necessities in some developing countries as a result of gender-based discrimination. Their decision to omit deprivations resulting from discrimination is based on a desire to avoid misclassifying a household as poor if the children within the household are deprived for other reasons; an alternative approach, focused on individual rather than household resources, would be to class children as deprived irrespective of whether the cause of their deprivation is discrimination or lack of household resources, on the basis that in either scenario the child lacks access to the resource. In line with this latter approach, UNICEF[4] have taken the view that if a child lacks a socially perceived necessity, regardless of whether an adult says they lack it because they cannot afford it, then it is an abrogation of child rights and should be treated as a deprivation. These issues require careful theoretical consideration, and the approach taken must be driven by the particular theoretical basis, definition of poverty and needs of the specific research. Elsewhere we have explored the potential to use the consensual method of poverty measurement with children (aged 8–16) themselves, with promising results suggesting that comparing children's and adults' reports on children's needs can offer a broader insight into their living conditions (Main and Bradshaw, 2012; Main, 2013).

Theoretically, then, there are viable rationales for opposite approaches to enforced and non-enforced lacks for children in the adult-reported PSE-UK 2012 data. Pragmatically, the effects of such approaches can be tested through comparing the rates of deprivation based on parentally reported enforced versus non-enforced lacks, and the kinds of children determined to be in poverty when alternative deprivation criteria are used – that is, when all lacks, rather than just enforced lacks, are counted as deprivations. In order to assess the potential impact of adult misclassification of items as lacked and not wanted when children do in fact want them, we explored differences between deprivation rates on each item or activity and among children lacking multiple items and activities based on consideration of enforced lack (want but cannot afford) and other lack (lack for other reasons). For most items, differences were found to be very small (<5%), indicating that few adults report children as lacking these for any reason other than being unable to afford them. Exceptions include:

- outdoor leisure equipment (10%)
- construction toys (23%)
- pocket money (14%)
- money to save (6%)

Among the activities, we found comparatively high levels of discrepancy between enforced and non-enforced lack: all but celebrations on special occasions had differences over 5%:

- hobby (7%)
- school trip (13%)
- toddler group (23%)
- clubs (19%)
- day trips (13%)
- holidays (9%)

For some of these items and activities (for example toddler group) it would be very difficult to ascertain whether parental reports truly reflect children's preferences, due to both the young age of child to which the activity is applicable and the purpose of the activity, which may meet both parental and children's needs. Others, however, such as pocket money and school trips, would lend themselves to testing through comparing parental and children's reports, since these items are particularly relevant to older children who have been demonstrated to have the capacity to respond to such questions (see Main and Bradshaw, 2012).

Using indices of deprivation based on summing, first, enforced lacks and, second, all lacks, it is possible to examine whether substantial differences in the classification of children as poor or deprived would occur based on these different choices. To compare these groups, we established thresholds based on classifying similar proportions of children as deprived, and compared the characteristics of children experiencing deprivation based on these alternative approaches.

Logistic regression can be used to examine the odds of being in poverty based on household employment status, family type, child age, ethnicity and housing tenure type. Findings indicate that:

- Household employment status and the child's age retained significant links to deprivation when enforced lack definitions were used, but not when all kinds of lack were counted.
- No clear pattern of difference between the two approaches was evident based on family type.
- Differences based on ethnicity were also unclear, but Pakistani/ Bangladeshi children were more likely to be deprived when all lacks were counted, an association which was not statistically significant when only enforced lacks were included.
- Children in socially or privately rented accommodation were more likely to be deprived than children in owner-occupied accommodation irrespective of the method for calculating deprivation.

On the whole, there is little evidence that there would be substantial differences in findings based on using the enforced lack approach as opposed to counting all lacks as deprivations. However, the rather substantial differences between rates of enforced lacks compared to all lacks for some items and activities highlights the importance of considering this issue, since children and parents may differ in their assessments of whether children are deprived or not. Our finding that household employment status was significantly associated with enforced lack but not with all lacks is not surprising, given that more employment in children's households is likely to be associated with higher income, meaning that lacks may be more likely to be a result of choice rather than necessity. However, it does not necessarily follow that the choices are those which children themselves, rather than parents, would make. Given that children are exposed to environments outside of their homes, and may encounter peers with access to resources which they themselves lack, it is entirely possible that children may be sensitive to lacking items and activities whether or not the reason for this lack is low income. This indicates that similar future studies could benefit from the inclusion, as far as practicably possible, of children. This inclusion should be in defining what items and activities are considered necessities, and in reporting on whether they have or lack socially perceived necessities. Based on our own concurrent research noted above (Main and Bradshaw, 2012), we believe there is a strong case for considering that children aged 8 and over have the capacity to respond to these types of question in survey settings.

Child poverty and social exclusion

Based on the three measures of child poverty available in the PSE-UK 2012 which are detailed in the Introduction, child poverty rates were:

- deprivation, based on children's access to child-specific personal and household non-income resources: 21%;
- income poverty, based on the after-housing-costs equivalised income of the household in which children live: 33%;
- PSE poverty, based on a combination of income and deprivation: 27%.

For the remainder of this chapter we focus on PSE poverty rates. Table 6.2 presents details of PSE poverty rates (the proportion of people who are poor) and composition (the proportion of the poor in each category), according to various socio-demographic characteristics. Significant differences between different social groups in their risk of exposure to poverty are detailed in the text below. Child poverty rates were found to differ in relation to several characteristics:

- *Household employment status:* Child poverty rates were highest in households containing no adults in paid work, including those in which adults were unemployed (47%) or inactive[5] (60%). The rate was lowest in households in which all adults worked full time (13%). However, in line with official poverty statistics (Shale et al, 2015), almost two thirds of poor children (60%) lived in households containing at least one adult in paid work – and only 6% lived in households with unemployed adults (with 34% living in households with inactive adults). Indeed, 12% of poor children lived in households within which all adults were in full-time employment, emphasising the need to look beyond activation to low pay and precarious employment in policy efforts to address child poverty.

- *Family type:* Child poverty rates were highest among lone parents, and especially lone parents with three or more children, with an 80% child poverty rate for this family structure. Having three or more children was also associated with an increased risk of child poverty for couple families, rising from a rate of 18% for couples with one or with two children, to 30% for couples with three or more children. However, 54% of poor children lived in couple families. This poses a challenge to the focus in Conservative proposals on family stability and structure rather than income in the diagnosis of poverty – such a change will likely result in the risk of misclassifying poor children as non-poor and vice versa based on a characteristic which does not provide a good proxy for living standards. The high poverty rates among families with three or more children is a matter for concern given recent policy developments limiting or proposing to limit access to benefits for families with three or more children (including the benefits cap, tax credits and child benefit). Such developments are highly likely to increase vulnerability to poverty for this already vulnerable group.

- *Child's age:* Differences in child poverty rates by age were not particularly large, ranging from 19% among 16–17-year-olds to 30% among 5–10-year-olds. Reflecting this, the composition of child poverty by age is similar to that of the population as a whole.

- *Ethnicity:* Child poverty rates were highest among children from Black African-mixed (44%), Black Caribbean-mixed (44%) and Pakistani/Bangladeshi (43%) ethnic groups. Children from Asian Indian backgrounds had the lowest rate at 9%. White British children matched the national poverty rate, at 27%. Chapter five of this volume presents more detailed findings relating to ethnicity.

- *Tenure:* Perhaps unsurprisingly, the highest poverty rate was found among children in socially rented accommodation, at 57%. Rates were also very high among children in private rented accommodation at 42%. Children in owner-occupied accommodation had the lowest poverty rates at 10%. In total, over three quarters of children – 78% – lived in rented accommodation, highlighting the prohibitive cost of home ownership for families on limited incomes.

In addition to overall deprivation, it is possible to use the material deprivation items to form indices representing domains within which children may experience deprivation.[6] These include food,[7] clothes,[8] participation,[9] development,[10] environment,[11] finance,[12] family[13] and individual.[14] Children lacking one or more of the items included in each domain are treated as deprived within that domain. The proportions of children deprived in each domain are detailed in Figure 6.1. The use of these domains may offer insight into how

Table 6.2: Poverty rates and composition of poor children by socio-demographic characteristics (%)

		PSE poverty		Total
		Rate	Composition	composition
	All FT	13	12	23
	Some FT, some PT	21	12	15
Household	Some FT, no PT	16	19	30
employment	All PT, no FT	43	11	6
status	Some PT, no FT	18	6	8
	No work, unemployed	47	6	3
	No work, inactive	60	34	14
	One adult, one child	44	9	6
	One adult, two children	39	11	7
	One adult, 3+ children	80	20	7
Family type	Two adults, one child	18	10	16
	Two adults, two children	18	22	32
	Two adults, 3+ children	30	22	21
	Other	15	6	11
	0–1	22	9	11
	2–4	28	18	18
Age of child	5–10	30	36	32
	11–15	29	29	28
	16–17	19	7	11
	White British	27	78	80
	White Other	30	5	4
	Black Caribbean/mixed	44	3	2
	Black African/mixed	44	5	3
Ethnicity	Asian Indian	9	1	3
	Pakistani/Bangladeshi	43	5	3
	Asian Other	16	2	3
	Other	28	2	2
	Owner	10	22	58
Tenure	Social renter	57	55	26
	Private renter	42	23	15
	Other	10	0	1
Total rate		**27**		

Note: Own analysis of PSE-UK 2012 data; shaded cells indicate <20 unweighted cases.
FT – full-time; PT – part-time.

parents prioritise children's needs when resources are tight – it appears that parents are likely to prioritise basic survival needs such as food and clothing, over more social and developmental needs relating to family and children's participation in wider society.

Figure 6.1: Proportion of children deprived on each domain

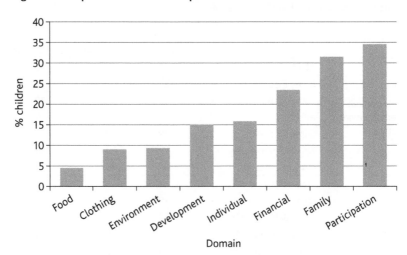

Note: Own analysis of PSE-UK 2012 data.

Child poverty, social exclusion, and outcomes

In this section we examine the associations between poverty and child-specific indicators of social exclusion and outcomes. Child-specific social exclusion indicators in the PSE-UK 2012 covered access to services for children and parents. Four possible negative outcomes for children were included – having had an injury or accident at home requiring A&E treatment; having been bullied; having special educational needs; and having been excluded from school. These questions were asked about all children within the household rather than about each child, so associations were explored between child poverty and living in a household where at least one child had experienced these outcomes. Here and in the next section, we use logistic regression to determine the odds of poor children/parents experiencing a particular issue, compared to non-poor children/parents. Odds ratios are provided, and can be interpreted as follows: an odds ratio of 1 indicates equal odds, below 1 indicates lower odds, and above 1 indicates higher odds.

Overall, child poverty was found to have significant links with missing out on a range of services and vulnerability to certain negative outcomes. This confirms that growing up in poverty impacts children beyond a simple lack of material resources, as social resources are less likely to be provided for these children and they are more likely to be exposed to social harms. Children experiencing poverty according to the PSE definition (that is, low income and deprivation) were significantly more likely to be excluded from all services other than public transport to school. The strongest association was with lack of access to nurseries, playgroups or mother and toddler groups. Regarding harms which children were vulnerable to, poor children were no more likely to have had an injury requiring emergency medical attention, or to have special educational needs. However, they were more likely to have been bullied, and to have been excluded from school – which may relate to the social stigma experienced by poor children and poor families. Results are shown in Table 6.3.

Table 6.3: Children's experiences of exclusion and negative outcomes

	% excluded overall	% excluded if poor	Odds if poor	
Service exclusion				
Facilities to safely play/spend time nearby	27	41	2.6	*
School meals	12	17	1.9	*
Youth clubs	26	34	1.8	*
After school clubs	12	20	2.4	*
Public transport to school	13	15	1.3	NS
Nurseries/playgroups/mother and toddler groups	6	17	11.4	*
Negative outcomes				
Injury or accident at home requiring A&E	20	23	1.2	NS
Child has ever been bullied	34	44	1.8	*
Child has special educational needs	16	17	1.2	NS
Child has ever been excluded from school	8	13	2.6	*

Note: Own analysis of PSE-UK 2012 data; NS – not statistically significant; * significant at the $p<0.05$ level; ** significant at the $p<0.01$ level.

Poor children, poor families?

Policy rhetoric under the previous Conservative-led Coalition (2010–15) and now the Conservative (2015–) governments has positioned child poverty as a problem stemming from parental (in) action and behaviours, rather than a structural problem requiring a redistributive response (see chapter one and Conclusion). A strong advantage the PSE poverty measure has over income-based poverty measures is that it allows for an examination of intra-household distributions of resources. Comparing poverty rates between adults and children, and for adults between those who live in households with children and those who do not, we begin to develop a more nuanced understanding of how different social groups allocate their resources, and especially how resources are shared within children's households. Such an understanding can provide evidence to test claims that parental behaviours, rather than low income, are the cause of child poverty. Poverty rates for these groups, compared to a baseline population rate of 22%, were:

- 21% among all adults
- 27% among children
- 15% among adults living in households which did not contain children
- 32% among adults living in households which did contain children

Thus, while poverty rates are higher for children than for adults as a whole, adults who live with children face the highest risk of poverty among these groups. That is, based on a combination of both income and the resources they have access to, adults living with children are more likely to be going without than the children they live with. Breaking this down again so that we can compare adults and children within households, based on classing adults as poor if any adult in the household was poor, and children as poor if any child in the household was poor, we found that:

- 56% of children lived in households where neither children nor adults are poor
- 27% of children lived in households where both children and adults are poor
- 16% of children lived in households where children are not poor but adults are poor
- 1% of children lived in households where children are poor but adults are not poor

This reinforces the above point that adults are more likely to be going without than children. While most children have a poverty status that is congruent with that of the adults they live with, among those who do not a much higher proportion live in what we might term 'incongruent protected' situations – where there is poverty in their household but they are not exposed to it – than in 'incongruent exposed' situations – where there is poverty in their household which they are exposed to but which they adults they live with are not (Main and Bradshaw, 2014). A reasonable interpretation of this may be that adults are attempting to protect the children in their households from exposure to poverty, often at the expense of their own living standards.

To test this hypothesis further we examined economising behaviours among adults living in households containing children, comparing those adults who lived in households containing poor children, to those living in households where children were not poor. Adults in households with poor children were significantly more likely to engage in the whole range of economising behaviours,[15] compared to adults in households with non-poor children. Examining the proportion of adults engaging in economising behaviours, and the odds of adults in households with poor children economising compared to adults in households with children who were not poor, we found:

- 69% skimped on their own food so that someone else could have enough, odds of 5.0:1
- 56% bought second-hand instead of new clothes for themselves, odds of 2.8:1
- 82% continued to wear worn-out clothes, odds of 3.3:1
- 66% cut back on visits to the hairdresser or barber, odds of 4.3:1
- 59% postponed visits to the dentist, odds of 2.3:1
- 87% spent less on their hobbies, odds of 2.9:1
- 92% cut back on social visits, odds of 3.6:1

Thus evidence points to almost all adults acting in protective ways towards their children, with children exposed to poverty as a result of a lack of household resources, rather than irresponsible or unskilled parenting. This point is taken up in greater detail in chapter seven, which covers parents' experiences of poverty and social exclusion.

Conclusion

In this chapter we have detailed the main findings relating to child poverty from the PSE-UK 2012 survey. The importance of child poverty to children's lives in the present, and to the adults they will become, is well documented; similarly, that child poverty is a serious problem in the UK has been established in a range of cross-national studies (Adamson, 2013). A range of policy interventions under the 1997–2010 Labour administrations, focusing both on redistribution towards families with children and activation of parents, resulted in declining poverty rates among children. More recently, though, the Conservative-led Coalition and subsequent Conservative governments have implemented austerity measures justified by arguments of economic necessity and by a reconceptualisation of the nature and causes of poverty. Families with children have been among those who have lost out most, through reductions to both incomes and services (Reed and Portes, 2014). Progress towards reducing child poverty in the UK has halted, and we are beginning to see increases (DWP, 2017). In addition, the vulnerability of families with children to future economic shocks has increased.

The Child Poverty Act's receipt of Royal Assent in 2010 was preceded by over a decade of concerted policy effort. While these efforts were only equivocally successful, substantial progress was made (Bradshaw, 2011; Piachaud, 2012; Lupton et al, 2013). Furthermore, Lewis (2011) noted a broad political consensus on the 'pillars' forming the basis on which eradicating child poverty would be achieved, including redistribution, activation/work intensification and upskilling workers. Changes introduced under the Conservative-led Coalition and subsequent Conservative governments, while broadly based around these same pillars, reflect a different emphasis which mirrors a different underlying explanation of poverty. That is, while individual explanations of poverty (which, in contrast to structural explanations, focus on individual shortcomings rather than social structures as the cause of poverty) were evident in some Labour policies, they dominate Conservative policy and rhetoric. While the Labour goals of increasing work intensity may be seen as rooted in a desire to 'make work pay', Conservative policies have increasingly been framed along the lines of 'ensure social security does not pay'. This emphasis is evident in the combined impact of their reform of working-age social security, which has included variously the abolition, freezing and cutting of different benefits (see Main and Bradshaw, 2014, 2016), and the rhetoric around child and working-age poverty, which has been framed in terms of 'overly generous' benefits 'trapping' poor families into 'dependence' (Joint Public issues Team, 2013; see also Main and Bradshaw, 2016). As a result, the role of redistribution has significantly declined since 2010, and several analyses of the distributional consequences of austerity have concluded that families with children are among the main losers (Cribb et al, 2013; Office of the Children's Commissioner, 2013; Reed and Portes, 2014; Lupton et al, 2015).

Alongside the shift in focus of economic policy noted above, discussions of child poverty have simultaneously shifted from a focus on increasing incomes as the best route to poverty reduction, to upskilling poor parents and altering parental behaviours, which have been positioned as among the root causes of child poverty (see Main and Bradshaw, 2014, 2016). An examination of perceptions of children's necessities and the intra-household distributions of resources between adults and children, presented in this chapter, provides a strong challenge to these narratives. Particularly of note are the findings that 60% of poor children live in households with at least one adult in paid work, emphasising the need for redistributive policies going beyond activation; and that 69% of adults in households with poor children are skimping on food, emphasising the alarming sacrifices poor parents are making in order to provide for their children. Current policies and policy proposals which stress parental skills and limit access to benefits for families represent a worrying development and are likely to result in increasing child poverty rates.

While the PSE-UK 2012, as a cross-sectional study, cannot offer insight into trends in child poverty rates, it contributes to our understanding of the nature and extent of child poverty in the early days of the 2010–15 Coalition, and some comparisons can be drawn with earlier studies. Comparing perceptions of necessities for children in 2012 and 1999, we find that in most cases there is a high level of stability in terms of what adults deem to be children's necessities. However, it is also clear that in some aspects of children's lives – for example their access to technologies such as the internet – new necessities are emerging which reflect broader social trends. The capacity to examine poverty in a manner which takes into account shared household resources such as income, but also considers children's differing needs compared to adults based on their unique status as both beings with needs in the present and becomings who require resources to develop towards adulthood, is a notable strength of the PSE approach. The resulting characteristics of the PSE poverty measure allow for the comparison of poverty experiences within households, allowing for the development of a strong challenge to current policy approaches detailed above. Simultaneously, we argue that this approach could be further developed through the inclusion of children themselves in future similar studies, addressing some of the possible limitations highlighted, for example, by UNICEF.

Many of the findings presented here are familiar. The characteristics of poor children reaffirm many previous findings, for example about the associations between child poverty and ethnicity. Regarding household work status, our findings echo official statistics (Shale et al, 2015), which show that most poor children live in households containing at least one adult in paid work. In contrast, our analysis of intra-household sharing represents a development, confirming with quantitative data the findings of qualitative studies which show parents to be sacrificing their own needs to provide for their children (such as

Ridge, 2002). Child deprivation rates would be much higher, and the depth of deprivation experienced by children more severe, if parents were not sacrificing their own living standards for the sake of their children. Our findings point to the need for a refocusing of policy on poverty reduction through redistribution, considering the needs both of children and parents.

Notes

[1] Child poverty rates based on children living in households with an income below 60% of the national median rose from 13% (before housing costs – BHC)/14% (after housing costs – AHC) in 1979 to 27% (BHC)/34% (AHC) in 1996/7 – see Bradshaw et al, 2017).

[2] Rates fell from 27% (BHC)/34% (AHC) in 1996/7 to 18% (BHC)/27% (AHC) in 2010/11.

[3] Non-overlapping confidence intervals, used to indicate a statistically significant difference.

[4] See: www.unicef-irc.org/publications/710; www.unicef-irc.org/publications/744

[5] 'Inactivity' is used here in the sense of labour market activity – this of course does not capture the wide range of activities which adults classed as 'inactive' are engaged in.

[6] These indices, as evident below, are not independent – i.e. they contain overlapping items.

[7] Including three meals; fruit; meat.

[8] Including coat; shoes; clothes; trousers.

[9] Including celebrations; hobby; clubs; day trips; holiday; leisure.

[10] Including books; study; games; computer; Lego; school trips.

[11] Including garden; bedroom.

[12] Including pocket money; saving money.

[13] Including holiday; day trips; celebrations.

[14] Including hobby; clubs; school trips; leisure.

[15] One of the PSE economising questions, regarding contributing to a pension fund, was not included in this analysis because of missing data as many respondents noted that this question was not relevant for them.

References

Adamson, P. (2013) *Child well-being in rich countries: A comparative overview*, Innocenti Report Card 11, Florence: UNICEF.

Bradshaw, J. (2011) 'Child poverty', in N. Yeates, T. Haux, R. Jawad and M. Kilkey (eds) *In defence of welfare: The impacts of the spending review*, London: Social Policy Association, 17–19.

Bradshaw, J., Chzhen, Y. and Main, G. (2017) 'Children and the crisis: UK', in B. Cantillon, Y. Chzhen, S. Handa and B. Nolan (eds) *Children of austerity: Impact of the Great Recession on child poverty in rich countries*, Oxford: Oxford University Press.

Brewer, M., Clark, T. and Goodman, A. (2002) *The government's child poverty target: How much progress has been made?* Institute for Fiscal Studies Commentary 88, London: Institute for Fiscal Studies.

Carr, J., Councell, R., Higgs, M. and Singh, N. (2014) *Households below average income: An analysis of the income distribution 1994/95–2012/13*, London: DWP.

Cribb, J., Hood, A., Joyce, R. and Phillips, D. (2013) *Living standards, poverty and inequality in the UK: 2013*, London: Institute for Fiscal Studies.

DWP (Department for Work and Pensions) (2017) *Households below average income: An analysis of the UK income distribution*, London: DWP.

Gordon, D. (2017) 'Producing an "objective" poverty line in eight easy steps', PSE-UK paper, www.poverty.ac.uk/sites/default/files/attachments/Steps-to-producing-the-PSEpoverty-line_Gordon.pdf

Gordon, D. Nandy, S., Pantazis, C., Pemberton, S. and Townsend, P. (2003) *Child poverty in the developing world*, Bristol: Policy Press.

Harker, L. (2006) *Delivering on child poverty: What would it take?*, A report for the Department for Work and Pensions, Cm6951, London: The Stationery Office.

Joint Public Issues Team (2013) *The lies we tell ourselves: Ending comfortable myths about poverty*, A report from the Baptist Union of Great Britain, the Methodist Church, the Church of Scotland and the United Reformed Church, http://csc.ceceurope.org/fileadmin/filer/csc/Social_Economic_Issues/Truth-And-Lies-Report.pdf

Lewis, P. (2011) 'Upskilling the workers will not upskill the work: why the dominant economic framework limits child poverty reduction in the UK', *Journal of Social Policy* 40:3, 535–56.

Lloyd, E. (2006) 'Children, poverty and social exclusion', in C. Pantazis, D. Gordon and R. Levitas (eds) *Poverty and social exclusion in Britain*, Bristol: Policy Press.

Lupton, R., Hills, J., Stewart, K. and Vizard, P. (2013) *Labour's social policy record: Policy, spending and outcomes 1997–2010*, Social Policy in a Cold Climate Report 1, June, http://sticerd.lse.ac.uk/dps/case/spcc/rr01.pdf

Lupton, R., Burchardt, T., Fitgerald, A., Hills, J., McKnight, A., Obolenskaya, P. et al (2015) *The coalition social policy record: Policy, spending and outcomes 1997–2010*, Social Policy in a Cold Climate Report 4, January, http://sticerd.lse.ac.uk/dps/case/spcc/RR04.pdf

Mack, J. and Lansley, S. (1985) *Poor Britain*, London: George Allen and Unwin.

Main, G. (2013) *A child-derived material deprivation index*, unpublished PhD thesis, University of York.

Main, G. and Bradshaw, J. (2012) 'An index of child material deprivation', *Child Indicators Research* 5:3, 503–21.

Main, G. and Bradshaw, J. (2014) 'Children's necessities: trends over time in perceptions and ownership', *Journal of Poverty and Social Justice* 23:3, 193–208.

Main, G. and Bradshaw, J. (2016) 'Child poverty in the UK: measures, prevalence and intra-household sharing', *Critical Social Policy* 36:1, 38–61.

Malone, C. (2014) 'Poverty has not doubled it is greed that has grown', Mirror, 21 June, www.mirror.co.uk/news/uk-news/poverty-not-doubled-greed-grown-3738335

Office of the Children's Commissioner (2013) *A child rights impact assessment of budget decisions: Including the 2013 Budget, and the cumulative impact of tax–benefit reforms and reductions in spending on public services 2010–2015*, www.childrenscommissioner.gov.uk/content/publications/content_676

Piachaud, D. (1981) 'Peter Townsend and the Holy Grail', *New Society*, 10 September.

Piachaud, D. (2012) 'Poverty and social protection in Britain: Policy developments since 1997', *Journal of Policy Practice* 11:1–2, 92–105.

Reed, H. and Portes, J. (2014) *Cumulative impact assessment*, Research report 94, Landman Economics and the National Institute of Economic and Social Research for the Equality and Human Rights Commission.

Ridge, T. (2002) *Childhood poverty and social exclusion*, Bristol: Policy Press.

Shale, J., Balchin, K., Rahman, J., Reeve, R. and Rolin, M. (2015) *Households below average income: An analysis of the income distribution 1994/5–2013/14*, London: DWP.

Townsend, P. (1979) *Poverty in the United Kingdom: A survey of household resources and standards of living*, Harmondsworth: Penguin.

SEVEN

The cost of children: parents, poverty, and social support

Esther Dermott and Marco Pomati

Introduction

Parental behaviour and parents in general have not been of interest in previous poverty surveys; a fact reflected in their omission from publications based on earlier Poverty and Social Exclusion (PSE) research. What justifies their inclusion this time is a changing popular, political and policy climate which has placed parents and their behaviours as centrally important to current and future levels of poverty in the UK. Parents are now framed as both the cause of, and potentially solution to, child poverty in a way not previously witnessed (Dermott, 2013).

Parents' experience of poverty and social exclusion

Parents are generally at higher risk of poverty than non-parents because of the added financial cost of children (Misra et al, 2012). In the UK, it has been argued, that this is at least partly due to a process of 'defamilization' (Lewis and Giullari, 2005), which has meant that private formal childcare plays a significant part in many families' organisation of care (albeit as an element of complicated mixture of provision alongside other family members, state providers, and voluntary organisations; Daly, 2011). The UK has among the highest costs for childcare of any country in Europe, equivalent to 26.6% of family income (Norman, 2014); significantly more mothers in the UK say that they do not work or work part-time because childcare services are too expensive (European Commission, 2013). Lone mothers have consistently been an even poorer group than parents as a whole (Bradshaw et al, 2000; Dermott and Pantazis, 2014; Dermott and Pomati, 2016a), as initiatives to encourage or coerce them into the labour market have largely failed to generate sufficient income to overcome poverty (Harkness, 2013).

Social exclusion is a broader concept than low income or deprivation and covers a range of dimensions, including access to services, social support and relationships, and access to social and economic participation (Levitas et al, 2007). It refers to the way in which disadvantage can include various forms of disconnection from the community; 'The implications of the concept of social exclusion for research on parenting are that research should ... [include] factors such as connectedness with the local community and ... access to mainstream services and transport' (Katz et al, 2007, p 6). However, in practice, social exclusion has been viewed primarily in relation to exclusion from the labour market (Levitas, 2005). This is perhaps most evident with respect to the longstanding international political concern with the employment rates of lone mothers, accompanied by a range of policy interventions to increase their levels of labour market involvement (Land, 2001; Haux, 2013). In the UK this has been framed as a way of reducing extremely high levels of poverty among this group and their children in order to reduce costs to the state (Berrington, 2014). Yet, from qualitative sociological research on families and the networks of support that they offer, we know that parents' social connections and communities are extremely important as parents rely on close relatives and peers for advice as well as practical support. This may take a whole range of forms: from the role of female relatives offering emotional and social support (as Mitchell and Green, 2002, title their article 'I don't know what I'd do without our mam'), to relying on grandparents for 'wraparound' informal childcare (Bryson et al, 2012), to facilitating leaving home transitions (Holdsworth, 2004), to direct financial support for those managing on limited resources (Daly and Kelly, 2015), to peer sharing websites (such as Mumsnet) for ideas on how to deal with anything from childhood illness to planning holidays to divorce arrangements. Capturing the extent and nature of these social relations and support is therefore valuable.

Parenting and poverty

The shift in parenting culture has been well documented in sociological studies of parent–child relationships (for example, Lee et al, 2014). Sharon Hays's (1996) work traced the rise and establishment of 'intensive parenting' in the US, characterised by child-centred, labour-intensive and expensive mothering. Authors such as Frank Furedi in *Paranoid parenting* (2001) took up this theme and suggested that it was equally applicable in the UK. The expansion of parenting manuals as a sub-genre of self-help books and proliferation of websites, blogs and magazines offering 'how to' guides are testament to an ongoing high public profile around a wide range of parental issues; from demographic concerns over who is having children and when, to debates over access to reproductive technologies, to heated debates over parenting styles.

In the UK, these broader debates about the nature of parenting gained further ground due to a political shift in family policy during the New Labour government, which saw parents gaining attention as among the key actors in the fulfilment of New Labour's campaign to improve social mobility and children's educational standards (Henricson, 2012). The Coalition government between 2010 and 2015 and latterly, since 2015, the Conservative government, have further promoted the idea that what parents do in the home has a major role in the life chances of their children (Field, 2010; Cameron, 2016) which, as a consequence, justified intervention in this sphere. Policy and research interest has shifted from estimating the importance of family form (especially a stable nuclear household arrangement) on outcomes for children in the 1980s and 1990s to the relationship between parenting (that is, the practices of parents) and children's educational achievements. The emphasis has been placed particularly on parent–child activities that are associated with educational development, such as reading and direct engagement with schools. Evidence suggests that parents have bought into this discourse: surveys commissioned by the Department for Education show that the percentage of parents who felt very involved in their child's school life increased from 30% to 50% between 2001 and 2007, and that parents are also more involved in activities such as reading and playing games compared to the beginning of the millennium (Peters et al, 2008).

The most recent shift in policy discourse has made an explicit link between educational underachievement of the poorest children in UK society and the behaviour of their parents. Although increasing involvement in parenting activities has not been associated with a narrowing in achievement gap between children from different backgrounds, the idea that parents can transcend household income has become engrained in policy circles (see for example then Prime Minister David Cameron's speech in 2016). Being brought up in a low-income household is associated with a substantial disadvantage in school (Hills et al, 2010). The school attainment of children eligible for free school meals (FSM) remains considerably lower than the average: the government indicators for GCSEs show a gap of 27 percentage points between those eligible for FSM and those who are not (DfE,

2015), with very little progress between the early 2000s and 2014. Recent research by Mills (2015) also shows a similarly large gap between children from higher managerial and professional homes and those from routine employment or not in employment at all (with 90% and 50% of boys passing five GCSEs respectively). The downplaying of the importance of economic inequalities means that individuals are blamed for their own disadvantage and parents with low incomes are blamed for failing to do the best for their children and for increasing the likelihood that their children will grow up in poverty and in turn become poor adults. A belief in the importance of parenting practices is used to suggest that it is parents who are living in poverty that are the problem. In one of the most influential reports on poverty and life chances in the UK, Frank Field noted that: 'Something more fundamental than the scarcity of money is adversely dominating the lives of these children. Since 1969 I have witnessed a growing indifference from some parents to meeting the most basic needs of children, and particularly younger children, those who are least able to fend for themselves' (Field, 2010, p 16). This goes against available evidence, which suggests that low-income parents (and particularly mothers) tend to protect their children from the impact of poverty by prioritising their children's needs over their own (Middleton et al, 1997; Ghate and Hazel, 2002; Bennett, 2008; see also chapter six in this volume). In 2011, Daly and Kelly (2015) interviewed 51 families in Northern Ireland and found that parents on low incomes felt under substantial pressure to preserve children's development and learning, as well as protecting them from the shame experienced in school by failing to keep up with their peers' consumption. Although there has been an increasing focus on parental activities in general there has been a focus on the poorest families (Gillies, 2008).

Parents in the UK receive relatively limited financial support from the state which is directed specifically to childcare needs. Child benefit which is a (near) universal scheme pays £20.70 a week for the eldest or only child and £13.70 for each additional child; for those earning over £50,000 per year, the entitlement is means tested and reduced on a sliding scale. However, the entitlement to 15 hours of free childcare a week for 3- and 4-year-olds (for 38 weeks of the year), which was introduced in 2013, has since been extended to include some disadvantaged 2-year-olds, and from September 2017 working parents are eligible for up to 30 hours care for their children. For lone parents, the age of the youngest child, which determines whether lone parents are entitled to claim a more generous form of welfare support (rather than unemployment benefit), has been reduced over the years from

16 to 5. Recently, the government has re-emphasised its view that providing parents with additional money has a limited ability to reduce poverty or improve parenting and instead asserted the value of other forms of parenting training. David Cameron announced in January 2016 that 'we now need to think about how to make it normal – even aspirational to attend parenting classes' and that vouchers would be provided to incentivise parents to enrol on such schemes. Even before this statement, Daly (2013) noted considerable growth in the number of parenting support programmes.

Parents as a whole have been under-studied and recent discourse around social mobility, educational attainment and the home learning environment suggests that now is a pertinent moment to analyse parents' material circumstances alongside specific parenting behaviours. There is therefore a need to map out the extent of poverty and social connectedness among parents to add to the picture of relative advantage and disadvantage across the population as a whole, as well as to explore the relationship between poverty and parenting practices which has dominated political and popular discourse in recent years. This chapter addresses both of these demands.

Measures

Using the Poverty and Social Exclusion Survey 2012 (PSE-UK 2012) we provide analysis of the extent of poverty and social support among parents; parents' economising practices; the situation of parents with regard to providing educational resources for children; and extent to which parents engage in a range of 'good' parent–child activities. This chapter focuses mainly on comparing the experiences of couple and lone parents, and between parents who are living in poverty and those who are not. We first provide analysis of the extent of poverty among parents using the 'PSE poverty' measure which combines income poverty and material deprivation. This measure, with its origins in Peter Townsend's work on relative poverty and Mack and Lansley's (1985) development of consensual poverty, defines living standards based on relative income *and* the extent to which individuals and households lack socially perceived necessities (see chapter one of this volume for details on how this is calculated). We also use an income-only measure of poverty (60% of the median equivalised household income after housing costs) to minimise the overlap between our definition of poverty and economising practices and child deprivation. We also examine social contact and social support as one element of social inclusion/exclusion by looking at the extent to which parents say that they lack adequate practical and/ or emotional support.

We then explore economising practices by examining how parents say they have cut back in the 12 months prior to the survey in order to reduce living costs, as well as the neighbourhood characteristics of parents who are in poverty. Given the focus on educational attainment as a potential route out of poverty for children and engagement with schools as a requirement of 'good' parents, we look at the living standards of parents who cannot afford certain educational resources, which are viewed either as necessities or desirable, for at least one child. One of the best indicators of children's educational advantage in international studies is living standards items as measured by the number of books in the household (Schulz, 2006) and we therefore particularly highlight the circumstances of those parents who cannot afford suitable books for their children.

In relation to parenting practices, we explore the relationship between 'good parenting' activities and socio-economic background. We focus on six activities which span across family meal habits, leisure and educational activities (see Table 7.1). Specifically, we explore how often parents and children jointly: have meals; play games and sport; watch television together; read or talked about reading; help or talk about homework. Finally, we look at whether parents have attended school parents' evenings in the last 12 months. The aim here is to explore the popular claim that it is what parents are doing in terms of specific forms of involvement which varies across income and class position.

Poverty, social contact, and social support

Looking first at overall levels of poverty (Table 7.2) the PSE poverty measure indicates that 61% of lone parents are living in poverty with a further 7% either being vulnerable to poverty (having a low income but not deprived of necessities) or rising (currently with high levels of deprivation but with an adequate level of income). This confirms what is already known about the extremely high levels of poverty experienced by this group of mainly women. While it is the figure for lone parents that stands out, it is also notable that the level of poverty among couple parents, at 28%, is higher than the figure for adults in general (22%) and for non-parents (16%), again confirming the cost of having children.

The significance of the role of paid work as the route out of poverty for adults has been frequently repeated by recent UK governments

Table 7.1: Frequency of parenting activities

Education
- In the last 12 months, have you (or your partner) attended a school parents' evening? (Yes/No)
- In the past year, have you employed a private tutor for your child/children? (No; Yes to assist children with mainstream school subjects and/or to teach children other skills)
- How many days in the past 7 days have you, or your partner read stories with your child/children or talked with them about what they are reading? (Never/Some (1–3) days; Most (4–6) days/Every day)
- How many days in the past 7 days have you, or your partner helped with or discussed homework with your child/children? (Never/Some (1–3) days; Most (4–6) days/Every day)

Leisure
- How many days in the past 7 days have you, or your partner played games with your child/children eg computer games, toys, puzzles etc.? (Never/Some (1–3) days; Most (4–6) days/Every day)
- How many days in the past 7 days have you, or your partner done sporting or physical activities with your child/children? (Never/Some (1–3) days; Most (4–6) days/Every day)
- How many days in the past 7 days have you, or your partner watched TV with your child/children? (Never/Some (1–3) days; Most (4–6) days/Every day)

Family mealtimes
- How many days in the past 7 days have you, or your partner eaten an evening meal with your child/children? (Never/Some (1–3) days; Most (4–6) days/Every day)

Table 7.2: Percentage of parents living in PSE poverty

	Family type (%)	
	Lone parent	Couple
Poor	61	28
Rising/vulnerable	7	8
Not poor	32	65
N=2,642	490	2,152

(Bailey, 2016). Exploring poverty at the household level by family type and employment status shows that those people who are not in work do emerge as most likely to be in poverty, followed by households whose members are not in full-time work. More than half of households whose adults are either inactive or unemployed are in poverty and around half of working families with adults not in full-time work and with children are in poverty. However, the financial struggle of families with children is actually starkest when looking at poverty rates for full-time workers. Among lone parents, full-time work is far from a sure way out of poverty: 30% of all single-parent households in full-time work are in poverty, compared to 15% of singles without children, 10% of couples with children and 5% of couples without children. So while being in full-time employment decreases the chances of parents being poor, it is certainly not the solution. As Bailey (2016) argues, the idea that labour market participation can resolve poverty relies on people having access to particular kinds of well remunerated work; and it is this work which may be more difficult for those with childcare responsibilities to access.

In terms of the ability to access practical or emotional support, there are differences between lone and couple parents. There are some clear and statistically significant differences between couple and lone parents in terms of those who report they would get 'not much' support during a personal crisis, if they were ill in bed, in need of advice, if they had relationship problems, needed someone to look after the home or had a serious personal crisis: 11% of couple parents report low levels of support if in need of someone looking after the home, compared to 19% of lone parents. Lone parents are also significantly more likely to report low levels of support for household and gardening jobs and when ill in bed (25% compared to 8% for couple parents). Given that lone parents are the sole adult in a household (in our measure of lone parenthood), this finding seems to indicate that parents tend to rely on those they live with for practical help, while emotional support may be forthcoming from outside of their household.[1] Indeed this disparity in being able to access practical help emerges despite the finding that lone parents are most likely to be engaged in frequent contact outside the household with both relatives and friends. Around 50% of all lone parents see relatives every day, and 40% see friends just as regularly; compared to lower levels of everyday contact with friends and relatives of around 30% or below for couples with and without children. The lower levels of support experienced by lone parents may therefore be a sign of lower availability of help *within* the household, which cannot be met by outside help despite high levels of social contact.

Economising and educational resources

The economising practices of parents show, unsurprisingly, a strong correlation with income. Parents on a low income are more likely to have cut back in the last year across the board: skimping on food so that others would have enough to eat, buying second-hand rather than new clothes, as well as curtailing their expenditure on eating out, hobbies, hairdressers, clothes and visits to the dentist. Figure 7.1 shows that those with incomes below 60% of the equivalised median

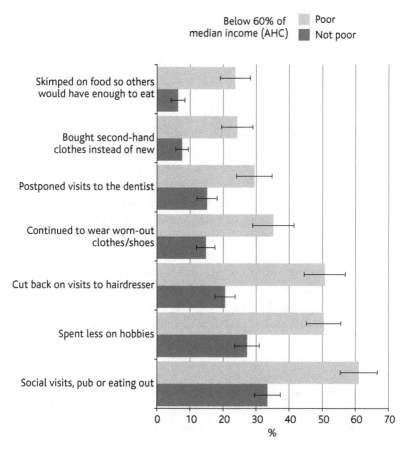

Figure 7.1: Percentage of parents economising by household poverty status (with 95% confidence intervals – CI)

household after housing costs (AHC) are at least twice as likely to economise often on any of these items than those whose income is higher. If we inspect the whole income distribution, those in the bottom income quartile are roughly four times more likely than those in the top quartile to skimp on food so that others in the household would have enough to eat. Given that lone parents have much higher rates of poverty than couple parents, it is unsurprising that they are also substantially more likely to economise than parents living as couples. This is in line with what we might expect as those with fewer material resources are forced to cut back more and go without, but it goes against the political narrative that poorer people are profligate spenders who would have an acceptable standard of living if they were able to manage their finances better (for example, Iain Duncan Smith quoted in *The Guardian*, 2014). As Main and Bradshaw (this volume) indicate in chapter six, these economising practices of parents do make a difference to the lives of children. There is a significant proportion of families in the UK in which children are not materially deprived, even though the household as a whole is classed as poor.

In cutting back to protect the living standards of their children the vast majority of parents – regardless of their household income – are able to provide their children with key educational resources (Table 7.3). (Note that we use an income-only measure here rather than 'PSE poverty' measure as some of the educational items were used as markers of deprivation to calculate the combined PSE poverty measure.) Only 2% of parents report that they do not have books suitable for their child's age because they cannot afford them, suggesting this is a very extreme form of deprivation. This is borne out by analysis of the living standards of these parents. Those who cannot afford suitable books on average lack ten necessities, compared to a median of two for those who say that they can afford appropriate books for children. Virtually all of these parents do not go on holiday away from home for one week a year because they cannot afford it and almost half (45%) have skimped on food often so that other others in the household would have enough to eat. They are also much more likely (84% compared to 38%) to report dogs and dog mess as a problem in their area, as well as seven times more likely (73% compared to 13%) to report that there are drug dealing activities locally. This seems to corroborate Ghate and Hazel's (2002) findings that parents on very low incomes were much more likely to live in areas unsuitable for their children to play. There is, then, a deprived group of parents who have extremely limited financial resources they can use to support children's educational and social activities, and this may be exacerbated by living in communities which are under-resourced.

However, it is still the case that on average low-income households have restricted access to educational resources. Around 25% of parents who are 'income poor' cannot afford at least one of: school trips at

Table 7.3: Percentage of parents who cannot afford educational items by income poverty status

		School trip (%)	Computer and internet for homework (%)	Suitable place to study (%)	Suitable books (%)	Lacking at least one item (%)
Below 60% median household income after housing costs	No	4	4	4	1	10
	Yes	11	10	6	3	25

least once a term; computer and internet for homework; a suitable place at home to study or do homework; adequate books. While 10% of parents who do not qualify as poor on the income measure say that cannot afford at least one of these items. Similarly, there is a gap in terms of the ability of parents to pay for children's clubs or activities (such as attending a drama group or football training), which may not be categorised as necessities but are widely valued as offering children social benefits and skills. Fifteen per cent of parents below the income poverty line compared to less than 5% of those parents above this threshold say that these are unaffordable. Again, there is no evidence that these parents claim that children's activities are beyond their means while they spend money on themselves.

Parenting activities

Given the constrained material circumstances of poorer parents, we might expect to find significant differences in terms of the frequency and types of parent–child activities that are undertaken. However, our analysis indicates a lot of overlap in the frequency of good parenting activities among couple and lone parents, and across income groups. As shown in Figure 7.2 over half of all parents say they spend four or more days a week eating a meal with their children, watching TV together, reading and helping children with their homework, and playing games. The only exception is sporting activities which a minority (c. 30%) of parents do most or every day. As might be anticipated, the frequency of activities such as playing games and assistance with homework varies strongly according to the age of the youngest child in the household. When this variable is accounted for, levels of parent–child activities are markedly similar. In addition, the overwhelming majority of parents said that they had attended a parents' evening in the last year.

There are no statistically significant differences between couple and lone parents, with the exception of playing sports (9% of lone parents compared to 17% for couple parents) and eating a meal together (90% and 83% respectively). We might speculate that the difference in playing sports reflects a gendered dimension to mothering and fathering activities as the vast majority of lone parents are women. The figures for eating together might reflect a requirement to share meals due to more limited finances.[2] Overall, the levels of parental activities are very similar across both groups.

We also find very weak evidence of differences in parenting across the income distribution. Parents in non-poor households are marginally more likely to report undertaking parental activities. However, the

Figure 7.2: Percentage of parents reporting they undertake parent–child activities most days or every day by family type (first set of bars) and poverty status (second set), 95% CI

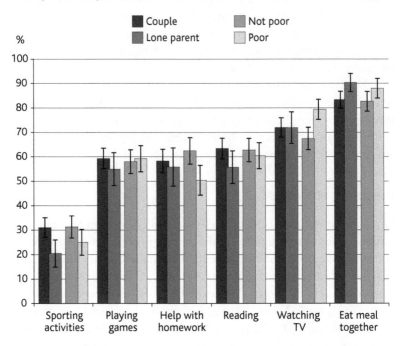

differences are very small and not statistically significant, except for watching TV. Similarly, we do not find major differences across the income distribution, except that parents at the very top of the income distribution are significantly less likely to watch TV and eat meals with their children most or every day; more than 75% of parents in the bottom quartile watch TV together with their children 'often' compared to 60% of those in the top quartile (Figure 7.3). Elsewhere (Dermott and Pomati, 2016b) we speculate in more depth on the reasons for these differences. We suggest that the figures for television viewing may be explained by the range of social activities available to those with different incomes, and that differences between parents' reporting of eating a meal together may be due to a combination of the time schedules of middle-class children engaged in activities outside the home and the work schedules of their parents. In addition, those in the top income quintile are marginally more likely to help with homework, which may reflect a higher level of engagement with formal educational achievement. The findings echo Hartas's analysis of the Millennium Cohort Study (2014) which analysed answers from

Figure 7.3: Percentage of parents reporting they undertake parent–child activities most days or every day by income quartile, 95% CI

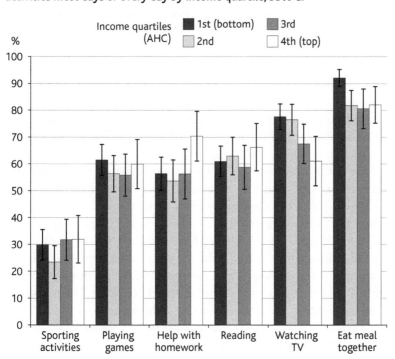

parents with children of the same age. She found that parents from different socio-economic background engaged with various learning activities roughly equally; overall there was no clear divide between the frequencies of 'good parenting' activities based on poverty level. There is, then, no indication of a group of poor parents who are failing to engage in a range of 'good' parenting practices (see also Dermott and Pomati, 2016b).

Conclusion

The first conclusion from the analysis of parents in the PSE study is that having children increases the chances of being poor in the UK today. Parenthood is expensive, and the combined effect of the costs of childcare, loss of income and limited state support means that becoming a parent may be a 'trigger' event for poverty. Viviana Zelizer's book *Pricing the priceless child* (1985) traced the rise of societies in which children are 'emotionally priceless' but economically a drain on household resources: it seems likely that many households with children will continue to experience significant material deprivation. It is single parents who, as in the PSE-GB 1999 survey (Bradshaw et al, 2000), stand out as having exceptionally high poverty rates: even full-time employment is often not sufficient to keep these families out of poverty. In a period when expectations of good parenting have increasingly become time intensive and financially expensive (Hays, 1996) this may be even more of an acute problem. The relative inability of poorer parents to provide an increasing number of commonly accepted resources in order to support their children's development, and especially educational progress, is however often labelled as an individual failing rather than a societal fault.

The second conclusion is that parents do prioritise their children's needs. Parents do their best to ensure that children have the items and activities that the population think of as necessities, and engage in parent–child activities associated with 'good' parenting. There is significant evidence of self-sacrifice and only the most severely deprived households have children who suffer from a lack of educational tools such as adequate books. Most parents have very similar levels of engagement in parent–child activities. The measures of good parenting we use are not comprehensive – and in any case the extent to which a list of specific activities can adequately capture 'good parenting' is contestable (Dermott, 2015) – but this degree of coherence in parenting practices perhaps reflects an adherence to similar views about the importance of those 'good' parenting activities that receive a high public profile (see also Dermott and Pomati, 2016b). Where differences between income groups do emerge, these may reflect different levels of access to the resources of educational capital and time that, although related, cannot be directly read off from income. These results therefore confirm the importance of measuring levels of deprivation and inequality more broadly than income allows, but also the importance of material resources for achieving adequate living standards for parents and their families.

Notes

[1] See also Dermott and Pantazis, chapter four this volume, on gendered differences to emotional and practical support.

[2] The question referred to either the respondent or their partner (if applicable) eating an evening meal with their child so the difference should not be due simply to greater flexibility for the respondent because of having another adult in the household who can undertake the activity.

References

Bailey, N. (2016) 'Exclusionary employment in Britain's broken labour market', *Critical Social Policy* 36:1, 82–103.

Bennett, F. (2008) 'How low-income families use their money', in J. Strelitz and R. Lister (eds) *Why money matters: Family income, poverty and children's lives*, London: Save the Children.

Berrington, A. (2014) 'The changing demography of lone parenthood in the UK', ESRC Centre for Population Change Working Paper 48, Southampton: CPC.

Bradshaw, J., Levitas, R. and Finch, N. (2000) 'Lone parents, poverty and social exclusion', PSE-GB 1999 Working Paper 11, www.bris.ac.uk/poverty/pse/99PSE-WP11.pdf

Bryson, C., Brewer, M., Sibieta, L. and Butt, S. (2012) *The role of informal childcare: A synthesis and critical review of the evidence*, London: Nuffield Foundation.

Cameron, D. (2016) Prime Minister's speech on life chances, 11 January, www.gov.uk/government/speeches/prime-ministers-speech-on-life chances

Daly, M. (2011) 'What adult worker model? A critical look at recent social policy reform in Europe from a gender and family perspective', *Social Politics* 18:1, 1–23.

Daly, M. (2013) 'Parenting support policies in Europe', *Families, Relationships and Societies* 2:2, 159–174.

Daly, M. and Kelly, G. (2015) *Families and poverty: Everyday life on a low income*, Bristol: Policy Press.

Dermott, E. (2013) 'Poverty versus parenting: an emergent dichotomy', *Studies in the Maternal* 4:2, www.mamsie.bbk.ac.uk/

Dermott, E. (2015) 'Displaying and doing family life: what is "good parenting" and who says so?', paper presented at European Sociological Association Conference, Prague, 25–28 August.

Dermott, E. and Pantazis, C. (2014) 'Gender and poverty in Britain: changes and continuities between 1999 and 2012', *Journal of Poverty and Social Justice* 22:3, 253–69.

Dermott, E. and Pomati, M. (2016a) 'The parenting and economising practices of lone parents: policy and evidence', *Critical Social Policy* 36:1, 62–81.

Dermott, E. and Pomati, M. (2016b) '"Good" parenting practices: how important are poverty, education and time pressure?', *Sociology* 50:1, 125–42.

DfE (2015) *GCSE and equivalent attainment by pupil characteristics, 2013 to 2014 (Revised)*, London: Department for Education, https://www.gov.uk/government/uploads/system/uploads/attachment_data/file/399005/SFR06_2015_Text.pdf

European Commission (2013) 'Q&A: Report on childcare provision in the Member States and study on the gender pension gap', Press release database, http://europa.eu/rapid/press-release_MEMO-13-490_en.htm

Field, F. (2010) *The foundation years: Preventing poor children becoming poor adults*, London: Cabinet Office.

Furedi, F. (2001) *Paranoid parenting*, London: Allen Lane.

Ghate, D. and Hazel, N. (2002) *Parenting in poor environments: Stress, support and coping*, London: Jessica Kingsley Publishers.

Gillies, V. (2008) 'Childrearing, class and the new politics of parenting', *Sociology Compass* 2:3, 1079–95.

The Guardian (2014) 'Duncan Smith outlines plans for prepaid benefits cards in place of cash', 29 September, www.theguardian.com/politics/2014/sep/29/duncan-smith-prepaid-benefits-cards-cash-payments

Harkness, S. (2013) 'Women, families and the "great recession" in the UK', in *Social Policy Review 25*, Bristol: Policy Press.

Hartas, D. (2014) *Parenting, family policy and children's well-being in an unequal society*, London: Palgrave Macmillan.

Haux, T. (2013) 'Lone parents and activation – towards a typology of approaches', *Journal of International and Comparative Social Policy* 29:2, 122–33.

Hays, S. (1996) *The cultural contradictions of motherhood*, New Haven, CT: Yale University Press.

Henricson, C. (2012) *A revolution in family policy*, Bristol: Policy Press.

Hills, J.C., Brewer, M., Jenkins, S., Lister, R., Lupton, R., Machin, S. et al (2010) *An anatomy of economic inequality in the UK: Report of the National Equality Panel*, London: Government Equalities Office/CASE, LSE.

Holdsworth, C. (2004) 'Family support during the transition out of the parental home in Britain, Spain and Norway', *Sociology* 38:5, 909–26.

Katz, I., Corlyon, J., La Placa, V. and Hunter, S. (2007) *The relationship between parenting and poverty*, York: Joseph Rowntree Foundation.

Land, H. (2001) 'Lone mothers, employment and childcare', in J. Millar and K. Rowlingson (eds) *Lone parents and employment: A cross-national comparison of recent policy developments*, Bristol: Policy Press.

Lee, E., Faircloth, C., Bristow, J. and MacVarish, J. (2014) *Parenting culture studies*, London: Palgrave Macmillan.

Levitas, R. (2005) *The inclusive society? Social exclusion and New Labour*, Basingstoke: Palgrave Macmillan.

Levitas, R., Pantazis, C., Fahmy, E., Gordon, D., Lloyd, E. and Patsios, D. (2007) *The multidimensional analysis of social exclusion*, Bristol: University of Bristol.

Lewis, J. and Giullari, S. (2005) 'The adult worker model family, gender equality and care: the search for new policy principles and the possibilities and problems of a capabilities approach', *Economy and Society* 34:1, 76–104.

Mack, J. and Lansley, S. (1985) *Poor Britain*, London: Allen Unwin.

Middleton, S., Ashworth, K. and Braithwaite, I. (1997) *Small fortunes: Spending on children, childhood poverty and parental sacrifice*, York: Joseph Rowntree Foundation.

Mills, C. (2015) 'Is class inequality at KS4 decreasing?', Working Paper Centre for Social Investigation, Oxford: Nuffield College, http://csi.nuff.ox.ac.uk/wp-content/uploads/2015/03/CSI_11_Class_Inequalities.pdf

Misra, J., Moller, S., Strader, E. and Wemlinger, E. (2012) 'Family policies, employment and poverty among partnered and single mothers', *Research in Social Stratification and Mobility* 30:1, 113–28.

Mitchell, W. and Green, E. (2002) '"I don't know what I'd do without our Mam": motherhood, identity and support networks', *Sociological Review* 50:2, 1–22.

Norman, H. (2014) 'UK childcare in the European context', Policy@ Manchester policy briefing, March www.policy.manchester.ac.uk/media/projects/policymanchester/992_Policy@Manchester_UK_Childcare_briefing_v5.pdf

Peters, M., Seeds, K., Goldstein, A. and Coleman, N. (2008) *Parental Involvement in children's education*, DCSF Report RR034, London: Department of Children, Schools and Families.

Schulz, W. (2006) 'Measuring the socio-economic background of students and its effect on achievement on PISA 2000 and PISA 2003', paper presented at the Annual Meeting of the American Educational Research Association (AERA), San Francisco, 7–11 April.

Zelizer, V. (1985) *Pricing the priceless child*. Princeton, NJ: Princeton University Press.

EIGHT

A worsening picture: poverty and social exclusion and disabled people

Pauline Heslop and Eric Emerson

Introduction

There have been mixed messages in recent years about UK policies for and about disabled people. On the one hand, the disability strategy *Fulfilling potential: Making it happen for disabled people* (Department for Work and Pensions, 2013), updated in 2014, sets out the government's view of a society where disabled people can realise their aspirations and fulfil their potential. On the other hand, campaigns to strengthen and protect disabled people's rights made the headlines when the national budget in 2016 was described as a 'sugar-coated assault on disabled people' by *The Guardian* newspaper (*The Guardian*, 2016). A string of reforms over recent years, including a change from Disability Living Allowance to Personal Independence Payments (PIP), changes to Employment Support Allowance, and cuts to social care funding have all left disabled people at increased risk of poverty and social exclusion.

In this chapter we present our analysis of the Poverty and Social Exclusion Survey 2012 (PSE-UK 2012) data in relation to disabled people in the UK. First, we look at how people have defined themselves as disabled, before moving on to exploring their experiences of low income, deprivation and poverty.

The precise extent of poverty and social exclusion among disabled people can, in many ways, be considered a 'wicked problem'. 'Wicked problems' are unique social or cultural problems that are difficult or impossible to define, let alone solve. They do not have simple causes, or solutions, and because of complex interdependencies, the effort to solve one aspect of a wicked problem may reveal or create other problems. The use of term 'wicked' is in relation to the problem's resistance to definition, measurement or resolution, rather than in relation to being evil.

So what makes the issue of poverty and disabled people a 'wicked problem'? First, there is no clear way of defining and therefore counting disabled people. Theoretical, policy and people's own perceptions of who is 'disabled' differ. Second, measuring poverty in disabled people is problematic as it frequently does not take account of the additional costs that disabled people incur because they are disabled. Let us first explore these aspects in a little more detail.

Defining 'disabled people'

Theoretical definitions have moved away from a 'medical model' in which disability is equated with biological inadequacy, to a 'social model' in which 'impairment' refers to a physical or mental condition, while 'disability' refers to the social disadvantages associated with being impaired due to society's failure to facilitate the full participation of people with impairments. More recently a bio-psycho-social model has attempted to incorporate elements of both the medical and social models, emphasising the interaction between health conditions and personal and environmental contextual factors (World Health Organization, 2001). In contemporary theoretical models, therefore, disability is not an attribute of a person but the result of an interaction between a person with impairment and their social, environmental and cultural milieu.

In policy terms, the Equality Act 2010 set outs the legal framework for the rights of disabled people in England and Wales. It defines a person as disabled if they have a physical or mental impairment which has a substantial and long-term adverse effect on their ability to carry out normal day-to-day activities. The phrase 'long-term' means that the effect of the impairment has lasted or is expected to last for 12 months or more. This definition enables a broad interpretation of who might be 'disabled'. It is akin to the social model of disability by emphasising the relationship between a person's impairment and their ability to carry out normal day-to-day activities, but in addition explicitly treats some medical conditions as disabilities, including cancer, HIV infection, multiple sclerosis and severe disfigurement. Under the Equality Act 2010, a person may be disabled in the present, by a condition that once existed but is no longer present (for example, an episode of mental illness), or by a condition that may appear in the future (for example, a person with a genetic predisposition to Huntington's disease). Internationally, the United Nations (UN) Convention on the rights of disabled people has a broader definition again, recognising that 'disability is an evolving concept and that disability results from the interaction between persons with impairments and attitudinal and environmental barriers that hinders [sic] their full and effective participation in society on an equal basis with others' (Preamble, Point 5). Here the adverse effects are not limited to 'day-to-day' activities; rather it is a person's full and effective participation in society that is the issue. A similar perspective is evident in the World Health Organization's *International Classification of Functioning, Disability and Health* (ICF) (World Health Organization, 2001).

Lay perceptions of who is or is not disabled usually take a narrower focus. They are often informed by media representation, discriminatory prejudices arising from pity, fear or otherness, and unconscious norms and social factors. As a result, one person may consider themselves to be 'disabled', while a second with a similar condition and set of circumstances may think that they are not. The Office for National Statistics (ONS) Opinions Survey in 2012 asked those who came under the Equality Act definition of disability if they perceived themselves to be disabled, and only a quarter did so. People who were least likely to think of themselves as disabled were those who were working; those who had higher levels of qualifications; those with medium to high income; those with dexterity impairment or with breathing, stamina or fatigue conditions; those who described the cause of their health condition as being natural ageing; and women. There is also variation in the self-reporting of disability between countries, in part reflecting the economic, social and cultural differences between nations. MacInnes et al (2014) report that there is a higher rate of self-reporting of disability in wealthier countries, and a tendency for southern countries to report less disability.

Given the diverse ways in which disability is described and understood, measuring disability in a consistent way has been problematic, and different studies have used different survey questions and designs leading to a lack of comparable data over time (for example, Mont 2007). In 2009, work began on a project to harmonise disability data in national household surveys and administrative data sources. A final set of standardised questions about long-lasting health conditions and illnesses (including impairment and disability) was agreed for use in national surveys in 2011, and updated in 2015, by the ONS in the UK. The statistical measure of disability (although the term 'disability' is not used in the questions) was agreed to be the following:

Do you have any physical or mental health conditions or illnesses lasting or expected to last 12 months or more? Coded 1 ('Yes')

AND

Does your condition or illness\do any of your conditions or illnesses reduce your ability to carry out day-to-day activities?
Coded 1(Yes, A Lot') OR Coded 2 (Yes, A Little')

Disabled people in the PSE-UK 2012

The PSE-UK 2012 identified disabled people as being those who reported a longstanding physical or mental health condition or illness lasting or expected to last for 12 months or more and whose condition or illness reduced their ability to carry out day-to-day activities. This was in line with the ONS' harmonised question for use in large-scale surveys, and akin to the Equality Act definition of disability. A fifth (22%) of respondents to the survey would be considered as 'disabled' using this definition.

However, in addition to this group are a number of respondents who reported that they had a longstanding physical or mental health condition or illness lasting or expected to last for 12 months or more, that this did not reduce their ability to carry out day-to-day activities, but did limit their ability to participate in society 'a little', 'quite a lot' or 'a lot'. Including them in the 'disabled' group aligns the operational definition of disability more closely with the broader UN Convention on the Rights of Persons with Disabilities definition of disability and the World Health Organization's ICF. This increases the overall prevalence of disability from 22% to 24%. A review of the age- and gender-specific prevalence of disability for both the ONS' harmonised question, and for the modified version that includes limitations to social participation, shows an association between increasing prevalence of disability with increasing age, and a greater proportion of women who are disabled in each of the age bands to age 64. Including those reporting limitations to social participation due to a longstanding impairment increases the risk of disability in all age groups from 25–34 onwards, especially among women in the 25–34 age group.

In order to align the data with an international readership, we have included in the 'disabled' group those with a longstanding condition or illness that reduces their ability to carry out day-to-day activities or that limits their ability to participate in society. Two thirds of these disabled people reported more than one longstanding health condition or illness; a quarter reported that they had four or more longstanding conditions or illnesses (29% of men and 23% of women). The most commonly reported conditions were mobility impairments (46.7% of disabled people), and problems with pain or discomfort (44.0% of disabled people).

Understanding poverty in relation to disabled people

The second aspect that makes the issue of poverty and disabled people a 'wicked problem' is in the definition of poverty itself in relation to disabled people. Other authors in this book have considered measures of low income (less than 60% median income after housing costs), deprivation (lacking and wanting three or more generally agreed necessities of life), and poverty (combined low income and deprivation) in relation to population groups. This is not quite so straightforward a picture with disabled people because they often encounter additional financial costs that are either greater than the costs for non-disabled people or simply not experienced by non-disabled people. Hence, disabled people are likely to have lower disposable income than non-disabled people, and be less able to meet their needs. Examples of additional financial costs include travel by taxi or specialist transport options that are more expensive than those incurred by disabled people, and specialist equipment or aids that are not needed by non-disabled people.

Estimation of these costs varies considerably, from as little to a few pounds a week to over a thousand pounds a week. Despite best efforts to estimate the additional costs of disabled people either explicitly (using expenditure diaries), or implicitly (by comparing the living standards of disabled and non-disabled people on similar incomes), the heterogeneity of impairments experienced by disabled people and the varied level and nature of the additional costs required have made such measurement difficult. Thus, any comparison of income between disabled and non-disabled people is potentially misleading if it does not also take into account the potential for disabled people incurring additional costs because they are disabled. A report for the Joseph Rowntree Foundation by MacInnes et al (2014) suggested that the lack of adjustment in official poverty statistics for the additional costs that disabled people incur results in a 'missing million' of people in poverty living in households with a disabled person.

Comparison of low income between disabled and non-disabled people

We are starting from the premise, therefore, that a direct comparison of low income between disabled and non-disabled people will underestimate poverty in disabled people by not taking into account additional expenditure associated with disability. Even so, the proportion of disabled adults with low income (the proportion with an equivalised household income after housing costs below 60% of the national median) was substantially more, at 30.4% than in non-disabled adults at 21.0%. Such a comparison between disabled and non-disabled adults, however, needs to address the confounding effects of age (disability increases with age while poverty decreases with age) and gender. We have done this by stratification of analyses (as is illustrated in the figures in this chapter) and by adjusting for age and gender when calculating risk estimates. Figure 8.1 shows the proportion of disabled men and women in income poverty compared with non-disabled men and women, demonstrating the increased proportion of disabled adults in income poverty at all ages until the oldest age groups, with a peak at age 35–44 years. The odds of a disabled adult being in receipt of low income were more than twice that of a non-disabled adult (odds ratio = 2.06 [1.74–2.45], p<0.001) when risk estimates are adjusted for age and gender.

Figure 8.1: The proportion of disabled men and women in receipt of low income compared with non-disabled men and women, by age group

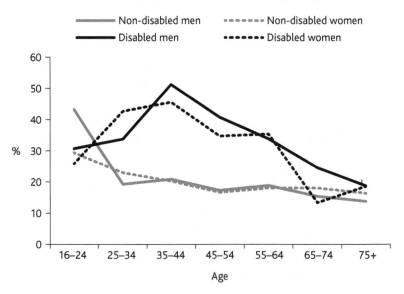

Comparison of deprivation between disabled and non-disabled people

As other chapters have described, the consensual approach to measuring poverty takes into account the public's perceptions of minimum needs, and the term 'deprivation' refers to those with an enforced lack of three or more of what the public perceives to be 'necessities' in contemporary society. First, we look at the prevalence of disabled adults being unable to afford each of the 25 items that the public perceive to be 'necessities', before reporting the risk of disabled people being unable to afford three or more of these.

Overall, disabled adults were significantly more likely than their non-disabled peers to be unable to afford each of the 25 necessities. Table 8.1 shows the prevalence and risk of disabled adults being unable to afford individual necessities. As Table 8.1 shows, just under half of disabled adults reported that they would be unable to meet an unexpected but necessary expense of £500, compared with 31% of non-disabled people, a three-fold risk when adjusted for age and gender. A similar proportion of disabled people (43%) reported that they were not able to make regular savings of at least £20 a month, compared with 28% of non-disabled people, a risk for disabled people of 2.72 times when adjusted for age and gender.

Disabled men and women were unable to afford a greater average (mean) number of necessities than non-disabled people: the mean number of unaffordable items was 3.6 for disabled people and 2.1 for non-disabled people. This difference ameliorated slightly with increasing age at the age groups for 65 years and older, but never equalised. The exception for this general pattern was disabled men up to the age 35–45 age group for whom the mean number of necessities that they could not afford rose with age, before reducing to approximately the level of disabled women from age 55 years.

We defined deprivation in the PSE-UK 2012 as lacking due to being unable to afford three or more generally agreed necessities of life. Here, 43% of disabled adults were unable to afford three or more of the 25 'necessities' of life, compared to 30% of non-disabled adults. Figure 8.2 shows the proportion of disabled and non-disabled men and women unable to afford three or more of the 25 'necessities' of life. At all ages, disabled people were more frequently deprived. Among disabled people, deprivation increased with age up to age 35–44 and then declined; in the 25–44 age groups deprivation was higher among men. Among the non-disabled population, deprivation declined monotonically with age; at younger

Table 8.1: Prevalence and risk of disabled adults being unable to afford individual necessities

Item	% cannot afford		Risk			
	% disabled	% non-disabled	Unadjusted		Adjusted (age, gender)	
Unexpected but necessary expense of £500	44.6	31.1	1.79***	(1.53–2.08)	2.99***	(2.50–3.56)
Regular savings (of at least £20 a month) for rainy days	43.3	27.8	1.98***	(1.67–2.34)	2.70***	(2.24–3.24)
Enough money to replace or repair broken electrical goods	35.3	23.6	1.77***	(1.49–2.09)	3.16***	(2.59–3.86)
Regular payments into an occupational or private pension	34.4	25.5	1.53***	(1.31–1.80)	2.27***	(1.91–2.70)
Enough money to keep your home in a decent state of decoration	27.2	17.5	1.76***	(1.47–2.09)	2.64***	(2.15–3.24)
All recommended dental work/treatment	20.2	16.1	1.32*	(1.07–1.63)	1.95***	(1.55–2.45)
Taking part in sport/exercise activities or classes	19.8	9.9	2.24***	(1.75–2.86)	3.24***	(2.50–4.21)
Household contents insurance	18.6	9.3	2.08***	(1.69–2.57)	3.80***	(3.00–4.81)
Appropriate clothes to wear for job interviews	15.0	5.8	2.89***	(2.23–3.75)	4.15***	(3.16–5.44)
Heating to keep home adequately warm	14.0	4.8	3.22***	(2.47–4.20)	4.38***	(3.28–5.84)
A damp free home	13.8	11.5	1.23	(0.93–1.61)	2.11***	(1.63–2.73)
A hobby or leisure activity	13.5	7.3	1.99***	(1.52–2.61)	2.91***	(2.18–3.89)
Two pairs of all-weather shoes	13.5	5.4	2.71***	(2.08–3.34)	4.78***	(3.56–6.42)
Fresh fruit and vegetables every day	12.8	4.0	3.56***	(2.61–4.86)	5.73***	(4.18–7.14)
Meat, fish or vegetarian equivalent every other day	9.1	2.5	3.86***	(2.70–5.54)	5.32***	(3.75–7.76)
A table, with chairs, at which all the family can eat	7.4	3.8	2.03***	(1.38–3.00)	3.49***	(2.42–5.03)

(continued)

Table 8.1: Prevalence and risk of disabled adults being unable to afford individual necessities (continued)

Item	% cannot afford		Risk		
	% disabled	% non-disabled	Unadjusted		Adjusted (age, gender)	
Visiting friends or family in hospital or other institutions	6.9	2.7	2.73***	(1.84–4.04)	3.38***	(2.29–5.00)
A warm waterproof coat	6.8	3.0	2.36***	(1.70–3.28)	3.57***	(2.44–4.99)
Attending weddings, funerals and other such occasions	6.7	1.7	4.15***	(2.63–6.55)	6.58***	(4.08–10.61)
Celebrations on special occasions such as Christmas	6.7	2.0	3.50***	(2.28–5.38)	4.66***	(3.06–7.09)
Two meals a day	4.7	1.3	3.82***	(2.33–6.26)	5.39***	(3.17–9.18)
Telephone at home (landline or mobile)	3.2	1.0	3.26***	(2.01–5.31)	4.85***	(2.94–7.99)
Washing machine	2.2	0.5	4.74***	(2.78–8.07)	5.55***	(2.95–10.44)
Curtains or window blinds	2.2	0.9	2.59***	(1.40–4.82)	3.92***	(2.08–7.37)
TV	0.5	0.1	4.18*	(1.27–13.80)	5.86**	(1.71–20.13)

Note: *p<0.05, **p<0.01, ***p<0.001.

Figure 8.2: The proportion of disabled and non-disabled men and women unable to afford three or more of the 25 'necessities' of life, by age group

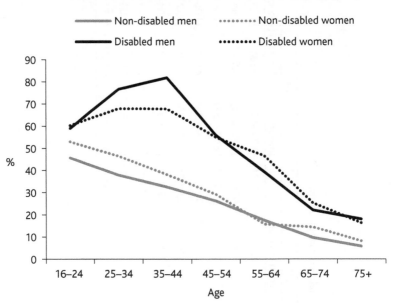

ages deprivation was slightly higher among women. Overall, the odds of a disabled person experiencing deprivation were more than three times the odds for a non–disabled person (odds ratio = 3.12, 2.60–3.74, p<0.001, large effect size) when risk estimates were adjusted for age and gender.

Comparison of poverty between disabled and non-disabled people

We have reported above that the odds of a disabled adult being in receipt of low income were more than twice the odds for a non-disabled adult, and the odds of a disabled person experiencing deprivation were more than three times the odds of a non-disabled person once risk estimates had been adjusted for age and gender. This is consistent with, and supports, the argument that income-based measures of poverty underestimate the prevalence among disabled people by not taking into account the additional expenditure associated with disability, such as additional travel costs or the cost of necessary equipment or aids. A similar association has been reported for children (Emerson and Hatton, 2007). Our definition of poverty in the PSE-UK 2012 is, however, based on combined low income (an equivalised disposable income after housing costs below 60% of the national median) and deprivation (lacking and wanting three or more generally agreed necessities of life). Once again, we remind the reader that this will underestimate poverty in disabled people, not only by not taking into account additional expenditure associated with disability but also by possibly omitting some perceived necessities of life for disabled people, such as a mobile phone, the ability to pay people to do small jobs around the home, or enhanced home security.

The overall prevalence of poverty in disabled adults was 20.7% and in non-disabled adults was 11.8%. Figure 8.3 shows the proportion of disabled and non-disabled men and women in poverty. It illustrates a more pronounced inverted U-shaped curve when looking at poverty in disabled men and women, compared with measuring income alone, or deprivation alone. There was a steep increase in poverty to the age group 35–45, more so for disabled men than disabled women, and then a more gradual tailing off to the oldest age group. By comparison, poverty in non-disabled men and women peaked at the youngest age group before steadily declining with age. The odds of a disabled adult being in poverty were more than three times those of a non-disabled person (odds ratio = 3.19 [2.56–3.98], p<0.001) when risk estimates were adjusted for age and gender.

Figure 8.3: The proportion of disabled and non-disabled men and women in poverty, by age group

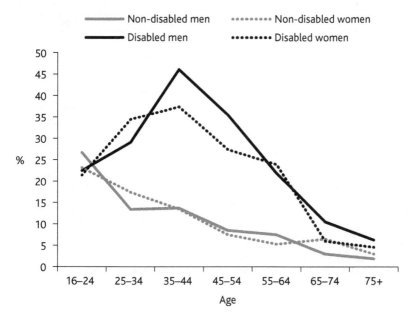

Risk of being in poverty by impairment group

We have identified above that the odds of a disabled adult being in receipt of low income and/or experiencing deprivation were significantly greater than those of a non-disabled person once risk estimates had been adjusted for age and gender. However, not all impairment groups experience similar odds of being in poverty. Table 8.2 highlights the risk of being in poverty for people with different identified impairments. What must be remembered is that disabled people may have one or more impairment and the interaction of different impairments may be more than the sum of individual parts. In addition, people with different impairments may require different levels of additional costs to ameliorate their conditions. Nevertheless, Table 8.2 indicates that the odds of being in poverty are highest for people with social or behavioural impairments compared with non-disabled people at more than six-fold, although the confidence intervals are wide. The odds are more than five-fold for people with learning impairments and mental health needs, and more than four-fold for those with memory or dexterity impairments.

Table 8.2: Risk (Odds Ratio corrected for between group difference in age and gender, with 95% CI) of being in poverty for disabled people with specific impairments

Impairment group	Odds ratio	95% CI
Socially/behaviourally	6.67	2.72–16.39
Learning/understanding/concentrating	5.93	3.66–9.60
Mental health	5.09	3.51–7.37
Memory	4.32	2.83–6.60
Dexterity	4.11	2.88–5.86
Hearing	3.98	2.39–6.63
Vision	3.92	2.43–6.30
Chronic illness	3.84	2.75–5.37
Mobility	3.57	2.63–4.81
Stamina/breathing/fatigue	3.49	2.49–4.91
Long-term pain/discomfort	3.40	2.58–4.49
Other	2.55	1.71–3.80

Notes:
Reference group = non-disabled people.
Target group = identified as disabled and mentions specific impairment. Participants can identify multiple impairments.

Social exclusion and disabled people

Social exclusion refers to a person's ability to participate in social, economic, political and cultural life and their relationships with others. Levitas et al (2007) in their report for the Social Exclusion Taskforce defined social exclusion as:

> a complex and multi-dimensional process. It involves the lack or denial of resources, rights, goods and services, and the inability to participate in the normal relationships and activities, available to the majority of people in a society, whether in economic, social, cultural or political arenas. It affects both the quality of life of individuals and the equity and cohesion of society as a whole. (2007, p 9)

There are many potential drivers at structural and individual levels that cause or generate social exclusion, such as an increase in single-person households, an ageing society, in-migration, cuts to social services, unemployment, critical life events and low household income. Describing these drivers as causes per se is usually difficult. Nevertheless, associations and correlations between such drivers and social exclusion can often be demonstrated. What may then not be clear is the relationship of the association, nor whether it is the driver itself or a factor associated with the driver that is associated with social exclusion.

Alongside an understanding of the drivers of social exclusion is a recognition that some groups in society are more vulnerable to social exclusion than others. Children, young people, women, people from ethnic minority groups and disabled people are all more likely to be vulnerable to social exclusion (Barnard and Turner 2011; Dermot and Pantazis 2014; MacInnes et al, 2014; Main and Bradshaw 2014). In these groups, the structural effects of discrimination or lack of empowerment are important drivers.

Discrimination and a lack of empowerment are common aspects of a disabled person's experience. As we have already seen, the UN definition of disability is that it results from the interaction between an individual with an impairment and the attitudinal and environmental barriers that hinder their full and effective participation in society on an equal basis with others. In this respect, all disabled people could be said to experience some degree or other of social exclusion. What is at issue for disabled people is the added complexity and impact of other risk factors for social exclusion over and above their disabled status, and the additional impact of these.

Our definition of social exclusion therefore refers to its multidimensional process. In the light of this, we were able to identify from PSE-UK 2012 data the proportions of disabled and non-disabled people who reported that in the past year they had been treated less favourably by people in positions of authority because of any of a range of personal characteristics. We found a significant difference between disabled and non-disabled people on the basis of disability, social class, religion, age, 'other' characteristic and 'any' characteristic once adjusted for age and gender. When adjusted for age and gender, there was a four-fold risk of disabled people reporting being treated less favourably on the grounds of social class (odds ratio = 4.27 [2.95–6.20]), a three-fold risk of being treated less favourably on the grounds of religion (odds ratio 3.39 [1.66–6.92]) and a two-fold risk on the basis of 'other' characteristics (odds ratio 2.36 [1.71–3.23].

The Bristol Social Exclusion Matrix (B-SEM) is a familiar tool for exploring the range of data on social exclusion available in existing data sets and administrative sources. The three main areas in which the domains fall are those of resources, participation and quality of life. Within each of these three domains are a number of indicators of social exclusion as follows:

- *resources*: economic, access to services, social, cultural;
- *participation*: economic, social, cultural, civic and political;
- *quality of life*: health and well-being, living environment, and crime, harm and criminalisation.

In this chapter we do not have the capacity to look at the full range of almost 40 individual measures of social exclusion. Instead, we are looking at a commonly reported indicator in each of the domains, as reported by individual respondents of the PSE-UK 2012. The one exception is the lack of availability of a cultural indicator in the 'resources' domain. In addition, another measure of social exclusion is the availability of practical or emotional support when needed. B-SEM includes 7 such forms of support with a composite score of less than 15 indicating a low level of social support, which we also consider.

Table 8.3 summarises the domains and indicators, and presents data comparing disabled and non-disabled people. It shows that for each indicator, the odds of a disabled person experiencing that aspect of social exclusion were significantly greater than those of non-disabled people.

Table 8.3: Commonly reported indicators of social exclusion, and comparison of disabled and non-disabled people

Domain	Indicator	Question	% disabled adults		% non-disabled adults		Age and gender-corrected odds ratio [CI]	Sig (p-value)
			M	F	M	F		
Resources	Economic	In arrears on any bills last year	21.4	26.1	20.2	19.5	2.46 [1.99–3.06]	<0.001
	Access to services	Lacks adequate access to 3 or more of 12 services*	25.7	29.3	19.6	19.7	1.53 [1.26–1.85]	<0.001
	Social	Less than monthly contact with family or friends (excl. text/email contact)	18.1	17.5	10.9	7.6	2.05 [1.63–2.59]	<0.001
	Cultural	Not available						
Participation	Economic	Not in paid employment (working age people only)	70.4	71.0	28.6	35.1	4.05 [3.34–4.90]	<0.001
	Cultural	Does not use any of the 5 listed social and cultural facilities†	32.6	32.3	20.2	18.4	1.74 [1.46–2.08]	<0.001
	Social	Participates in 5 or fewer of 14 common social activities‡	45.2	43.5	19.6	25.5	2.90 [2.43–3.46]	<0.001
	Political and civic	Not a member of any of 12 listed organisations§	58.6	57.8	41.5	44.6	1.97 [1.69–2.31]	<0.001
Quality of life	Health and well-being	Fair/bad or very bad general health	73.9	75.0	12.3	11.8	17.96 [14.91–21.63]	<0.001
	Living environment	Home not in 'good' state of repair	35.8	34.6	29.6	27.8	1.77 [1.48–2.11]	<0.001
	Crime, harm and criminalisation	Experienced harassment or discrimination	17.5	13.6	9.4	9.3	2.51 [1.99–3.16]	<0.001
Availability of support	Low social support	Social support score less than 15¶	32.7	27.2	21.6	20.2	1.85 [1.52–2.23]	<0.001

(notes overleaf)

Notes to Table 8.3:

* Doctor, dentist, optician, post office, Citizen's Advice Bureau or other advice services, chemists, corner shop, medium to large supermarkets, banks and building societies, pub, bus services, train or tube station.

† Library; public sports facility; museums and galleries; evening classes; public or community hall.

‡ A hobby or leisure activity; a week's holiday a year; friends and family for a meal or drink once a month; going out socially once a fortnight; celebrations on special occasions; a meal out once a month; holidays abroad once a year; visits to friends and family in other parts of the country; going out for a drink once a fortnight; attending weddings, funerals; visiting friends and family in hospitals/other institutions; attending church, synagogue, mosque or other places of worship; going to the cinema, theatre or music event once a month; taking part in sport/exercise activities or classes.

§ For example, sports, leisure or social club; trade union; campaigning group.

¶ Respondents were asked how much support they would get on seven items: a lot (score 3), some (score 2), not much (score 1), none at all (score 0): being ill in bed and needing help around the home; needing practical help around the home such as moving heavy furniture; needing someone to look after home or possessions while away; needing a lift somewhere in an emergency; needing advice about an important life-change; being upset because of relationship problems or feeling depressed; serious personal crisis.

The greatest disparity between disabled and non-disabled people was in relation to health and well-being: the age and gender-corrected risk of a disabled person reporting that their general health was fair/bad or very bad was 17.96 times that of a non-disabled person. The second greatest disparity was in relation to employment, where the risk of a disabled adult reporting that they were not in paid employment was over four times that of a non-disabled adult. On other indicators of social exclusion, disabled people experienced more than twice the risk of non-disabled people in relation to participating in 5 or fewer of 14 common social activities (2.90); experiencing harassment or discrimination (2.51); being in arrears on any bills in the last year (2.46); and having less than monthly contact with family or friends (excluding text or email contact) (2.05).

The conclusive nature of poverty and social exclusion in relation to disabled people

This chapter presents a conclusive picture of poverty and social exclusion among disabled people in the period 2010 to 2013. Our analysis has been of disabled adults, rather than households with disabled people, because households of different size and composition have different needs and add an additional layer of complexity. Although PSE-UK 2012 data would enable us to make possible adjustments to reflect the age and gender of household members, we have no precise equivalence scale that we can use to take account of the impact of a disabled person on a household's experience of poverty. Further, our analysis is based on the cross-sectional PSE-UK 2012 which provides a snapshot of disabled people at a particular time point. There are advantages and disadvantages to this approach. On the one hand, this captures the position of disabled people at an equivalent time during a period of social reform. On the other hand, it ignores 'disability trajectories' (Burchardt 2000) and the flows in and out of disability over the lifetime of a person.

Our conclusions in relation to disabled individuals, however, are stark. The odds of a disabled adult being in poverty were more than three times those of a non-disabled person when risk estimates were adjusted for age and gender. The odds of a disabled person being socially excluded from a range of indicators was significantly more than those for non-disabled people for each of the 11 indicators. Analysis of comparable data examining the experiences of deprivation and disadvantage in households with a disabled person from 1999 to 2012 concluded that the experiences of deprivation and disadvantage for households with disabled people had considerably worsened over the 12 years to 2013 (Heslop and Gordon 2015). We echo their conclusions that disabled people now appear to be among the 'poorest of the poor'.

The question that this raises is 'why?' Why have policies failed to sufficiently create, let alone sustain, a society where difference is accommodated and disabled people are protected from poverty and social exclusion? Goodley et al (2014) lay the blame on today's 'neoliberal-ableism' and its narrow conceptions of personhood, which have resulted in a disproportionate impact on disabled people. McKee and Stuckler (2011) attribute the assault on universalism and the demise of the welfare state by the Coalition government of the time to the drive to reduce the national deficit: 'The deficit must be reduced, and so, one by one, benefits are removed and groups are pitted against each other' (2011, p 3). Duffy (2013) from the Centre for Welfare Reform argues that there is an in-built bias in the current democratic and welfare system towards protecting perceived universal services and cutting those perceived by the public as being for 'other people', particularly when supported by the rhetoric of 'shirkers', 'scroungers' or 'cheats'.

What is evident is that social policies up to 2013 have significantly worsened the social and economic circumstances of disabled people, and more recent welfare reforms (see Unison, 2013) that affect disabled people are highly unlikely to ameliorate this situation; indeed they are likely to intensify poverty and social exclusion in relation to disabled people even further. There is some evidence about this emerging already. The Family Resources Survey (Shale et al, 2015) shows that the percentage of people living in households where at least one member was disabled, and whose equivalised household income was less than 60% median income after housing costs, rose from 27% in 2012–13 to 30% in 2013–14. This equates to an increase of 300,000 people in 'disabled households' with a household income at less than 60% median income after housing costs. It was the fourth year that the proportion of disabled households living in poverty rose, from a low of 23% in 2008/2010.

With regard to social exclusion, evidence continues to support our findings about disabled people being excluded from a range of aspects of contemporary life to a greater extent than non-disabled people. A review of primary research evidence led by Scope in 2015 concluded that 'large sections of the population hold negative attitudes towards disabled people', and that men in general were more likely to hold negative attitudes compared with women, especially among younger age groups (Aiden and McCarthy, 2015, p 17). Moreover, attitudes towards people with less 'visible' impairments tended to be much more negative. From 2013/14 to 2014/15, there was a 25% increase in hate crimes recorded by the police in England and Wales that were motivated by a person being disabled (Corcoran et al, 2015). However, campaigners suggest that disability hate crime is still 'massively' under-reported and that victims are failing to receive justice.

So what of the future for disabled people? We have persuasive evidence about increasing poverty and social exclusion in relation to disabled people that shows no sign of abatement or amelioration. The potential for this to cause what has been described as 'social death' for disabled people is very real – in other words they are at risk of becoming ever more excluded from society because of hardening discriminatory attitudes, the shame of living in relative poverty, and an inability to live an independent life without appropriate support. Pelham (2014) argues that we are approaching a 'tipping point' for disabled people in terms of poverty and social exclusion. What could pull us back from this is an increased awareness of the negative impact of benefit changes on disabled people and their families, the future-proofing of service provision for disabled people, attaching equal value to disabled people as to other citizens, and an emphasis on the dignity, respect and rights of disabled people.

References

Aiden, H. and McCarthy, A. (2015) *Current attitudes towards disabled people*, London: Scope, www.scope.org.uk/Scope/media/Images/Publication%20Directory/Current-attitudes-towards-disabled-people.pdf

Barnard, H. and Turner, C. (2011) *Poverty and ethnicity: A review of evidence*, York: Joseph Rowntree Foundation.

Burchardt, T. (2000) 'The dynamics of being disabled', *Journal of Social Policy* 29:4, 645–68.

Corcoran, H., Lader, D. and Smith, K. (2015) Hate Crime, England and Wales, 2014/15. Statistical Bulletin 05/15. Home Office, London. https://www.gov.uk/government/uploads/system/uploads/attachment_data/file/467366/hosb0515.pdf

Department for Work and Pensions (2013) *Fulfilling potential: Making it happen for disabled people*, www.gov.uk/government/uploads/system/uploads/attachment_data/file/320745/making-it-happen.pdf

Dermot, E. and Pantazis, C. (2014) 'Gender and poverty in Britain: changes and continuities between 1999 and 2012', *Journal of Poverty and Social Justice* 22:3, 253–69.

Duffy, S. (2013) 'Briefing on how cuts are targeted', Centre for Welfare Reform, London, www.centreforwelfarereform.org/library/by-date/briefing-on-how-cuts-are-targeted.html

Emerson, E. and Hatton, C. (2007) 'The socio-economic circumstances of children at risk of disability in Britain', *Disability & Society* 22:6, 563–80.

Goodley, D., Lawthorm, R. and Runswick-Cole, K. (2014) 'Dis/ability and austerity: beyond work and slow death', *Disability & Society* 29:6, 980–4.

The Guardian (2016) 'Budget 2016: a sugar-coated assault on disabled people and local democracy', 18 March.

Heslop, P. and Gordon, D. (2015) 'Trends in poverty and disadvantage among households with disabled people from 1999–2012: from exclusion to inclusion?', *Journal of Poverty and Social Justice* 22, 209–26.

Levitas, R., Pantazis, C., Fahmy, E., Gordon, D., Lloyd, E. and Patsios, D. (2007) *The multi-dimensional analysis of social exclusion*, Bristol: University of Bristol, http://dera.ioe.ac.uk/6853/1/multidimensional.pdf

MacInnes, T., Aldridge, H., Bushe, S., Tinson, A. and Born, T.B. (2014) *Monitoring poverty and social exclusion 2014*, York: Joseph Rowntree Foundation.

Main, G. and Bradshaw, J. (2014) *Child poverty and social exclusion: Final report of 2012 PSE study*, York: University of York, www.poverty.ac.uk/sites/default/files/attachments/PSE-Child-poverty-and-exclusion-final-report-2014.pdf

McKee, M. and Stuckler, D. (2011) 'The assault on universalism: how to destroy the welfare state', *British Medical Journal* 343, d7973.

Mont, D. (2007) *Measuring disability prevalence*, Washington, DC: World Bank.

Office for National Statistics (2015) Harmonised concepts and questions for social data sources: Primary principles. Long-lasting health conditions and illnesses, impairments and disability. Newport: Office for National Statistics, Newport, www.ons.gov.uk/methodology/programmesandservices/harmonisationprogramme/primarysetofharmonisedconceptsandquestions

Pelham, C. (2014) 'Overview: the future of disability', in C. Wood and R. Scott (eds) *'How far we've travelled, and how far we have to go...' The future of disability*, London: Demos.

Shale, J., Balchin, K., Rahman, J., Reeve, R. and Rolin, M. (2015) *Households below average income: An analysis of the income distribution 1994/95–2013/14*, London: Department for Work and Pensions, www.gov.uk/government/uploads/system/uploads/attachment_data/file/437246/households-below-average-income-1994-95-to-2013-14.pdf

UN (United Nations) (2006) UN Convention on the Rights of Persons with Disabilities, www.un.org/disabilities/convention/conventionfull.shtml

Unison (2013) 'Welfare reform changes affecting disabled people', www.unison.org.uk/content/uploads/2013/07/On-line-Catalogue217093.pdf

World Health Organization (2001) *International classification of functioning, disability and health*, Geneva: World Health Organization.

NINE

Devolution and North/South division: poverty and social exclusion in the countries and regions of the UK

Mike Tomlinson

Introduction

The focus of this chapter is on the spatial analysis of poverty and social exclusion in the UK, drawing on the Poverty and Social Exclusion Survey 2012 (PSE-UK 2012) and other data. The growing interest in the geography of poverty reflects the longstanding concern with regional economic and labour market imbalances as well as the politics of devolution in its various guises. The chapter critically appraises the contemporary policy frameworks for tackling spatial variations in poverty. The traditional debate between area-based interventions and anti-poverty strategies targeted on selected individuals and groups is revisited in the context of both the new 'war against the poor' and the prospects of devolution, including the 'revolution in the way we govern England' (Osborne, 2015), whether through the 'Northern Powerhouse', city regions or elected mayors. The implications of the UK leaving the European Union (EU) – 'Brexit' – are touched on where relevant.

Geographies of poverty

While there is a strong tradition of studying the spatial distribution of poverty in the UK, this has been hampered by a lack of consistent measures and policy goals, making assessments over time difficult (Dorling et al, 2007, p 2). There are two main traditions, the first based on measures of deprivation derived largely from administrative sources (Beatty and Fothergill, 2014) but also from the Census (see Tunstall and Lupton, 2003), and the second based on sample surveys of income. The PSE-UK 2012 survey falls into the latter tradition, but its strength lies in combining income data with deprivation and a wide range of measures of social exclusion.

Multiple deprivation indices are principally used for targeting resources towards areas of greatest need (Smith et al, 2015, pp 69–73), whether this involves the distribution of financial support or the rationing of services as English local authorities struggle to manage a 23.4% per capita cut in overall funding between 2009/10 and 2014/15, with more to come (Innes and Tetlow, 2015). These cuts have been, and will be, applied very unevenly: 'on the whole, more deprived areas and those that saw faster population growth have seen larger cuts. Further cuts planned for 2015–16 will generally be focused on the same local authorities that have lost over the last five years' (Institute for Fiscal Studies, 2015). Further, people in the poorest local authorities have been hardest hit by the post-2010 welfare reforms which, by 2020–1, will have resulted in a cumulative loss to claimants of £27 billion per year (Beatty and Fothergill, 2016).

Sample surveys of income such as the Family Resources Survey (FRS), used to calculate income-based 'at-risk-of-poverty' measures, are only suitable for broad geographies such as GORs (Government Offices for the Regions, which formally closed in 2011 but are still retained for statistical reporting purposes), though there are efforts to derive estimates of income poverty for small areas by linking survey data to administrative and/or Census data (Dorling et al, 2007; Fry, 2011; Fenton, 2013). But the FRS does have the advantage of providing a continuous series of household income poverty statistics for the countries and regions of the UK since 1994/5, except in the case of Northern Ireland, which only has a suitable sample size from 2002/3.

The FRS – the basis of the income data in the PSE-UK 2012 survey – is also used for measuring regional gross disposable income per head (RGDI) at various Eurostat-defined geographies (NUTS 1, 2 and 3),[1] based on groupings of administrative areas – NUTS 1 corresponds to the old GORs (discussed further below). The NUTS geographies are not only used for comparable income poverty and deprivation data across all EU countries but also provide the basis of eligibility for European Regional Development Fund and European Social Fund support under the three categories of 'less developed', 'transition' and 'more developed' regions.[2] Cornwall and West Wales & the Valleys are the only areas of the UK in the 'less developed' category (less than 75% of the average EU GDP per head). West Wales & the Valleys is due to receive almost a fifth (18.6%) of the UK's total allocation of structural funds for the 2014–20 period (€10.8 billion) (Department for Business, Innovation and Skills, 2014). Brexit potentially threatens the collection and reporting of comparable UK statistics on income and living conditions, and social protection, required under EU law, and as yet there is no discussion of what (if any) policies will replace the EU regional programmes post-Brexit.[3]

The debates surrounding geographies of poverty have changed very little in recent years. On the one hand is the view that poverty is insufficiently concentrated geographically to justify area-based interventions, as the majority of poor people do not live in 'poor areas'. Area-based policy interventions, which enjoyed a renaissance under the Blair governments (1997–2010) were often dismissed by social policy universalists as going back to 'gilding the ghetto' (Community Development Project, 1977), a form of residualism avoiding the delivery of resources to individuals and families on a categorical basis of need. As Burrows and Bradshaw (2001, p 1348) put it, 'there is little in the way of reliable evidence on the efficacy, or otherwise, of area-based approaches to the alleviation of poverty and associated detrimental outcomes'. On the other hand, the notion of a 'poor area' as meaning something over and above a collection of people on low incomes who live there, has strong support (Carley et al, 2000; Spicker, 2001). Pragmatically, area-based interventions, especially if they are targeted on small geographies highly ranked on deprivation indices, can effectively target those in poverty. But this may only be one consideration in the use of area programmes, 'which will continue to be supported by other rationales, such as belief in the existence of area effects, as a rationing mechanism, or to pilot programmes for wider use' (Tunstall and Lupton, 2003, p 28).

One of the issues is whether poverty becomes more spatially dispersed or concentrated as overall rates increase or decline. During the 1970s, the level of PSE-defined poverty declined and poverty appeared to become less spatially concentrated. But as poverty rates rose in the 1980s and 1990s, 'more and more people became concentrated in enclaves of high poverty' (Dorling et al, 2007, p 31). Using deprivation measures and smaller areas, Rae (2012) observed a similar trend: as poverty declined between 1999 to 2005, there was a decrease in the spatial concentration of economic deprivation. In contrast, a rise in overall unemployment rates appears to result in a reduction in unemployment differences between regions (Green, 1997).

Economic disparities

Work on the geographies of poverty is part of the broader discussion of uneven economic development across the UK, the short-hand for which is the North/South divide in terms of regional GDP, average incomes, employment and unemployment rates, and the structure of the labour market in terms of sectors and skills (Bachtler, 2004; Rowthorn, 2010; Gardiner et al, 2013). Some commentators (for example, Haugen, 2005) regard regional differences and inequalities as 'inevitable' and 'acceptable'. The economic dominance of the South East over other places, according to the supporters of neo-liberalism, is proof that the new market capitalism of Thatcher and Reagan worked: 'here was entrepreneurialism, here were sunrise industries, here there were few trade unions.... In "the north", by contrast, people were still mired in corporatism, weighed down by labourism, trade unions, sunset industries' (Allen et al, 1998, p 2). In the language of austerity economics, some regions are state-dependent 'Cuban-style' economies, hugely subsidised by London and the South East (Centre for Economics and Business Research, 2012; Tomlinson, 2016). Nor has the collapse of the banking sector and subsequent recession fulfilled the predictions that it would be 'grim down south' (Lee, 2012) as London continues to benefit from the 'metropolitanisation of gains and a nationalisation of losses' (Leaver, 2013) and benefits disproportionately, even exclusively, from large-scale infrastructure projects (Chakrabortty, 2014). In fact, far from fading away, there has been 'a growing "North–South Divide" in output and employment growth over the past four decades, even if London is included as part of the "South"' (Gardiner et al, 2013, p 897). A somewhat neglected aspect of this discussion is the extent to which recent social security benefit cuts have further exacerbated regional inequalities. Beatty and Fothergill (2013, p 16) estimate that by 2014/15, the average loss was £560 per working-age adult per year in the North West and North East regions compared to £370 in the South East.

Most accept the need for some level of state intervention to address continuing inequalities and the problems that the pull of London creates. The thinking behind the Barlow Report (1940) has 'shaped the official mindset of politicians, planners and policy makers for generations' (Morgan, 2002, p 798), though barely survives given the relative decline of UK regional policies. Similarly, the core rationale of EU structural funds is to 'correct' regional imbalances and reduce economic and social disparities between member states. Part of the UK 'regional' problem became politically devolved to Wales, Scotland and Northern Ireland from the 1970s onwards. One of the 'unintended consequences' of this (Travers, 1999) was a growing English nationalism in the poorer English regions (Tomlinson, 2002, p 71) as the limitations of English centralism became more apparent.

Some commentators link the Brexit referendum result, particularly in England, directly to austerity policies (Dorling, 2016), as there were stronger leave majorities in areas with lower public spending (Harrop, 2016).

It is widely recognised that the UK is now 'one of the most spatially centralised nations, politically, financially and economically, in the OECD group' (Martin et al, 2015, p 9). Local tax revenues account for only 4.9% of total tax revenues in the UK compared to 36.9% in Sweden and 12.9% in France (OECD, 2013). Even in relation to spending, UK local authorities are responsible for remarkably little of total public spending and under the Coalition government's austerity programme (2010–15) the proportion fell from 17.1% to 13.9% (Innes and Tetlow, 2015, p 5). But the main point is that the UK (alongside Ireland and Greece) is highly centralised in terms of both public *and* private finance. Following deregulation in the 1980s, regional banking supporting regional industry has been replaced by a handful of centralised banks which are mainly engaged in mortgage lending (about 40% of loans), or lending to other financial institutions and property companies. The centralisation of financial and political power explains 'the scale of spatial imbalance in the UK [which] has increased faster than in other major European countries. The increase in the disparities in regional shares of GDP in the UK has far outstripped that in France, Spain, Italy and Germany, and also (at state level) that in the United States' (Martin et al, 2015, p 3).

The geography of income inequality

One way of looking at regional inequalities is to compare the average disposable household income per head of the richest NUTS 2 area with the poorest, using Eurostat data that controls for national purchasing power differences. On this basis, Croatia has the lowest regional inequality with a richest-to-poorest area ratio of 1.03. The ratio is 1.14 for Ireland and 1.45 for Germany. While the lowest UK region, West Midlands, has an average income per inhabitant (€13,200 in 2013) that is above the highest regions in Croatia and Poland (and the same as Attiki, the richest area in Greece), the UK has the widest inequality between regions of any country, with a richest-to-poorest area ratio of 2.87. The West Midlands was also the poorest NUTS 2 region of the UK in 2005 and at that point in time, the ratio of the richest area average – Inner London West – to the West Midlands was 2.44. So even in this relatively short period – albeit one that includes the recent recession – regional inequalities have widened.

At the level of NUTS 1 areas of the UK, the widening inequalities from 2007, the year prior to the recession, up to 2014 are very clear.[4] In real terms the average disposable income per head grew by 4.3% in London (with the highest average) but declined by 6.7% in Northern Ireland (with the lowest). The ratio of the London average to the Northern Ireland average rose steadily from 1.44 in 2007 to 1.61 by 2014. Between 2007 and 2014, Wales, the area with the second worst average income, saw no real growth. The North East, which has the third worst average gross disposable income per head, saw a 2.9% increase in real terms but was still only 64% of the London average. By 2014, the average disposable income per head in Northern Ireland was just 62% of the London value.

Data for average disposable income per head are available down to NUTS 3 level – there are 173 such areas in the UK. The poorest area is Leicester in the East Midlands region where real average disposable income per head dropped by 5% between 2007 and 2014. Average income per head fell furthest – by 10.9% – in the West and South of Northern Ireland, the sixth poorest NUTS 3 area in the UK (author's calculations from ONS, 2016). In contrast, the richest NUTS 3 area saw an astonishing real growth in average income per head of 15.5%, such that the gap between Leicester and Kensington & Chelsea and Hammersmith & Fulham grew from a ratio of 3.13 to 3.81 in the space of eight years. The 20 richest areas were more likely to have experienced positive average income growth than the 20 poorest areas, 14 of which saw negative or zero growth.

The growing geographical inequalities described above are reflected to some extent in changes in income poverty rates. The published data at GOR/NUTS 1 level is averaged over three years and between 2004/5–2006/7 and 2011/12–2013/14, relative income poverty (before the deduction of housing costs – BHC) fell by two percentage points across the UK as a whole, from 17% to 15%. The rate for the North East and East Midlands fell the most, by four percentage points in each case, while Northern Ireland's rate shows no change over the period. But income poverty rates (BHC) for working-age adults rose in five of the areas, fell in four, and stayed the same in three areas. The gap between the lowest and highest poverty rates of working-age adults increased from seven percentage points (South East and West Midlands) to nine percentage points (South East and Northern Ireland). The gap between the South East and eight other NUTS 1 areas widened (author's calculations from FRS).

However, when housing costs are removed (after housing costs – AHC), the picture is rather different, with much less variation between the areas. Over the period, poverty rates for all individuals rise in Wales and Northern Ireland, fall in six areas, including Scotland, and remain the same in four areas. London has the highest poverty rate for all individuals (27%) while the South East, South West, East of England and Scotland all have the lowest rate (18%). For working-age adults, the AHC income poverty rate rises over the period in every NUTS 1 area, and by three percentage points in the case of Northern Ireland. The South East has the lowest poverty rate at the beginning and end of the period, a position shared with East of England by 2011/12–2013/14. While poverty has increased for working-age adults on the AHC measure, the gap between the areas with the highest and lowest income poverty rates remains the same at eight percentage points.

Spatial variation in poverty and social exclusion

The PSE-UK 2012 survey data includes a variable for the NUTS 1 areas but the number of cases (c.11k) is less than half of those in the FRS (c.29k). The annual income data for regions in the FRS is regarded as 'too volatile' (Carr et al, 2014, p 38) and so is presented as three-year averages. Given that the PSE-UK 2012 survey income data is based largely on data collected for the FRS, we may assume that at NUTS 1 area level the PSE income data is equally (or more) volatile. Table 9.1 compares the income poverty rates from the FRS (2010/11) and PSE-UK 2012 surveys. The PSE-UK 2012 survey values (BHC) for three areas – the North West, East Midlands and London – lie outside the confidence intervals of the FRS 2010/11 results. The PSE results (AHC) for London and the North West are also outside of the FRS confidence intervals, along with Eastern England and the South East. The PSE results appear to be overestimating income poverty for the South East, Eastern and especially the North West, and underestimating poverty in London (and the East Midlands for the BHC measure).

For a North/South of England analysis, the limitations of the data mean it is necessary to amalgamate regions with little sensitivity to the sort of precision that Dorling has brought to the task. He draws a line which wriggles its way from the Bristol channel to Grimsby, on a south-west/north-east axis (see Dorling, 2010, pp 24–5). The best fit of NUTS 1 areas to this line places the South West, South East, London, East of England and East Midlands areas in the 'South' and West Midlands, North West, Yorkshire and Humberside and the North East regions in the 'North'. Analysts sometimes present the 'South' with and without London, recognising that it is a special case

Table 9.1: Proportion of individuals living in households below 60% of median income, by region (%)

	FRS 2010/11	Confidence intervals		PSE-UK 2012 survey
		Lower	Upper	
Before housing costs				
North East	18	16	20	18.8
North West	18	16	19	23.4
Yorks and Humberside	20	19	22	19.9
East Midlands	16	15	18	14.4
West Midlands	19	18	21	19.9
Eastern	13	12	14	13.9
London	16	15	17	14.3
South East	11	10	12	11
South West	14	13	16	14.4
Wales	18	16	20	20.3
Scotland	15	13	16	15.5
Northern Ireland	20	17	23	18.8
After housing costs				
North East	20	18	22	19.5
North West	22	21	24	28.3
Yorks and Humberside	24	22	26	22.2
East Midlands	19	17	21	18.5
West Midlands	23	22	25	24.3
Eastern	17	16	19	20.4
London	28	27	30	26.4
South East	17	15	18	18.9
South West	20	18	21	21.4
Wales	23	21	25	23.6
Scotland	17	16	19	16.6
Northern Ireland	20	17	23	19.9

Note: Shaded regions have PSE values that lie outside the FRS confidence intervals.

Source: FRS 2010/11 and PSE-UK 2012 survey

both as an economic driver and a place of huge wealth, and as a site of the highest levels of poverty at NUTS 1 level (Gardiner et al, 2013). Another issue is whether there are sufficient data to present Wales separately or whether to include it in 'the North'. Scotland and Northern Ireland were oversampled for the PSE-UK 2012 survey, accounting for 23% and 19% of individual cases respectively. The sample for Wales was only 2.9% of the total (just under 350 cases). However as a country of the UK with its own parliament and government, whatever the limits of Welsh devolution, it is desirable to present results for Wales wherever possible.[5]

For the purpose of analysing the PSE-UK 2012 survey data, the GOR areas are amalgamated as described in Table 9.2. The English regions are merged into North and South, with two variants for the South – with and without London. Wales, Scotland and Northern Ireland are retained as separate entities.

Table 9.2: Distribution of GORs

GOR – 12	GOR – 6	GOR – 5
North East	North of England	North of England
North West		
Yorks and Humberside		
West Midlands		
East Midlands	South of England (without London)	South of England (with London)
Eastern		
South East		
South West		
London	London	
Wales	Wales	Wales
Scotland	Scotland	Scotland
Northern Ireland	Northern Ireland	Northern Ireland

Income poverty and deprivation

The first PSE-UK 2012 survey results presented in Table 9.3 are for income poverty (first column), using the conventional threshold of 60% of the median household income. Wales has the highest income poverty, followed by the North of England, London and Northern Ireland. The inclusion of London raises the poverty rate for the South of England by 1.5 percentage points, though it remains the lowest, second only to Scotland.

Table 9.3 also gives the results for a number of deprivation measures. For the PSE measure, 44 items relevant to adults and children are used and two thresholds – three and five or more items – are shown in the Table 9.3. The PSE items for adults and children were established by means of focus groups (Fahmy et al, 2011), which informed an attitudinal survey into the public's perceptions of necessities. Items were included as 'necessities' if supported as such by a simple majority, and are statistically valid, reliable and additive. Views on necessities are remarkably consistent across social categories such as gender, age, marital status and ethnicity, and by health status, employment status, occupation and so on (Kelly et al, 2012; Mack et al, 2013). More

Table 9.3: Relative income poverty and deprivation by area

% of all individuals	PSE at-risk-of-poverty (AHC)	Deprived of 3 or more PSE items	Deprived of 5 or more PSE items	Child Poverty Act deprivation	EU material deprivation
North of England	28.7	37.0	24.5	20.0	19.6
South of England (with London)	23.8	32.8	20.1	18.1	17.3
South of England (less London)	22.3	31.2	18.1	16.1	16.0
London	28.0	37.3	25.9	23.8	21.1
Wales	31.1	35.4	23.5	37.5	24.3
Scotland	19.9	28.4	16.1	14.7	17.0
N Ireland	26.7	34.7	21.1	22.1	22.4

Source: PSE-UK 2012 survey

important for the concerns of this chapter, there appear to be very few significant variations between Scotland, Northern Ireland and the rest of the UK (with the exception of attitudes towards attending a place of worship – 55% think this is a necessity in Northern Ireland compared to only 30% in Great Britain) (Gannon and Bailey, 2013; Mack et al, 2013).

Wales has the highest proportion of individuals (adults and children) below the deprivation threshold used for the Child Poverty Act measure, the current EU measure (deprived of three or more of nine items) and the proposed EU2020 measure (not shown). However, London and the North of England exceed the rate for Wales using the PSE deprivation measures. Scotland has the lowest deprivation under the Child Poverty Act measure and under the two PSE measures given in Table 9.3.

Deprivation rates by specific deprivation domains (groupings of items under food, clothing, household goods and so on) were calculated and the North of England is most deprived on household goods and information. Wales is highest for food deprivation, followed by the North. London is lowest on food deprivation but highest on social deprivation and poor housing conditions. Northern Ireland comes out the worst on financial deprivation. Scotland has the lowest deprivation for every domain except food.

Poverty – combined income and deprivation

In Table 9.4, three measures that are based on both low income and deprivation are presented. The first two columns use the PSE-UK

Table 9.4: Combined income and deprivation poverty measures by area

% of individuals	Child Poverty Act: combined low income and material deprivation	Child Poverty Act: combined severe low income and material deprivation	PSE consensual poverty
North of England	13.0	6.4	25.4
South of England (with London)	8.7	2.4	20.9
South of England (less London)	7.9	2.2	19.1
London	10.8	2.9	26.4
Wales	18.0	(n<20)	25.3
Scotland	10.6	5.8	17.8
N Ireland	12.3	3.7	24.3

Source: PSE-UK 2012 survey

2012 data to calculate the Child Poverty Act measure for poverty and severe poverty (below 50% median household income plus deprivation), and the final column shows the results for PSE consensual poverty. There are a number of points to note from Table 9.4. First, Scotland has around 2.5 times the rate of severe poverty (Child Poverty Act measure) than the South of England, but has the lowest rate of consensual poverty of any area. Second, London has the highest rate of PSE consensual poverty, even though the PSE income poverty rates reported in Table 9.1 were below the FRS rates (BHC and AHC) and outside of the confidence intervals. A third point is that the Child Poverty Act measure results in rates well below (in some cases less than half) the PSE consensual poverty measure.

So far, the results presented have been based on all individuals. Table 9.5 breaks down the PSE consensual poverty rates into those for children (aged under 18), working-age adults and older persons (aged 65 or more). The male/female rates are also shown. For every area, the rates of child poverty are higher than those for working-age adults, which in turn are very much higher than the rates for older people. On the PSE poverty measure over one in three children in Wales and London are living in poverty. Even in the South of England (less London), one in five children are living in poverty. In terms of gender, in every area except Wales, women have higher rates of PSE poverty than men, however neither the gender difference for Wales nor London is statistically significant (risk ratios not shown). The higher male poverty rates in Wales are likely to be associated with high male rates of long-term sickness – the PSE-UK 2012 survey found 16.0% of working-age men in Wales were long-term sick compared to 7.0% of all men.

Table 9.5: PSE consensual poverty for social categories by area

% of individuals	All individuals	Children	Working-age adults	Older adults (65 and over)	Male	Female
North of England	25.4	30.3	27.8	10.7	24.6	26.2
South of England (with London)	20.9	24.7	22.3	10	20.1	21.8
South of England (less London)	19.1	21.4	21.0	9.0	18.7	19.5
London	26.4	34.1	25.8	14.6	24.3	28.4
Wales	25.3	34.4	26.9	(n<20)	28.8	22.1
Scotland	17.8	22.5	18.8	8.2	16.3	19.2
N Ireland	24.3	27.3	25.5	14.3	22.9	25.7

Source: PSE-UK 2012 survey

The North/South divide

In this section, the PSE-UK 2012 survey data are used to test the consistency of the North/South divide in England. For the purposes of the analysis, London is included in the South of England (but Wales and Scotland are not included in the North). Risk ratios with confidence intervals are calculated for a range of income poverty measures, deprivation and combined income and deprivation measures (see Table 9.6).

Except for three of the measures – Child Poverty Act deprivation, PSE housing conditions deprivation and social deprivation – people in the North of England are more at risk of poverty and deprivation than people in the South, significantly so at the 95% confidence level. For example, people in the North have 1.5 times the risk of absolute poverty (Child Poverty Act measure) than people in the South of England. They are 1.5 times at risk of food deprivation, albeit from a low base. On the severe low income and deprivation Child Poverty Act measure, people in the North have 2.65 times the risk of poverty. Northern children are 1.23 times as likely to be at risk of PSE poverty and working-age adults 1.25 times.

Social exclusion across the UK

For this last section, the Bristol Social Exclusion Matrix (B-SEM) (Levitas et al, 2007) is used as the basis for selecting variables from the PSE-UK 2012 survey to represent the three broad dimensions of social exclusion (Resources, Participation and Quality of Life) and their sub-

Table 9.6: Relative risk of poverty in the North compared to the South of England (including London)

	Risk ratio	95% confidence interval	
		Lower	Upper
Income poverty			
At-risk-of-poverty (BHC – Modified OECD)	1.632	1.499	1.776
At-risk-of-poverty (AHC – Modified OECD)	1.179	1.1	1.264
Child Poverty Act absolute poverty	1.532	1.421	1.651
At-risk-of-poverty (PSE equivalisation)	1.206	1.127	1.291
Deprivation			
Child Poverty Act deprived	1.1	0.975	1.24
EU material deprivation	1.135	1.042	1.236
EU2020 deprived	1.452	1.232	1.712
PSE deprived 5 or more items	1.222	1.129	1.323
PSE food deprivation	1.506	1.295	1.751
PSE clothing deprivation	1.25	1.117	1.399
PSE housing conditions deprivation	1	0.932	1.072
PSE social deprivation	1.006	0.925	1.094
Poverty, income + deprivation			
Child Poverty Act: combined low income and material deprivation	1.504	1.272	1.778
Child Poverty Act: combined severe low income and material deprivation	2.652	1.985	3.544
PSE consensual poverty	1.213	1.126	1.306
PSE child poverty	1.23	1.071	1.412
PSE working-age poverty	1.246	1.139	1.363

Note: All risk ratio values are statistically significant *except* the three shaded values.
Source: PSE-UK 2012 survey

divisions, as shown in Table 9.7. While it is not possible here to reflect the full complexity of the B-SEM approach, the spread of variables, 23 in all, chosen to represent the domains, provides a comprehensive basis for assessing the relative picture of poverty and social exclusion across areas of the UK.[6] The method for overall ranking broadly follows that of Bradshaw et al's (2007) league table of how well rich countries promote the well-being of children. Six areas – the North of England, the South of England (less London), London, Wales, Scotland and Northern Ireland – are ranked for each variable in order of the most (1) to least excluded (6) (see Table 9.8). In generating the rates and area ranking for each variable, the differences between areas were tested for statistical significance (using one-way Anova multiple comparisons).

Table 9.7: Social exclusion variables

Dimension	Domain	Selected indicators from PSE-UK 2012 survey
Resources:	Material/economic resources	PSE consensual poverty; deprivation of 5 PSE necessities
	Access to public and private services	Access to doctor, dentist, post office, bus, CAB, library, supermarket, corner shop, bank
	Social resources	How much support if: • ill in bed • need advice about an important change in life • upset because of relationship problems/ feeling a bit depressed and need someone to talk to
Participation	Economic participation	Non-employed ('inactive' or unemployed, age 16–65).
	Social participation	Talks to friends once a week or less; talks to relatives once a week or less
	Culture, education and skills	Can't afford to go out to the cinema, theatre or music once a month; age left school
	Political and civic participation	Contacted political representative; signed petition; member of organisation (political, social, cultural)
Quality of life	Health and well-being	Life satisfaction; long-term illness; feeling part of the community
	Living environment	Damp housing; satisfaction with area lived in; housing deprivation
	Crime, harm and criminalisation	Worried about home being broken into; physically harmed

Resources

For both PSE consensual poverty and households lacking five or more PSE deprivation items, Scotland has significantly lower rates than Wales, London and the North of England. Scotland is also least excluded for two of the social resources variables.

The proportions of households which are 'constrained' in their access to a range of public and private services were explored, following the work of Bramley and Besemer (2016). Of the statistically significant differences, the results for bus services stand out in that London households are much less constrained than everywhere else, with Northern Ireland households three times as likely to have constrained access to buses. In terms of North/South differences, households in the North are 1.3 times as likely to be constrained in their access to banks and 1.4 times in the case of Citizens' Advice services. A combined constrained access to services ranking is shown in Table 9.8.

The three indicators selected as markers of a lack of social resources were based on the survey question asking people how much support they would get in various circumstances (see Table 9.7). The rankings are based on those replying 'not much' or 'none at all'. Overall, one tenth of the adult population have very low or non-existent levels of social resources in relation to the three questions selected. People in the North are significantly more excluded when needing advice than those in the South.

While Table 9.8 shows London as the worst area for material/economic exclusion, it is the least constrained area for access to services. The North is worst off for access to services and two of the social support variables. Scotland is consistently low in the rankings across all the variables.

Participation

The lowest rate of exclusion from paid work ('inactive' or unemployed) was in the South of England (28%) and the highest, Wales (42%). The North was significantly different from the South and Wales was significantly different from Scotland and the South.

In Northern Ireland, 23% of adults talk to relatives once a week or less compared to 48% of Londoners who are significantly more isolated from relatives than people in all other areas. Those in the South are significantly less likely to talk to relatives than those in the North. In the North, 40% of adults talk to friends once a week or less compared to 29% in Wales. The North is significantly different from Wales, Scotland and the South.

No statistically significant differences between areas were found in the proportion of adults unable to afford to go out to the cinema, theatre or music once a month. The highest rate of adults who had left school at 16 or earlier was 60% in Wales and the North, and the lowest was for London at 36%. London was significantly different from all other areas. Northern Ireland had a significantly lower proportion of early school leavers (49.8%) than the North of England.

Only 11.7% of people in Northern Ireland said they had contacted a political representative in the last three years, compared to 15.3% in Scotland and there were no significant differences between areas. In the South of England, 33.4% had signed a petition in the last three years compared to 23.1% in Northern Ireland. The rate for the

Table 9.8: Ranking of social exclusion variables by area

| | Resources | | | | | | |
| | Material/economic | | | Access to services | Social resources | | |
Ranked from most excluded (1) to least excluded (6)	PSE consensual poverty	PSE consensual child poverty	Lacking 5 or more PSE deprivation items	Constrained use of 9 services	Support if ill in bed	Support if needing advice	Support if relationship problem
North of England	2	3	2	1	1	1	4
South of England*	5	6	5	3	3	5	5
London	1	2	1	6	2	3	2
Wales	3	1	3	2	6	2	1
Scotland	6	5	6	5	4	6	6
N Ireland	4	4	4	4	5	4	3

| | Participation | | | | | | | |
| | Economic | Social | | Culture, education and skills | | Political and civic | | |
Ranked from most excluded (1) to least excluded (6)	Excluded from paid work	Talks to relatives	Talks to friends	No cinema, theatre, or music	Left school at 16 or earlier	Contacted political representative	Signed petition	Member
North of England	2	3	1	3	1	3	3	3
South of England*	6	2	3	2	4	4	6	6
London	4	1	2	1	6	4	5	2
Wales	1	5	6	6	2	2	2	4
Scotland	5	4	4	5	3	6	4	5
N Ireland	3	6	5	3	5	1	1	1

(continued)

Table 9.8: Ranking of social exclusion variables by area (continued)

| | Quality of Life | | | | | | | |
| Ranked from most excluded (1) to least excluded (6) | Health and well-being | | | Living environment | | | Crime, harm and criminalisation | |
	Long-standing illness or disability	Overall life satisfaction	Low life satisfaction	Damp home	Area satisfaction	Housing deprivation	Fear of break-in	Physically harmed
North of England	3	1	2	3	2	4	3	4
South of England*	4	4	3	4	3	5	5	1
London	6	3	3	1	1	1	2	1
Wales	1	2	1	2	5	6	4	6
Scotland	2	6	5	6	4	2	6	3
N Ireland	5	5	6	5	5	3	1	5

Note: *Less London.

South of England was significantly higher than for the North, Wales and Northern Ireland. Regarding membership of a social or cultural organisation, rates were significantly higher for the South relative to the North and London.

No clear patterns stand out in the rankings shown for participation – three areas, London, Northern Ireland and Wales, contain rankings of both 1 and 6. One surprising finding is that Northern Ireland is ranked as most excluded in terms of political and civic participation, contrary to its reputation for high levels of political and civic engagement. All of the scores for the North of England lie in the top half of the most excluded rankings.

Quality of life

The North of England has a significantly lower average life satisfaction score than Scotland and the South. There were no significant differences in the proportions with 'low life satisfaction' scores (0–4 on a scale of 0–10). The PSE-UK 2012 survey showed that 42% of individuals in Wales have a longstanding illness or disability compared to 28% in London. Rates were significantly lower in London than in the North of England, Wales and Scotland.

There were significant differences in the proportion of households reporting problems with damp, ranging from 17.1% in London to 10.0% in Scotland – the latter is significantly better off than London, the South and the North. Households in London are significantly less satisfied with the area they live in than those in Northern Ireland and Wales. Overall housing deprivation (a composite of PSE deprivation items that relate to housing) is significantly lower in Scotland than in the North and London.

The extent to which people are 'very' or 'fairly worried' about their home being broken into is significantly less in Scotland (30.4%) than in Northern Ireland (47.3%), London (44.7%) and the North (40.5%). Over a fifth (21.3%) of people in London and the South report being physically harmed in the past year, significantly different from the North (16.9%) and Wales (12.7%).

London is top-ranked for the poor living environment variables and, along with the South, for the proportion of people reporting that they were physically harmed in the last year. Scotland has the lowest ranking for three variables – overall life satisfaction, damp housing and fear of break-in.

Overall social exclusion

Table 9.9 brings together the results for the three dimensions of social exclusion in the B-SEM by summing the ranks. The North of England is the most socially excluded area of the UK while Scotland is the least excluded. The overall ranking is the same as for resources but not quite the same as participation and quality of life. Wales is better ranked than Northern Ireland on participation while the quality-of-life rankings diverge the most from the overall pattern. Northern Ireland has the best quality-of-life score and London the worst.

Table 9.9: Overall rankings for social exclusion

Ranked from most excluded (1) to least excluded (6)	Overall ranking	Σ of all rankings	Σ of rankings for Resources	Σ of rankings for Participation	Σ of rankings for Quality of Life
North of England	1	55	14	19	22
London	2	60	17	25	18
Wales	3	73	18	28	27
N Ireland	4	88	28	25	35
South of England	5	94	32	33	29
Scotland	6	108	38	36	34

Conclusion

The data from the PSE-UK 2012 survey and other sources presented above show that country and regional differences in poverty and social exclusion across the UK are substantial and growing, even over the relatively narrow period since 2007. These differences are clearly related to what are generally referred to as 'regional economic imbalances', which are evident in inequalities in GDP, the structure of regional economies, different histories of occupational harm and unemployment, and latterly the differential impact of cuts in social security and local authority funding. For the post-war period up to the mid-1970s, regional imbalances were mediated both by explicit attempts to redistribute employment and investment away from the South and towards the North, and by the mediating effects of social security policies. But compensation via regional economic development – whether national or EU-led – has proved no match for deindustrialisation and the emergence of an economy dominated by London-based financial interests, services and rent, rather than manufacturing and public service. As the evidence in this chapter shows, the North of England has fared the worst from the devolution of regional policy and its relative decline in England, a predictable outcome in the wake of neo-liberal economic policies and the absence of an explicit goal of regional territorial justice (Morgan, 2006). The powers of devolved entities to compensate for the failures of economic development through income and service distribution remain limited. In recent years, the deliberate undermining of social security and other public services, especially working-age benefits for the long-term sick and disabled, has further weakened the prospects of reducing geographical inequalities in poverty. Brexit raises the prospect of 'taking control' by further compounding social (including 'racial') divisions and lowering the priority to address regional imbalances. It may even result in Scotland and Northern Ireland leaving the UK.

This is not to suggest that recent governments have no sense of the need to address the inequalities across the countries and regions of the UK. In some respects, the initiatives which devolve powers to the countries of the UK, especially Scotland, or the devolution to city regions and elected mayors, may be seen as a recognition of the need for greater decentralisation of economic governance away from Westminster and the Treasury. On the other hand, unless country and regional imbalances are mainstreamed in macro-economic policy and the whole range of public investment decisions, then devolution will amount to little more than devolving responsibility for austerity and public sector decline.

Similarly, devolution of powers over transport or health and social care spending to city regions is unlikely to impact on geographical inequalities in poverty, or to reduce poverty at all. The UK countries and English regions with the highest rates of long-term sickness and disability, and the highest reliance on in-work and out-of-work benefits, will continue to see increases in child poverty and working-age poverty as the impact of the welfare reforms of recent years are fully realised. Since the amendment of the Child Poverty Act 2010 by the Welfare Reform and Work Act of 2016, the UK government policy is to promote 'social mobility' rather than to eradicate poverty. The Scottish government objected to the new policy and succeeded in removing the obligation to appoint ministers to the Social Mobility Commission and for reporting requirements. But in going their own way – a Child Poverty (Scotland) Bill was introduced in February 2017 – and retaining an explicit commitment to anti-poverty strategies, it is questionable whether the devolved governments have the necessary revenue-raising and distributive powers to deliver effective country-level poverty reduction strategies. Mitigations of the worst effects of social security and tax credit cuts, such as the non-implementation of the 'bedroom tax' and other special provisions for Northern Ireland (Evason Report, 2016), the Discretionary Assistance Fund in Wales and the new legal duty to help *prevent* homelessness (under the Housing (Wales) Act 2014), or Scotland's focus on maximising financial entitlements are all important, but devolved anti-poverty strategies are as yet marginal to the overall Westminster control of income redistribution and employment law.

Notes

[1] NUTS 1, 2 and 3 – Nomenclature des unités territoriales statistiques, see http://ec.europa.eu/eurostat/web/nuts/overview

[2] The structural funds account for roughly 30% of the UK's receipts from the EU. The remaining 70% are agriculture-related payments, the biggest of which are to sugar companies and large land owners. (see http://farmsubsidy.openspending.org).

[3] The two relevant laws are (i) Regulation (EC) No. 1177/2003 of the European Parliament and of the Council of 16 June 2003 concerning Community statistics on income and living conditions (EU-SILC) and (ii) Regulation (EC) No. 458/2007 for the provision of European statistics on social protection.

[4] The following figures are calculated from ONS (2016) using 2014 values and Treasury deflators.

[5] According to NatCen's technical report: 'It was possible to boost the sample in Scotland and Northern Ireland to ensure that national comparisons within the United Kingdom could be made. As there were insufficient Primary Sampling Units (PSUs) in Wales in a single year's FRS it was not possible to boost the sample for Wales' (Maher and Drever, 2013).

[6] Access to the nine public and private services listed in Table 9.7 are combined into a single 'access to services' ranking.

References

Allen, J., Massey, D. and Cochrane, A. (1998) *Rethinking the region*, London: Routledge.

Bachtler, J. (2004) 'Regional disparities in the United Kingdom', in H. Karl and P. Rollet (eds) *Employment and regional development policy: Market efficiency versus policy intervention*, Hannover: Veri. der ARL, 36–49.

Barlow Report (1940) *Report of the Royal Commission on the Distribution of Industrial Population*, London: HMSO.

Beatty, C. and Fothergill, S. (2013) *Hitting the poorest places hardest: The local and regional impact of welfare reform*, Sheffield, Centre for Regional Economic and Social Research, Sheffield Hallam University.

Beatty, C. and Fothergill, S. (2014) 'The local and regional impact of the UK's welfare reforms', *Cambridge Journal of the Regions, Economy and Society* 7:1, 63–79.

Beatty, C. and Fothergill, S (2016) *The uneven impact of welfare reform: The financial losses to places and people*, Sheffield, Centre for Regional Economic and Social Research, Sheffield Hallam University.

Bradshaw, J., Hoelscher, P. and Richardson, D. (2007) 'An index of child well-being in the European Union', *Journal of Social Indicators Research* 80, 133–77.

Bramley, G. and Besemer, K. (2016) *Poverty and local services in the midst of austerity: final report of 2012 PSE study*, www.poverty.ac.uk

Burrows, R. and Bradshaw, J. (2001) 'Evidence-based policy and practice', *Environment and Planning* 33, 1345–8.

Carley, M., Campbell, M. et al (eds) (2000) *Regeneration in the 21st century: Policies into practice*, Bristol: Policy Press.

Carr, J., Councell, R., Higgs, M. and Singh, N. (2014) *Households below average income: An analysis of the income distribution 1994/95–2012/13*, London: Department for Work and Pensions.

Centre for Economics and Business Research (CEBR) (2012) 'One pound in five earned in London subsidises the rest of the UK – Northern Ireland, Wales and North East receive more than a fifth of their income as subsidies from outside the region', Data release, 13 February, www.cebr.com

Chakrabortty, A. (2014) 'What's that sucking sound? It's all the public money and private wealth being swallowed up in London', *The Guardian*, 10 February.

Community Development Project (1977) *Gilding the ghetto: The state and the poverty experiments*, London, Home Office Community Deprivation Unit.

Department for Business, Innovation and Skills (2014) 'EU Structural Funds: UK allocations 2014 to 2020', Policy paper, 30 April, www.gov.uk/government/publications/eu-structural-funds-uk-allocations-2014-to-2020

Dorling, D. (2010) 'Persistent North–South divides', in N.M. Coe and A. Jones (eds) *The economic geography of the UK*, London: Sage, 12–28.

Dorling, D. (2016) 'Brexit: the decision of a divided country', *British Medical Journal* 354, i3697.

Dorling, D., Rigby, J., Wheeler, B., Ballas, D., Thomas, B., Fahmy, E. et al (2007) *Poverty, wealth and place in Britain, 1968 to 2005*, York: Joseph Rowntree Foundation.

Eurostat (various years) *European statistics on regions and cities*, http://ec.europa.eu/eurostat/web/products-catalogues/-/KS-02-13-692

Evason Report (2016) *Welfare reform mitigations Working Group report*, Belfast: Northern Ireland Executive, January, www.executiveoffice-ni.gov.uk/publications/welfare-reform-mitigations-working-group-report

Fahmy, E., Pemberton, S. and Sutton, E. (2011) *Public perceptions of poverty, social exclusion and living standards: Preliminary report on focus group findings*, PSE Working Paper Methods Series 12, www.poverty.ac.uk

Fenton, A. (2013) *Small-area measures of income poverty*, LSE CASE paper 173, http://sticerd.lse.ac.uk/dps/case/spcc/WP01.pdf

FRS (Family Resources Survey) (various years) London: Department for Work and Pensions, www.gov.uk/government/collections/family-resources-survey--2

Fry, R. (2011) *Understanding household income poverty at small area level*, Office of National Statistics, Regional Trends 43.

Gannon, M. and Bailey, N. (2013) *Attitudes to the necessities of life in Scotland: can a UK poverty standard be applied in Scotland?* PSE Working Paper Analysis Series 5, www.poverty.ac.uk

Gardiner, B., Martin, R., Sunley, P. and Tyler, P. (2013) 'Spatially unbalanced growth in the British economy', *Journal of Economic Geography* 13, 889–928.

Green, A. (1997) 'Exclusion, unemployment and non-employment', *Regional Studies* 31:5, 505–20.

Harrop, A. (2016) 'Support for Brexit linked to unequal public spending', 20 September, Fabian Society, www.fabians.org.uk/support-for-brexit-linked-to-unequal-public-spending/

Haugen, J. (2005) 'The inevitability of regional variation in the UK', *The Park Place Economist* 13, 96–101, www.iwu.edu/economics/PPE.html

Innes, D. and Tetlow, G. (2015) *Central cuts, local decision-making: Changes in local government spending and revenues in England, 2009–10 to 2014–15*, London: Institute for Fiscal Studies.

Institute for Fiscal Studies (2015) 'Sharpest cuts to local government spending in poorer areas; same areas likely to lose most in next few years', Press release, 6 March, www.ifs.org.uk

Kelly, G., Tomlinson, M., Daly, M., Hillyard, P., Nandy, S. and Patsios, D. (2012) *The necessities of Life in Northern Ireland*, Working Paper Analysis Series 1, www.poverty.ac.uk

Leaver, A. (2013) 'The metropolitanisation of gains, the nationalisation of losses', openDemocracyUK, 25 September, www.opendemocracy. net

Lee, N. (2012) 'Grim down South? The determinants of unemployment increases in British cities in the 2008–2009 recession', *Regional Studies* 48:11, 1761–78.

Levitas, R., Pantazis, C., Fahmy, E., Gordon, D., Lloyd, E. and Patsios, D. (2007) *The multi-dimensional analysis of social exclusion*, Bristol: University of Bristol.

Mack, J., Lansley, S., Nandy, S. and Pantazis, C. (2013) 'Attitudes to necessities in the PSE 2012 survey: are minimum standards becoming less generous?', Working Paper Analysis Series 4, www.poverty.ac.uk

Maher, J. and Drever, E. (2013) Poverty and Social Exclusion Survey Technical Report, http://doc.ukdataservice.ac.uk/doc/7879/mrdoc/pdf/7879_pse_gb_2012_technical_report_final.pdf

Martin, R., Pike, A., Tyler, P. and Gardiner, B. 2015) *Spatially rebalancing the UK economy: The need for a new policy model*, Regional Studies Association, www.regionalstudies.org

Morgan, K. (2002) 'The English question: regional perspectives on a fractured nation', *Regional Studies* 36:7, 797–810.

Morgan, K. (2006) 'Devolution and development: territorial justice and the North–South divide', *Publius* 36:1, 189–206.

OECD (Organisation for Economic Co-operation and Development) (2013) Tax policy analysis, Revenue Statistics – taxes by level of government, http://www.oecd.org/tax/tax-policy

ONS (Office of National Statistics) (2016) *Regional gross disposable household income (GDHI): 1997 to 2014*, 25 May, www.ons.gov. uk/economy/regionalaccounts/grossdisposablehouseholdincome/bulletins/regionalgrossdisposablehouseholdincomegdhi/2014

Osborne, G. (2015) 'Building a Northern Powerhouse', 14 May, www. gov.uk/government/speeches/chancellor-on-building-a-northern-powerhouse

Rae, A. (2012) 'Spatially concentrated deprivation in England: an empirical assessment', *Regional Studies* 46:9, 1183–99.

Rowthorn, R. (2010) 'Combined and uneven development: reflections on the North–South divide', *Spatial Economic Analysis* 5:4, 363–88.

Smith, T., Noble, M., Noble, S., Wright, G., McLennan, D. and Plunkett, E. *The English indices of deprivation 2015*, London: Department for Communities and Local Government.

Spicker, P. (2001) 'Poor areas and the "ecological fallacy"', *Radical Statistics* 76, 38–79.

Tomlinson, M. (2002) 'Reconstituting social policy: the case of Northern Ireland', in R. Sykes, C. Bochel and N. Ellison (eds) *Social Policy Review 14: Developments and debates 2001–2002*, Bristol: Policy Press, 57–83.

Tomlinson, M. (2016) 'Risking peace in the "war against the poor"? Social exclusion and the legacies of the Northern Ireland conflict', *Critical Social Policy* 36:1, 104–23.

Travers, T. (1999) 'Will England put up with it?', *The Guardian*, Society section, 21 April, 2–3.

Tunstall, R. and Lupton, R. (2003) *Is targeting deprived areas an effective means to reach poor people? An assessment of one rationale for area-based funding programmes*, LSE CASE paper 70, London.

TEN

More similarities than differences: poverty and social exclusion in rural and urban locations

Nick Bailey and Maria Gannon

Introduction

This chapter focuses on the differences in poverty and social exclusion between rural and urban locations in the UK. It examines differences in material terms, including levels of poverty as well as broader measures of living standards. It also explores wider aspects of social exclusion. Given space constraints, we cannot look at all of the domains covered by the 2012 Poverty and Social Exclusion Survey (PSE-UK 2012) so we focus on one or two aspects for each of the three broad areas of resources, participation and quality of life. Under resources, we look at access to services as this is widely seen as problematic in more rural areas. For participation, we examine employment, because of its importance both as a form of participation but also as the key means to access resources. In relation to quality of life, we look at housing and neighbourhood environment: some aspects of housing quality are often seen as more problematic in rural areas while neighbourhood problems are more obviously an urban issue. Finally, we look at health and well-being as a domain with interesting differences which have perhaps been less discussed in the literature.

The differences we explore matter in two ways. The first is for judgements about the relative needs of different areas. In the UK, there has long been a strategy of distributing resources for local public services in a way which takes account of the relative needs of areas. This is apparent in the formulae used by national governments to allocate funding to local government and health services, for example. Measures which attempt to identify relative needs therefore attract close scrutiny with intense arguments about the biases which may arise from particular measures (Bailey et al, 2003; Bailey et al, 2016). One strength of the PSE-UK 2012 survey is that it allows us to compare locations

219

using multiple measures of poverty and hence to make more rounded judgements about the biases in each and hence about relative needs.

The second is about the nature of needs in different areas. Here the central issue is whether a single national policy approach to tackling poverty or social exclusion is appropriate, or whether the differences in the nature of problems require distinctive urban and rural policies to be developed. Again, the literature suggests these differences may be quite significant, implying the need for distinctive policy responses (Shucksmith and Philip, 2000).

In the next section, we explain how rural and urban locations are identified for the purposes of this analysis, building on official classification schemes used in different parts of the UK. After that, the chapter turns to look at the range of measures of poverty and deprivation which the PSE-UK 2012 survey provides, comparing urban and rural locations on each. It complements this with evidence on living standards more broadly in the following section. The chapter then examines some of the wider aspects of social exclusion, covering a selection of the domains from the B-SEM. The last part of the analysis examines the experience of being poor in different locations through questions on shame arising from poverty. In the concluding session, we discuss some of the broad implications for policy.

Identifying rural and urban contexts

We need to begin by deciding how to distinguish urban and rural locations. There is no official UK classification as each national government produces its own (Countryside Agency et al, 2004; NISRA, 2005; Scottish Government, 2012a). While each classifies small areas of the country[1] primarily on the basis of settlement size, they vary in other important details. The national classifications do not map onto each other in a simple way but there is enough similarity to produce a fourfold scheme for the purposes of this paper: large urban areas (population of the settlement greater than 100,000); other urban areas (population greater than 10,000); small towns (population above 3,000); and rural areas (population below 3,000). There are some minor differences in definitions and cut-offs used.[2]

Within the rural category, there may be important differences between places closer to or further from urban centres as such centres may offer greater access to employment opportunities and important services. As Scotland has more extensive rural areas, its classification distinguishes between 'remote' and 'accessible' locations, based on drive times to urban centres with a population of 10,000 or more.

Analysis of the Scottish data from the PSE-UK 2012 survey using that classification has shown some important differences between these two (Bailey et al, 2016). However, it was not possible to make the same distinction for the English and Welsh or Northern Irish cases so this aspect of rurality is not covered here. Those interested in these differences are referred to the Scottish analysis.

The UK is one of the most urbanised countries in the EU. Using our classification, just over half the UK population lives in large urban areas (52%) with most of the rest in other urban areas (27%). The remaining fifth are evenly split between small towns and villages or rural locations. Unusually, it is also a country where the rural population is growing faster than the urban and has been doing so for several decades (Eurostat, 2013). In other respects, demographic differences between urban and rural areas in the UK are similar to those in most of the rest of Europe (Eurofound, 2014). Urban areas tend to draw in large numbers of young adults, in part due to their function as centres for higher and further education but also because of employment and lifestyle opportunities. Rural areas tend to have an older population balance, partly as a result of the out-migration of younger adults but also because of inward retirement migration. In our sample, older people (55 or over) make up 35% of the population of small towns and rural areas, compared with 25% in large urban areas. By contrast, younger adults (18–34 years old) make up 24% of the population in large urban areas, compared with just 15% in rural areas. Children are present in roughly equal proportions across the hierarchy but more urban locations have more lone-parent households and fewer couples with children.

It should also be noted that, while we focus on urban–rural differences for the UK as a whole in this chapter, these differences vary across the country to some extent. We can see some of this variation in the demographics of urban and rural areas in the different nations. First, England and Wales are more urbanised than the rest of the UK. In Scotland, large urban areas make up only one third of the total (36%) compared to over half in England and Wales, but small towns are more important (23% compared with 11%). Northern Ireland also has fewer people in large urban areas (30%) but far more in rural areas (33%); this last is in spite of the use of a slightly lower cut-off limit for settlements to be judged 'rural' here, as noted above. In this respect, Northern Ireland has more in common with the Republic of Ireland, which is one of the least urbanised countries in Europe (Eurofound, 2014). Second, the composition of places in the same category varies across the UK. The demographic differences noted above are found most strongly in England and Wales, and least strongly in Northern

Ireland. In the latter case, demographic differences across the urban–rural hierarchy are quite limited.

Inevitably, England and Wales are going to dominate the UK analyses presented here because of their large share of the total population. We should not assume that the results are equally applicable in all part of the country. We do occasionally refer to results for the separate nations in this chapter and we have produced a detailed analysis for Scotland as noted above. A further study on the Northern Irish case would be a useful addition.

Poverty and deprivation

In the UK, poverty and deprivation have long been associated more strongly with urban areas than rural. In the early 20th century, cities were the locations which carried the legacy of rapid industrial growth over the previous hundred years, with high concentrations of slum housing, poor health and poverty. Later in that century, they were the locations hit hardest by deindustrialisation and increasing unemployment while, in the 21st, they are the locations where rising inequality is most apparent, with growing numbers of low-income households struggling to find stable, well-paid employment or to compete for access to housing. In rural areas, by contrast, there has been a tendency to play down or deny the existence of poverty and deprivation, emphasising instead an image based on the 'rural idyll' of a strong work ethic, self-reliance and cohesive communities (Cloke et al, 1995). Rural sociologists have struggled against these discourses in an effort to put rural poverty and social exclusion on the map but have shown that such disadvantage exists even in the most affluent rural areas (Shucksmith, 2003).

In this context, there is particular sensitivity about whether different measures of poverty provide a fair picture of the relative levels of need in different locations. One key comparison is between indirect measures based on low incomes and direct measures based on achieved living standards or deprivation (Ringen, 1988). Low-income measures suffer from a number of limitations, not least that income is only one measure of the resources available to a household. Such measures do not reflect inequalities in levels of savings or assets, including home ownership, nor of debts. From a rural perspective, a different concern has been that income-based measures may understate rural poverty because they do not take account of differences in the cost of living (Shucksmith and Philip, 2000), although it should be noted that the evidence on cost-of-living differences appears rather mixed, with some elements (notably fuel and transport) higher in rural areas but others (notably housing) lower (Bailey et al, 2016).

The PSE-UK 2012 provides a range of poverty measures which can be used to compare urban and rural locations. These include: low-income poverty measured before and after housing costs (BHC and AHC); adult deprivation (lacking three or more of the adult necessities); child deprivation (lacking three or more of the child or adult necessities); the PSE-UK 2012 combined poverty measure (deprived and on a low income); and three subjective poverty measures. A discussion of the relative merits of these various measures is provide in the first two chapters to the companion volume (Bailey and Bramley, 2017; Mack, 2017).

All eight measures are shown in Figure 10.1. Overall, we see significant levels of poverty in both rural and urban locations but, in general, progressively higher levels in more urban places (Figure 10.1). There are some important differences between measures, but overall the picture is quite consistent.

We can use this to shed some light on the debate noted above about the possible bias from using low-income measures. If rural costs of

Figure 10.1: Poverty and deprivation by urban–rural location

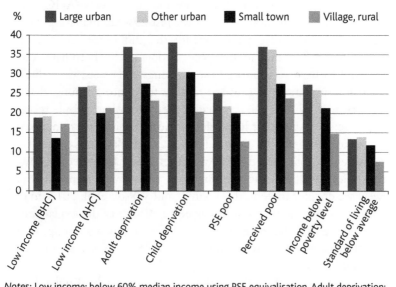

Notes: Low income: below 60% median income using PSE equivalisation. Adult deprivation: lacking 3 or more of the 22 adult necessities. Child deprivation: lacking 2 or more of the 22 child necessities. PSE poor: combined low income (AHC) and deprivation. Perceived poor: 'could genuinely say [they] are poor now' all or some of the time. Income below poverty level: housing income below the level respondent identifies as being necessary to keep a household like theirs out of poverty. Standard of living: believed to be below average. For full details, please refer to Bailey and Bramley (2017). Weighted cases around 11,500 (all), 8,200 (adults only) and 2,300 (children only), depending on measure.

living were higher, we would expect deprivation measures to show rural areas in a worse light relative to urban areas than low-income measures; deprivations assess what people can afford to do and hence reflect costs of living. In fact, deprivation measures show *urban* areas in a much worse light: they suggest there is more of a difference between urban and rural locations than low-income measures indicate. This is particularly true for child deprivation where rates in large urban areas appear to be almost double those in rural locations. If anything, therefore, we would argue that low-income measures appear to overstate rural poverty relative to urban, rather than understating it.

It is also worth noting that the low-income measure which takes account of housing costs (AHC) shows relatively more poverty in urban areas than the one which ignores this area of expenditure (BHC). Housing costs are a very substantial element of expenditure for the majority of households, with higher costs faced by those in urban locations where there is greater competition for land and housing.

One reason for this difference between low-income and deprivation measures might be demographics. Rural areas have a larger elderly population than more urban locations, as noted above, and this group is less likely to be deprived, even when in low-income poverty. For example, of the 25–34-year-olds in low-income poverty (AHC), 71% are deprived, but for those 65 and over just 29% are deprived. There might be a variety of explanations for this difference. On the one hand, it may reflect the fact that older people are likely to have fewer debts and to have accumulated more savings and assets, the value of which low-income measures fail to take fully into account, that is, low-income measures may overstate poverty for older people relative to younger. On the other hand, deprivation measures may understate poverty for older people if the elderly are more likely to say they lack necessities because they do not want them, perhaps reflecting lower expectations for generations brought up when living standards were lower (see chapter three in this volume and Wilson et al, 2017, in the companion volume for more discussion). Whatever the explanation, however, we find that controlling for differences in age composition does not change our view about the relative levels of poverty in urban and rural locations.

As noted above, the UK figures are dominated by England and Wales but we can produce separate analyses for Scotland and Northern Ireland. In Scotland, the picture is similar to the UK as a whole although rural areas appear somewhat less advantaged compared to their urban counterparts here; as Shucksmith and Philip (2000) note, there has been more substantial gentrification of rural areas in England.

On the low-income AHC measure, for example, rural poverty in Scotland is as high as in the urban areas, although on the deprivation measure it is still lower. If we use the Scottish urban–rural scale to separate more remote locations from accessible ones, there appears to be a particular problem of poverty in remote rural areas, where it is markedly higher than in remote towns (Bailey et al, 2016). In Northern Ireland, by contrast, the gradient runs in the opposite direction albeit relatively weakly. Again, this region appears to have a very different urban–rural geography to the rest of the UK, and one with more in common with the Republic of Ireland (Eurostat, 2013).

Separately from the poverty measures, respondents are asked about levels of borrowing (the number of different types of borrowing) and problems with debts or paying the bills as an indication of levels of financial stress in the household. The answers to these questions reinforce the picture provided by deprivation measures. Compared with those in rural areas, people in more urban areas report more types of borrowing and more problems with debt and with paying bills. This further strengthens the conclusion that deprivation measures provide the more reliable guide to relative levels of need in urban and rural locations. Measures of low-income poverty based on a snapshot of current incomes do not capture these aspects of negative resources in the form of debts, which may reflect incomes over a much longer period.

Living standards and inequality

Poverty measures obviously focus our attention on those with the fewest resources but the PSE-UK 2012 survey also lets us take a broader look at living standards across the income spectrum. Here we take a brief look at a couple of measures to see whether differences in poverty are reflected more generally in differences in living standards: do areas with more poverty tend to have less affluence as well or are there areas which are more polarised, with high levels of poverty alongside high levels of affluence?

The PSE-UK 2012 survey provides a range of questions which can be used here. In addition to the questions on the 44 'necessities' items which make up the deprivation scale, the survey asks about ownership of seven items which might be regarded as 'luxuries' – they are not identified as 'necessities' by the public and they are owned or consumed by less than half the population. These are: a second car, a second bathroom, a second home, a home security system, payments into a private pension scheme, private health insurance and a holiday abroad. The survey also asks people to assess the quality of their goods or consumption in seven areas: clothing and shoes, kitchen, furniture, home entertainment, car, entertainment and holiday accommodation.

The pattern with individual 'luxury' items is a little mixed because some of these items may be seen as more or less of a luxury depending on where you live. For example, people in rural areas are more likely to have a second car, reflecting the limitations of public transport services, while those in urban areas are more likely to have home security, reflecting differences in crime risks. The cost of some items may also vary between urban and rural locations so that it is a less reliable guide to living standards; a second bathroom is much more common in rural areas where housing costs tend to be lower.

Averaging across respondents' answers on the number of luxuries and the quality of goods, however, there is a consistent picture which differs to some extent from that provided by poverty measures. The highest levels of luxuries and of quality of items are found in rural locations where poverty is lowest, and these levels fall for small town and other urban areas where poverty tends to be progressively higher. In the large urban areas, however, the average level of luxuries and of quality of items is greater than in other urban areas even though levels of poverty are higher. There is evidence here, therefore, of greater polarisation within the large cities, with a larger proportion at both extremes.

This picture is further supported by some simple measures of income inequality such as income ratios. The 80/20 ratio, for example, shows how much larger the income (AHC) of someone at the 80th centile of the income distribution is than the income of someone at the 20th centile. For the UK as a whole, the 80/20 ratio is 3.28 but it is slightly higher in urban areas (3.41) and lower for others such as rural areas (3.08). Urban areas have the most inequality in the upper half of the income distribution, particularly at the very top. Rural areas have more inequality in the lower half. For example, the gap between those on median incomes and those on the 10th centile (the 50/10 ratio) is 3.17 in rural areas compared with 3.05 in large urban areas. It should be noted, however, that absolute incomes at both points are lower in urban locations.

Social exclusion

Resources: access to services

One of the key elements of the literature on rural poverty and exclusion is about problems of access to services, public and private, and transport. On transport, the rural dimension is particularly clear. Costs of transport combined with the limited availability of public transport can lead to isolation or a loss of opportunities, or to the diversion of a larger proportion of household resources to this area of expenditure, with consequences for other areas. There may be particular problems for people unable to drive or to afford a car, including both older people and young adults (Storey and Brannen, 2000; Hodge et al, 2002; Eurofound, 2014).

On services, the picture is perhaps more complicated because geographic distance is only one barrier to accessing adequate services. The quality of service also matters, as does the pressure or demand on that service. Geographic access is more of a problem in rural locations although it can still be an issue in urban locations, particularly for low-income households without access to a car. However, problems of service quality and demand pressures are often seen as more problematic in urban locations (Bramley and Evans, 2000). With public services, the main reason is that the funding formulae used to allocate resources for services fail to take sufficient account of needs. In England, the needs component in funding for local government services has been severely (and covertly) reduced in recent years (Hastings et al, 2015). With private services, poor access also reflects the low purchasing power of areas with high concentrations of deprivation.

The PSE-UK 2012 survey asks respondents about access to a wide range of services: 17 are general services which might be used by all households, while 5 are services for older people and 6 for children and young people. (For a detailed discussion, see chapter four in the companion volume, Bramley and Besemer, 2017). Here we take a broad approach to service exclusion that goes beyond geographic access, looking at whether people report that they find services inadequate, unavailable or inaccessible due to cost or affordability. The overall picture does show greater problems of service access in more rural areas, but it also shows some problems in urban areas as well as variation between different kinds of service (Figure 10.2).

The urban–rural gradient is most obvious in relation to the general services, with 69% of people in rural areas reporting problems accessing two or more of these services compared with 50% of those in urban areas. The differences are apparent for most of the individual services, but not all. While rural areas have greater problems in relation to most of the retail, leisure and health services, there are important services where problems are just as great in urban areas: access to doctors, post offices, community centres and pubs. Problems with public transport are particularly severe in rural areas, however, and these

Figure 10.2: Problems in access to services by urban–rural location

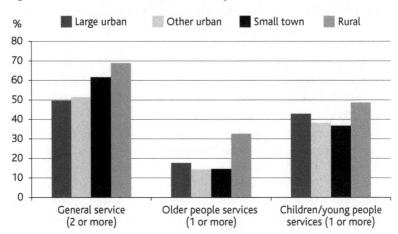

Notes: Questions on general services asked of all adults, while those on services for older people restricted to people 65 or older and those on children and young people restricted to households with children. Weighted cases: 9,088 (general services); 1,862 (older people); and 3,068 (children/young people).

services are of course important as a means of accessing many other kinds of opportunity. The picture is very similar if we look only at poor individuals or those with limiting long-term illnesses or disability.

With services for older people, problems of access are in general far less severe, with fewer than one in five older people reporting any problems. In this case, rural areas stand out, with nearly twice as many problems as any of the other type of area. This difference affects all five of the services for older people. In Scotland, where we can split the rural sample into finer sub-divisions, the problem is particularly severe in remote rural areas (Bailey et al, 2016).

Problems with services for children and young people appear much more acute than those for older people, with more than two in five families reporting difficulties in access. In this case, problems appear to be no worse in rural areas than in urban locations, but there is a slightly different mix of problems. In urban areas, problems are greater in relation to access to play facilities, whereas families in rural areas are more likely to report problems accessing youth clubs, after-school clubs or public transport to school.

Participation: employment

In the B-SEM framework, employment is seen as valuable for social inclusion not just for the resources it may bring but more directly as a form of participation: a social role which serves to integrate people into society. Several previous studies have suggested that the inclusionary benefits of paid work may be less in rural areas due to greater barriers to securing well-paid employment there. This is partly a problem of finding accessible employment which matches individual skills given the 'thinner' nature of rural labour markets (Phimister et al, 2000; Hodge et al, 2002). It may also be related to the nature of employment opportunities provided in the rural economy where there are more problems with low pay and seasonal fluctuations in demand, linked to the reliance on tourism and agricultural industries (Scottish Government, 2012b). In addition, rural commuting costs tend to be greater, reducing the returns from paid work, while the inadequacy of public transport may make running a car more of a necessity even for those with relatively low earnings (Shucksmith and Philip, 2000). There are particular problems for families needing childcare, since the economics of providing this service in rural areas are more challenging (Monk et al, 1999; RPIWG, 2001).

The PSE-UK 2012 provides data on current employment status as well as recent employment history. In terms of current employment, rural areas do not appear disadvantaged. The employment rate is slightly higher (76% of working-age people in rural areas, compared with 69% in large urban areas). While there are more people in rural areas working part-time, particularly men, the proportions working full-time are no different. At the household level, we can look at the extent to which working-age adults managed to maintain paid work over the whole of the previous 12 months – the household work-intensity rate. This captures the effects of any seasonal variations, with a value of 100% indicating that every working-age adult (excluding those in full-time education) worked full-time for the whole of the previous 12 months. Rural areas appear no different to urban: average household work intensities are 67% and 65% respectively. Finally, looking back over the previous five years, those in rural areas are no more likely to report having ever been unemployed than people in the large urban areas (19% versus 23% respectively).

While access to employment in rural areas appears no worse, the benefits of work appear to be greater. Of those in employment in large urban areas, over one in six is in poverty (17%) compared with fewer than one in eight in rural areas (12%). If we look in more detail at levels of employment for the household (Figure 10.3), we see that the difference stems from those with lower levels of work intensity, that is, households where not every adult has paid work. For those with high work intensity (greater than 80%), poverty risks are low everywhere.

Figure 10.3: Poverty rates by household work intensity and urban–rural location

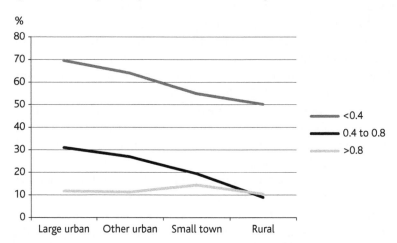

Notes: People below retirement age and not in pensioner households. Weighted cases = 5,009.

For households with lower work intensity, however, poverty risks are much lower in more rural locations.

Various factors might explain this difference. One interpretation is that the returns from paid work in rural areas are greater, relative to costs of living. This would be consistent with the evidence above on differences between measures of low-income poverty and deprivation. Another possibility is that the figures may be distorted by the migration of people at or near retirement to rural areas. Such households may have one or more members in paid work but also have the benefits of occupational pensions or other savings, reducing both the need to work and in-work poverty rates. A partial test for this is to remove older people (over 50, for example). When we do this, the picture remains the same so pre-retirement migration does not appear to be the explanation.

Quality of life: housing and neighbourhood

Housing quality and affordability have long been seen as a key problem in rural locations, particularly for older and lower income households. Social housing is relatively scarce, partly because of a more conservative politics in rural locations, which discouraged council house building in the past (Shucksmith and Philip, 2000). In the present day, land ownership patterns and planning restrictions can combine to limit supply of land for new housing, particularly for the smaller and cheaper units that might be accessible to younger people (Satsangi et al, 2010). In some areas, problems are exacerbated by competition from older and more affluent in-migrants, including second-home owners. Rural housing costs may also be driven up by heating costs, due to greater reliance on more expensive fuels and, in some cases, greater exposure to the weather.

For urban locations, housing problems are certainly present, especially in the south of England where demand pressures have driven prices up, but there has also been greater emphasis on problems associated with the neighbourhood environment. Across Europe, poorer urban neighbourhoods in particular are seen as being characterised by a range of physical and social problems (Eurofound, 2014).

On housing, the PSE–UK 2012 survey records overall satisfaction as well as the respondent's assessment of the state of repair (from various questions on specific disrepair problems as well as a general disrepair question) and whether the home was hard to heat (from various questions about cutting back on energy use as well as a question on whether home was too cold last winter). On the neighbourhood, it covers overall satisfaction with the area, as well as perceptions of: social problems (noisy neighbours, people disorderly in the street, insults or harassment, vandalism); problems associated with congestion or density (noise, pollution or traffic problems); and other environmental problems (lighting, parking or litter problems).

The results in Figure 10.4 tend to show modest differences in relation to housing, with urban areas slightly more problematic: higher dissatisfaction with housing, more people reporting disrepair and more reporting problems heating the home. There are more obvious

Figure 10.4: Housing and neighbourhood environment by urban–rural location

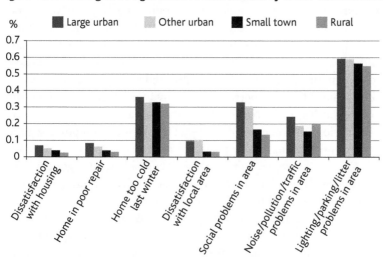

Notes: Weighted cases around 11,570 depending on the question.

differences in relation to the neighbourhood, with a much larger urban–rural gap in relation to satisfaction. This appears to arise from social problems in the area in particular, although problems related to the physical environment or amenity also tended to be worse in urban locations. Rural areas enjoy a relative advantage in this respect.

Quality of life: health and well-being

Health and well-being are the last aspects of the B-SEM which we examine in this chapter. Research has suggested that the population of rural areas is relatively healthy, with lower mortality rates (Shucksmith and Philip, 2000). Although there is a general gradient of improving health from urban to rural, however, the most remote rural areas are not so advantaged. The gradient also varies by condition, respiratory conditions being worse in urban areas, but suicides worse in rural ones, for example. Explanations may be about physical environment (especially air quality, a benefit of rural living widely identified by residents; Shucksmith and Philip, 2000) as well as social context. Selective migration may also play a role.

The PSE-UK 2012 survey captures several aspects of health and well-being. There are three questions on subjective well-being: general satisfaction with day-to-day activities, with feeling part of a community and with life overall. Respondents give ratings from 0 to 10, with high satisfaction taken as 9 or 10 (15% to 30% of the population, depending on the question). There are two further questions on general health and limiting health problems or disabilities. The first is based on a single question using a five-point scale and we contrast the highest ('very good' – 31%) with the rest. The second is constructed from separate questions identifying whether people are limited in daily tasks or activities by any health problem or disability. For ease of comparison, we contrast those with no limiting health problems or disabilities (76%) with the rest.

The main difference between subjective well-being questions and those on health or disability is that the latter are shaped much more by the biological processes of ageing. The proportion reporting good health or no limiting health problems or disabilities declines steadily with age; for example, half of 18–24-year-olds report good health compared with just 1 in 10 of those over 80. By contrast, subjective satisfaction rates tend to rise with age, peaking amongst those aged 65–74 before declining slightly. People who are poor report lower well-being and worse health on all the measures. (See chapter twelve in the companion volume by Tomlinson and Wilson, 2017, for a more detailed discussion of the PSE-UK 2012 evidence on well-being.)

There appears to be an important advantage for rural areas in relation to subjective well-being, although the origins of this are not clear. With the health- or disability-related measures, there are no differences between urban and rural locations but, with subjective well-being, people in more rural locations appear noticeably more positive (Figure 10.5). These differences persist even if we control for differences in age, gender and household types, or differences in incomes and deprivation.[3] If we look only at poor individuals, it is rural areas alone where people report higher well-being, with the other three all very similar. A variety of explanations might be made for this finding and it is not possible to test these using the PSE-UK 2012 survey. These might include features of the physical environment, such as proximity to green space, or the social environment, arising from social contacts and networks.

Figure 10.5: Health and well-being by urban–rural location

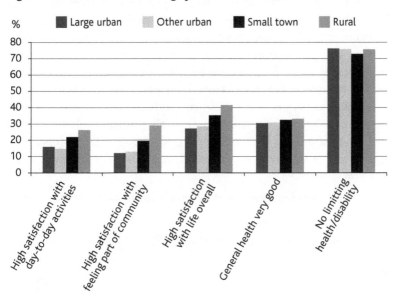

Note: Weighted cases between 8,335 and 8,397 depending on question.

Experience of poverty

For the final part of the analysis, we draw on PSE-UK 2012 data on the experience of poverty. In recent years, research has shown that shame and disrespect are common features of the experience of being poor. In a comparative study, Walker et al (2013) identify that, across many different countries, people who are poor report feeling a sense of shame and that this in turn has a range of harmful consequences, leading to 'pretence, withdrawal, self-loathing, "othering", despair, depression, thoughts of suicide and generally to reductions in personal efficacy' (2013, p 215). Lister (2004, p 99) provides a series of quotes from people with experience of poverty who argue that being shamed and disrespected are the worst aspects of being poor in their view.

Some studies have argued that the nature of rural communities makes poverty particularly shameful or stigmatising in those locations. This is due to the greater visibility or exposure which people in rural communities report, due to the smaller and more intimate communities which typify such areas. It may be further exacerbated by the fact that rural poverty conflicts with the idealised image of rural life where the work ethic and self-reliance are said to be particularly valued (Fabes et al, 1993, quoted in Shucksmith and Philip, 2000) so that poverty is interpreted to a greater extent as evidence of personal failure.

The PSE–UK 2012 survey asks respondents if they have ever felt embarrassed or been made to feel small because of poverty (respectively, feeling shame and being shamed). Taken together, these questions suggest that one in four people (26%) have felt shame due to poverty at some time in their life. We cannot say when or where this experience of poverty occurred but nevertheless it is interesting to compare experiences for those currently living in urban and rural locations. We can compare people with similar levels of current poverty, measured by level of deprivation (Figure 10.6). People with high levels of deprivation are much more likely to report having

Figure 10.6: Ever experienced shame by current deprivation and urban–rural location

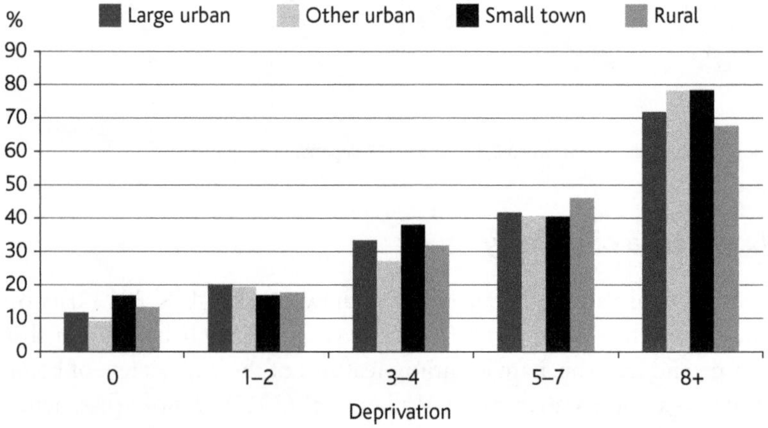

Note: Weighted cases = 8,127.

experienced shame. At very high levels of deprivation, such shame is reported by nearly everyone. On the basis of these data, poverty does not appear to be any more shameful in rural locations.

Discussion and conclusions

Overall, the results from the PSE-UK 2012 support many of our existing perceptions about urban–rural differences in the UK. The UK is one of the countries in Europe where urban areas perform slightly worse than rural ones across a number of dimensions of poverty and social exclusion, although it should be stressed that similarities are greater than differences (Eurofound, 2014). Of course, the four broad categories used here also serve to mask a great deal of variation within each. Some of that is regional – there is a rather different urban–rural gradient in Northern Ireland, for example. Some of it would be revealed if, as in Scotland, we could make finer distinctions within the rural category.

For policy, one of the most striking findings is how much the selection of poverty measures influences our perception of relative levels of need. In particular, the kind of low-income measure that policy analyses rely on most heavily tends to understate urban poverty compared with that in rural areas. We also note that the choice of measures influences perceptions of relative needs between social groups, notably differences by age. Together these analyses suggest that policy needs to take these differences more seriously. It is possible that deprivation measures contain their own biases, as the debate in relation to age variations suggests. Nevertheless, the limitations of low-income measures should be more readily acknowledged and alternatives more widely adopted.

In other respects, the main message for policy is the similarity of problems of social exclusion in urban and rural contexts. Claims for urban or rural exceptionalism do not find much support here. In some respects, urban areas appear to have slightly more problems; neighbourhood conditions and subjective well-being, for example. In others, it is rural areas where challenges are greater, most notably in transport and access to services. These differences do justify variations in the policy focus in urban and rural areas and the creation of secondary 'top-up' initiatives to address specific aspects of these. Overall, however, the analysis shows that similarities outweigh differences. In particular, poverty is equally shaming in urban and rural locations. The core to tackling poverty and social exclusion in all areas is concerted national policies to restore basic standards of living.

Notes

[1] The UK has been divided up into a set of small spatial units for the purposes of producing local or 'neighbourhood' statistics. These units are called Lower Super Output Areas (LSOAs) in England and Wales, Datazones in Scotland and Super Output Areas in Northern Ireland.

[2] To improve comparability, we use additional information to distinguish large urban areas from other urban areas in England and Wales. In Scotland, the threshold for large urban areas was 125,000 rather than 100,000. In Northern Ireland, the threshold for small towns started at 2,250 rather than 3,000. For details, see Bailey (2012).

[3] Logistic regression models with appropriate controls; results not shown.

References

Bailey, N. (2012) 'Contextual variables on the PSE-UK: a methodological note', Glasgow: University of Glasgow.

Bailey, N. and Bramley, G. (2017) 'Introduction', in G. Bramley and N. Bailey (eds) *Poverty and social exclusion in the UK: vol. 2 – The dimensions of disadvantage*, Bristol: Policy Press.

Bailey, N., Bramley, G. and Gannon, M. (2016) 'Poverty and social exclusion in urban and rural areas of Scotland', PSE-UK Working Paper, Bristol: PSE.

Bailey, N., Flint, J., Goodlad, R., Shucksmith, M., Fitzpatrick, S. and Pryce, G. (2003) *Measuring deprivation in Scotland: Developing a long-term strategy*, Edinburgh: Scottish Executive Central Statistics Unit.

Bramley, G. and Besemer, K. (2017) 'Poverty, local services and austerity', in G. Bramley, and N. Bailey (eds) *Poverty and social exclusion in the UK: volume 2 – the dimensions of disadvantage*, Bristol: Policy Press, pp 113–133.

Bramley, G. and Evans, M. (2000) 'Getting the smaller picture: small-area analysis of public expenditure incidence and deprivation in three English cities', *Fiscal Studies* 21:2, 231–67.

Cloke, P., Goodwin, M., Milbourne, P. and Thomas, C. (1995) 'Deprivation, poverty and marginal-ization in rural lifestyles in England and Wales', *Journal of Rural Studies* 11:4, 351–65.

Countryside Agency, DEFRA, ODPM, ONS, Welsh Assembly Government (2004) *Rural and urban classification 2004*, Cheltenham: Countryside Agency.

Eurofound (2014) *Quality of life in urban and rural Europe. 3rd EQLS policy brief*, Luxembourg: Publications Office of the European Union.

Eurostat (2013) *Eurostat regional yearbook 2013*, Luxembourg: Publications Office of the European Union.

Hastings, A., Bailey, N., Besemer, K., Bramley, G., Gannon, M. and Watkins, D. (2015) *The cost of the cuts: The impact on local government and poorer communities*, York: Joseph Rowntree Foundation.

Hodge, I., Dunn, J., Monk, S. and Fitzgerald, M. (2002) 'Barriers to participation in residual rural labour markets', *Work, Employment & Society* 16:3, 457–76.

Lister, R. (2004) *Poverty*, Cambridge: Polity Press.

Mack, J. (2017) 'Fifty years of poverty research', in G. Bramley and N. Bailey (eds) *Poverty and social exclusion in the UK: vol. 2 – The dimensions of disadvantage*, Bristol: Policy Press.

Monk, S., Dunn, J., Fitzgerald, M. and Hodge, I. (1999) *Finding work in rural areas: Bridges and barriers*. York: Joseph Rowntree Foundation/ YPS.

Northern Ireland Statistics and Research Agency (NISRA) (2005) *Report of the Inter-departmental Urban–Rural Definition Group*, Belfast: NISRA.

Phimister, E., Shucksmith, M. and Vera-Toscano, E. (2000) 'The dynamics of low pay in rural households: exploratory analysis using the British Household Panel Survey', *Journal of Agricultural Economics* 51:1, 61–76.

Ringen, S. (1988) 'Direct and indirect measures of poverty', *Journal of Social Policy* 17:3, 351–66.

RPWIG (Rural Poverty and Inclusion Working Group) (2001) *Poverty and social exclusion in rural Scotland*, Edinburgh: Scottish Executive.

Satsangi, M., Gallent, N. and Bevan, M. (2010) *Communities and planning in Britain's countrysides*, Bristol: Policy Press.

Scottish Government (2012a) *Scottish Government urban/rural classification 2011–12*, Edinburgh: Scottish Government.

Scottish Government (2012b) *Rural Scotland key facts 2012*, Edinburgh: Scottish Government.

Shucksmith, M. (2003) *Social exclusion in rural areas: A review of research*, London: DEFRA.

Shucksmith, M. and Philip, L. (2000) *Social exclusion in rural areas: A literature review and conceptual framework*, Edinburgh: Scottish Executive Central Research Unit.

Storey, P. and Brannen, J. (2000) *Young people and transport in rural areas*, Leicester: Youth Work Press/Joseph Rowntree Foundation.

Tomlinson, M. and Wilson, L. (2017) 'The poverty of well-being', in G. Bramley and N. Bailey (eds) *Poverty and social exclusion in the UK: vol. 2 – The dimensions of disadvantage*, Bristol: Policy Press.

Walker, R., Kyomuhendo, G.A., Chase, E., Choudhry, S., Gubrium, E.K., Nicola, J.Y. et al (2013) 'Poverty in global perspective: is shame a common denominator?', *Journal of Social Policy* 42:2, 215–33.

Wilson, L., Fahmy, E. and Bailey, N. (2017) 'Social participation and social support', in G. Bramley and N. Bailey (eds) *Poverty and social exclusion in the UK: vol. 2 – The dimensions of disadvantage*, Bristol: Policy Press.

Conclusion: innovating methods, informing policy and challenging stigma

Gill Main

The preceding chapters of this volume have detailed the ways in which poverty and social exclusion are very real and large-scale problems in the UK today. They have also examined the subtle variations in vulnerability to poverty and the impact poverty has on different groups within society. But the aim of this book – and of the 2012 Poverty and Social Exclusion Survey (PSE-UK 2012) research as a whole – is not simply to document poverty in the UK, but to challenge its prevalence and offer practical insights into how policy and practice may best work towards its end. As Piachaud (1987) enjoins us, any study of poverty must aim to change attitudes and social actions, if it is to be part of the solution and not part of the problem. As noted in the title, here I draw attention to three specific ways in which the PSE-UK 2012 in general, and this volume in particular, might contribute to achieving this aim:

- **Innovating methods:** accurate measurement of poverty is vital to its eradication. We do not claim that the PSE-UK 2012 is a panacea; but it does represent the latest developments in the field. These developments have built on work conducted by the founders of the consensual approach (Townsend, 1979; Mack and Lansley, 1985), and have depended upon the rigour of its critics (for example, Piachaud, 1987). Furthermore, the large sample size of the PSE-UK 2012 has enabled the fine-grained analysis of different population groups presented in this volume. While methodological developments will continue, an increased awareness of the groups within society which face the highest vulnerability to poverty, and the impacts of poverty on different groups, can only help in understanding and combating the problem.

- **Informing policy:** the ways in which poverty is conceptualised, defined and measured within the policy environment, and its prioritisation within policy agendas, are greatly variable over time. Significant changes in both the conceptualisation of poverty and its prioritisation as a social problem are evident in recent history, as detailed below. Studies such as the PSE-UK 2012 can help to inform policy approaches through testing the assumptions they draw on about the nature, causes and effects of poverty, and can help to promote its inclusion as a policy priority through highlighting the extent and nature of the problem, overall and for specific sub-populations.

- **Challenging stigma:** that those in poverty experience stigma and shame is nothing new; narratives of an 'undeserving' poor can be traced back through the centuries. However, recent shifts in UK policy, rhetoric and media have combined to create an atmosphere of extreme hostility and scapegoating towards those in poverty and/or vulnerable to social exclusion. Public compassion towards those in poverty, including via an understanding that recent policy changes increase the risk of poverty for all of us, is a vital step towards policy change. The PSE-UK 2012 can contribute to this through a combination of rehumanising those in poverty through hearing their stories, and providing robust data to challenge 'othering' narratives, whatever their source.

This volume adds to a large body of literature highlighting the structural factors which render particular population groups particularly vulnerable to poverty, and the structural barriers which too often prevent them from escaping poverty. Yet, repeatedly, social policies to reduce and eradicate poverty are subsumed by competing priorities such as a purported need for austerity (HM Treasury, 2015), and by ideologically motivated debates about the nature of poverty which disregard empirical evidence and expert opinion in favour of stigmatising rhetoric (Clark and Newman, 2012). This concluding chapter summarises the contribution of this volume in relation to the three themes detailed above, and presents suggestions in relation to directions for future research, via both further analysis of PSE-UK 2012 data and developments which could inform new studies.

Developing state-of-the-art poverty measures

The measures of poverty and social exclusion included in the PSE-UK 2012 draw on strong theoretical and empirical bases, detailed in chapter one. This is invaluable in providing data on the experiences of population groups of interest, and in examining where further theoretical and methodological innovation is indicated. Two issues arising from the chapters in relation to potential future developments are detailed here: the useful but problematic nature of households as a unit of measurement and/or analysis; and the tension between generating generalisable poverty measures and paying adequate attention to the specific needs of different social groups.

The value and problems of the household unit in poverty studies

The household is commonly used as a sampling unit, and as a unit for the purposes of measurement and/or of analysis, in studies of poverty. The shortcomings of relying on household-level measurement, and the somewhat different approach to the use of households in the PSE-UK 2012, are detailed in the Introduction and expanded upon in the chapters on disability, gender, and parents and children. Four problematic assumptions can be identified which underlie the use of households in poverty measurement:

- that resources are shared equitably between household members;
- that there is a high level of stability in household formation and structure;
- that individuals can be easily assigned to a single household; and
- that resources are not transferred between households.

The first of these assumptions is addressed comprehensively throughout this volume. The second is alluded to in the chapter on young people, in relation to the growing trend for young people to struggle to leave, or make multiple transitions out of and into their parental home (where this is an option for them). The latter two points are ripe for development through future research. In relation to the third assumption, the use of households as sampling units assumes that individuals can be assigned to a single household containing one or more people. The veracity of this assumption is challenged by growing numbers of individuals – children following parental separation or re-partnering – who are members of multiple households. Such children may live in multiple households comprising varying household structures and, furthermore, their lives may be better understood by considering the relevance of extended family members such as grandparents, who may provide extensive care, despite children not technically being members of their household (for example, Statham, 2011). Research with children emphasises the importance they place on links with disparate family members across the multiple households of which they are (or even may not technically be) a member (Davies,

2015). This links to the final assumption, about the transfer of resources between households. Some questions on transfers between households in the form of gifts were included in the PSE-UK 2012 but are not covered in this volume. In combination these issues present an important challenge in relation to the measurement of poverty – how can the experiences of people who may live across multiple households with varying access to income and other resources be captured? And, given the rapid fluctuations which may take place in people's needs, incomes and living arrangements (for example, in the lives of parents and children following parental separation), how can the fluidity of needs and living arrangements best be captured?

As noted in the Introduction, the inclusion of all adult household members represents an important innovation in understanding poverty at an intra-household level; one way in which the PSE-UK 2012 approach could be further refined to more fully account for the perspectives and experiences of all household members would be through the inclusion, where possible, of children as respondents. Allowing for children's perspectives in the classification of child-relevant items and activities as necessities, and for their reports on the deprivations and social exclusion they experience, would enhance knowledge on child poverty and social exclusion and would allow for intra-household comparisons between adults and children and between individual children. As the distribution of resources within a household relates not only to household-level availability, but also to social and cultural norms, interpersonal relationships, differing individual needs, shared and individual priorities, and power, such data would allow for a much more nuanced exploration of the vulnerability of different household members, and how vulnerability may relate to factors such as age, gender, disability and other relevant characteristics.

Consensual indicators and minority needs

The basis of the consensual approach to poverty measurement is that it is possible to establish a set of necessities which the majority of the population agree that no one should have to go without – as detailed in chapter one. This allows for the production of poverty measures which are not only scientifically valid and reliable, but also have the backing of popular consensus, lending them a high level of political credibility (see Gordon, 2006). However, several chapters in this volume highlight the tension between achieving a list of necessities which are approved by the general public and ensuring that the different needs of, and costs associated with membership of, sub-populations are adequately addressed. Two issues are of relevance here: whether a sub-population is considered to have different enough needs that a separate set of necessities is warranted; and if so who gets a say in determining the needs of that sub-population.

The manner in which the PSE-UK 2012 differentiates between adults' and children's needs, detailed by Main and Bradshaw (in chapter six), provides an example of how the different situations and requirements of a sub-population can be incorporated into the consensual approach. Many chapters in this volume raise the question of whether a similar differentiation would be valuable for other social groups – for example in relation to people with disabilities; young people; older people; and people living in urban and rural locations. However, adopting multiple lists of necessities based on different subgroup needs raises two issues. First, the public accessibility and potentially the political sway of a poverty measure may be lessened by increasing complexity and conditionality in understanding its basis. Second, judgements would be required about how to establish which specific subgroups require a separate set of necessities (and how would heterogeneity within these groups – for example, between people with vastly differing types of disability – be handled); and who gets a say in assessing the necessity or otherwise of specific items and activities for these groups. Issues of popular misunderstandings and prejudice (see, for example, DWP, 2014) may compromise the general public's capacity to offer meaningful insight on, for example, the needs of people with disabilities – and as Heslop and Emerson (chapter eight in this volume) note, 'disability' encompasses heterogeneous conditions which will be associated with specific and diverse additional needs. Thus, while there are no clear answers to this issue, future studies would benefit from a careful consideration of how the needs of diverse groups can be represented in order to minimise the risk of misclassification among subgroups likely to have different needs to the general population.

Informing policy

The timing of the PSE-GB 1999 and PSE-UK 2012 studies is notable in relation to policy – in 1999, Tony Blair's recently elected Labour government had begun the process of putting poverty, and particularly child and pensioner poverty, firmly onto the policy agenda. While Labour's track record on poverty across its time in office (1997–2010) was mixed (see Joyce and Sibieta, 2013), and transfers to working-age adults declined, substantial progress was made, including decreasing the differential risk of exposure to poverty for people at different stages of the life-course (see Lupton et al, 2013). In contrast, the economic crisis of 2007/8, followed by recession and the election of a Conservative-Liberal Democrat Coalition in 2010, resulted in a change in focus from poverty to national debt, and from social investment to austerity. These were the predominant conditions while the PSE-UK 2012 was in the field, and remain so at the time of writing. As such, the PSE-UK 2012, and comparisons between PSE-UK 2012 and PSE-GB 1999, can be used to produce information of high value to policy makers. Three ways in which the PSE-UK 2012 has provided policy-relevant evidence – in relation to the inequities of austerity politics, the status of different social groups, and the role of structural conditions in shaping people's vulnerability to poverty – are detailed below.

Austerity and its inequitable impacts

Several detailed accounts of the impact of the economic crisis and subsequent austerity measures, in the UK and across the world, are now available (for example, Beatty and Fothergill, 2014). The varied measures of poverty and social exclusion included in the PSE-UK 2012 can contribute to understanding the effects of austerity. This is examined in this volume in relation to older people, young people, children, parents, people with disabilities and people from minority ethnic groups. In relation to this last group, increasingly harsh policy approaches to immigration (see below for more on this) are framed as offering fairer opportunities for British nationals, but risk pushing immigrant and ethnic minority populations further into poverty. Specific details of policy changes adopted as part of the austerity agenda, and recommendations for their reversal, can be found in the chapters of this volume. The overarching message – that austerity has hit the most vulnerable hardest, and that living conditions among these groups are dangerously precarious – challenges both the ideological basis of austerity and its effectiveness as a policy strategy. This latter point is further confirmed by office for National Statistics (ONS) figures showing that the public sector debt as a percentage of GDP grew from 65.2% in May 2010, when the Conservative-Liberal Democrat Coalition took power, to 82.9% in July 2016.[1]

Intersecting identities, multiple dimensions

A major contribution of the PSE-UK 2012, and particularly the nuanced approach to poverty measurement which combines low income and deprivation, is its highlighting of the importance of intersecting aspects of identity. These can mediate or compound vulnerability to poverty and social exclusion. Despite the importance of these intersecting identities, the chapters presented in this volume are unanimous in their challenge to reductions and increased conditionality in social security provision as little support is found for claims about the 'undeserving' nature of any particular group of social security claimants: high levels of deprivation among those in poverty help to debunk claims that poverty is a lifestyle choice; and the attitudes and behaviours of the poor appear remarkably similar to those of the non-poor. Moves towards 'simplifying' the benefits system, for example through monthly payments of Universal Credit to the head of household replacing multiple benefit types, should be approached with caution: while decreasing the complexity of claiming is to be welcomed, monthly payments may prove extremely difficult to manage for people surviving on a day-to-day basis, and payments to one household member may exacerbate existing inequalities (see Tarr and Finn, 2012, for a detailed analysis of the Universal Credit plans).

The PSE-UK 2012 fieldwork was completed in 2012, two years after the formation of the Conservative-Liberal Democrat Coalition government. Since then, the UK has seen the election in 2015 of a Conservative majority government which has pursued yet more aggressive austerity measures. Continued austerity has been justified through rhetoric focused on contrasting the experiences of purportedly different groups at the lower end of the socio-economic spectrum, avoiding attention to the growing distance between those at the top and those at the bottom. Examples of this include pitting 'hard-working families', who deserve support through policy measures such as the new minimum wage for people aged 25 and over (confusingly referred to as the 'living wage'; see, for example, D'Arcy and Kelly, 2015) against 'troubled families' who purportedly cause havoc in their neighbourhoods and present a high cost to the taxpaying public (DCLG, 2013); and pitting UK national tax payers and social security recipients against 'benefit tourists' from within and beyond the European Union (Cameron, 2013). Both of these examples show a disregard for research evidence, which questioned the basis of estimates of the total number of 'troubled families' meeting policy criteria (Levitas, 2012) and the legitimacy of claims relating to the success of the programme (Crossley, 2015), and the existence of 'benefit tourists' (Metcalf, 2016). Indeed, recent figures released by the Department for Work and Pensions (DWP) show a substantial deterioration in social security provision for European Economic Area migrants following the implementation of more stringent residence and eligibility tests since December 2013 (DWP, 2016). Pitting disadvantaged groups against one another succeeds in distracting from the extraordinary and growing levels of inequality in the UK, perpetuated by tax breaks primarily benefiting the rich (Resolution Foundation, 2016). The example of 'benefit tourism' is particularly troubling in light of consistent evidence that popular perceptions of immigration are among the top issues influencing voters – including the 2015 general election (Ipsos MORI, 2015) and the more recent referendum on Britain's membership of the European Union (Ipsos MORI, 2016). Increases in racially motivated hate crimes following the referendum were confirmed by the police (BBC, 2016a), and the United Nations Committee on the Elimination of Racial Discrimination condemned the 'divisive, anti-immigrant and xenophobic rhetoric' employed by the campaigns (UNCERD, 2016). In light of the findings presented by Karlsen and Pantazis (chapter five this volume), especially relating to the increased risk of poverty for some ethnic minorities, including white Polish people, and the high risk of discrimination among these groups, recent trends are a cause for concern. A policy priority should be ameliorating the effects of poverty faced by minority groups, rather than exacerbating prejudice and discrimination.

The chapters in this volume have focused primarily on 'headline' indicators of poverty, including low income, deprivation and the PSE poverty measure. This valuable analysis provides only a fraction of the insight that the PSE-UK 2012 has the capacity to deliver; many more analyses are available through the companion volume on the various dimensions of poverty; the multitude of working papers available on the project website; two Special Issues of academic journals edited respectively by Eldin Fahmy and Christina Pantazis; Mary Daly and Grace Kelly's (2015) book on some of the qualitative research undertaken for the PSE-UK 2012 study; and Stewart Lansley and Jo Mack's (2015) book setting the PSE-UK 2012 in the context of three decades of research into poverty and social exclusion in the UK. Examining different dimensions of poverty and social exclusion can help to capture more precisely and accurately the differential vulnerabilities experienced by people and by social groups. Thus the PSE-UK 2012 highlights the policy importance of developing and maintaining a range of poverty and social exclusion measures, allowing for careful monitoring of poverty levels and the risks faced by diverse social groups.

Bringing structure to the policy debate

As noted in the Introduction, the focus of this volume is on structural conditions affecting vulnerability to poverty. Indeed, the findings presented here – which indicate strong disparities between different social groups in their vulnerability to poverty along the lines of characteristics such as age, gender, ethnicity and disability status – support this focus. Differences in vulnerability to poverty according to these characteristics point to structural barriers disproportionately impacting certain segments of the population; this is a problem whether policy commitment is to equality of opportunity or equality of outcome (a distinction which, while widely used, is highly problematic; see Calder, 2016). Yet policy interventions focus almost exclusively on individual agency, rather than social structure – whether through efforts to activate and/or upskill the workforce and thereby address a deficit in motivation or skills, or increase the number of hours people work. This is not a new trend – it was evident under the Labour government of 1997–2010 as well as the previous Conservative governments of 1979–97 (Lewis, 2011). A great deal has been written elsewhere about the changes in international political paradigms over the past three decades which have resulted in both increased vulnerability to poverty, and increased individualisation in national social policy responses (for example, see Arnold and Bongiovi, 2013). The findings presented here contribute to the body of literature challenging the individualised nature of policy portrayals of the causes of poverty, and the interventions arising from these. Little short of a paradigmatic shift in policy thinking on poverty, towards a more structural focus which addresses the multiple and intersecting barriers faced by vulnerable groups, rather than addressing perceived deficits in the groups themselves, is indicated.

Challenging stigma

The predominance of individualised explanations for poverty, noted above, helps to create an atmosphere of stigma around poverty and shame among people unlucky enough to experience it (Walker, 2014). Individualising policy rhetoric and stigmatising public perceptions of poverty can form a vicious cycle, creating a hostile environment for those in poverty as reflected by long-term declines in societal support for spending on social security, and distinctions in public attitudes between the 'deserving' poor – such as pensioners – and the 'undeserving' poor – such as the unemployed (Clery, 2015). An important role of the PSE-UK 2012, and of all poverty studies, is therefore to test the claims which create and perpetuate this stigma and challenge damaging attitudes which increase the harm done by poverty. The PSE-UK 2012 has demonstrable potential to contribute to challenging this stigma through testing and challenging the claims made in, or assumptions informing, policy rhetoric, offering an alternative narrative to popular presentations of poverty and, through ongoing work in communities, giving voice and power to people living in poverty.

Testing policy rhetoric and the assumptions underlying policies

Through the production of data on the resources, behaviours and experiences of a large and diverse sample, the PSE-UK 2012 provides rich information on the complexities of poverty and how those in poverty differ from, or are similar to, the rest of the population. Such analysis has fed not only into academic outputs from the study, but also into responses to various policy agendas and consultations – the full range of responses, on the topics of child poverty and children's services (Gordon, 2010, 2012; Bradshaw, 2013), the Troubled Families Programme (Levitas, 2012), budget and child poverty consultations in Northern Ireland (Daly et al, 2011; Tomlinson and Kelly, 2011) and fuel poverty (Fahmy, 2012) can be found in the 'policy responses' section of the PSE-UK 2012 website. In many of the chapters of this book – for example in relation to children, parents, young people, and disabled people – strong challenges are raised to current policy approaches based on testing the rationale used to justify particular interventions. Certainly, there is scope for further extending the impact of the PSE-UK 2012 through new analyses. The data from PSE-UK 2012 is freely available for academic analysis via the ESRC's UK Data Service[2], offering future researchers the opportunity to draw on a wealth of policy-relevant information with a strong potential for impact.

Challenging and changing popular narratives

Patrick's (2016: 2) analysis of the 'scrounger' narrative surrounding claimants of out-of-work social security benefits in and beyond the UK highlights the 'framing consensus on welfare'. Within this narrative, policy rhetoric, print media and television disseminate a shared message: that social security claimants (and in particular those on out-of-work benefits) are a threat to social order requiring discipline and control. Indeed, the term 'poverty porn' has arisen to describe the coverage through multiple media sources of sensationalised versions of the lives of the poor. Communicating the results of the PSE-UK 2012 widely in order to increase public understanding of the issues has been a significant and central feature of the project as a whole. Findings from the PSE-UK 2012 have been the subject of mainstream television programmes and media reports. In 2013 the ITV Tonight documentary *Breadline Britain* (ITV 2013), which depicted the lives of people across Britain who are affected by poverty, was watched by over 3 million viewers. Based on findings from the PSE-UK 2012, it emphasised that poverty in contemporary Britain is not restricted to a small minority and has increased over the last 30 years. In March 2016, the leading BBC documentary series *Panorama* broadcast *Too poor to stay warm*, which drew on PSE-UK 2012 work on fuel poverty and was seen by 2.4 million people (BBC, 2016b). The Radio 4 programme *Thinking Allowed* has had three episodes which drew on PSE-UK 2012: exploring the measurement of poverty; challenging the relationship between poverty and bad parenting; and exploring the extent of food poverty in the UK (BBC, 2015, 2016c). The website www.poverty.ac.uk, which provides access to all research outputs from the project, has had 1.5 million page views with visitors from all over the world. While media accounts of poverty remain dominated by negative and sensationalised portrayals, the importance of a strong research base to challenge these narratives cannot be overstated.

Ongoing work with communities

The PSE-UK 2012 incorporated many strands of work. This volume has focused on the research findings from the two quantitative surveys; as noted above, Daly and Kelly's (2015) book documents some of the qualitative strand of the research. In addition to these academic outputs, part of the PSE-UK 2012 involved collaborations with community groups, pressure groups, and organisations and networks working for poverty reduction across the UK. Details of this work can be found on the PSE-UK 2012 website.[3] Additionally, several participants in the qualitative and community strands of the PSE-UK 2012 kindly agreed to share videos documenting their experiences of poverty – also available on the PSE-UK 2012 website.[4] This innovative approach to academic research combines quantitative survey data, qualitative interview data, and collaborations with community groups. The resulting mass of data provides a compelling case for action to end poverty in the UK, across the broad range of social groups covered in this volume.

Concluding comments and recommendations

The PSE-UK 2012, as with previous PSE studies, takes a structural approach to examine the extent, nature, causes and effects of poverty in the UK. This is in contrast to the more individualised approaches that dominate everyday policy and media representations of poverty, which focus on what the poor should do (but, if we are to believe popular representations, usually do not do) to get themselves out of poverty. As the chapters in this volume have detailed, escaping poverty is much more complex and difficult to achieve in reality; and while all the population groups discussed are heterogeneous, some characteristics are associated with greater vulnerability than others, as a result of disadvantages inherent in social structures (for example, the discrimination experienced by certain ethnic groups, and the disadvantages associated with gender). To conclude, some key messages for different groups with a role to play in understanding and combating poverty are summarised:

- **For academics:** The ways that poverty is defined and measured can have important implications for research, and for the credibility of findings. Different research questions (for example, whether the focus is on household or individual experiences of poverty) and different population groups (for example, the experiences of children, of different ethnic groups and of disabled people) may require different indicators if their needs are to be adequately captured. A genuine understanding of access to resources, and the ways in which income does and does not translate into resources for different individuals and groups – stratified according to particular characteristics such as gender, age, and disability – will help in the production of high-quality poverty indicators.

- **For policy makers:** The dominant position within current policy rhetoric, that individual deficiencies are the cause of poverty and that the poor require upskilling and increased motivation to work, does not stand up to scrutiny. As noted in chapter one of this volume, of Levitas' three discourses on poverty, Moral Underclass Discourse and Social Inclusion Discourse have dominated policy approaches in recent years. A shift towards the Redistributive Discourse, with policies that help to ensure that those facing the greatest disadvantage receive the greatest support, is long overdue.

- **For practitioners:** Interventions into the lives of those living in poverty can be hugely beneficial – just as they can be for those facing other kinds of disadvantage. However, changes to the skills and attitudes of those in poverty will not create more and better paid jobs, and neither will they reduce the structural barriers – such as discrimination – faced by particular social groups. In some areas of life in which interventions have been promoted – such as parenting skills for those in poverty (see Dermott and Pomati, this volume) – there is little evidence that those in poverty are substantially different to anyone else. Rather, supporting people in poverty to access the resources to which they are entitled, combating discrimination and advocating individually and collectively for better provision are more likely to make a sustainable difference to the lives of those currently vulnerable to poverty.

- **For the media:** Responsible reporting on poverty, which accounts for the structural causes of poverty and does not 'other' those unlucky enough to be poor by engaging with stylised presentations of the 'deserving' versus the 'undeserving', is vital. This has a role in changing public perceptions of poverty and challenging policy rhetoric – with the potential to generate a 'virtuous cycle' whereby the softening of public attitudes and poverty eradication efforts become symbiotic.

As we complete this manuscript, the UK is on the brink of the 2017 general election. The outcome has the potential to consolidate the dominant economic policy of austerity, which will condemn ever increasing numbers of people to poverty, or to challenge this approach. The evidence presented in this volume is largely statistical in nature – behind these statistics are the real lives of increasing numbers of people who are experiencing (among other issues) hunger, cold, stigma and social isolation. Whatever view might be taken on the causes, this situation is patently not acceptable or excusable within the context of one of the largest global economies.

Notes

[1] Figures from: https://www.ons.gov.uk/economy/governmentpublic sectorandtaxes/publicsectorfinance/timeseries/hf6x/pusf

2   See: https://discover.ukdataservice.ac.uk/catalogue/?sn=7879&type=
    Data%20catalogue for the main survey and https://discover.ukdataservice.
    ac.uk/catalogue/?sn=7878&type=Data%20catalogue for the omnibus
    survey.

3   See: http://poverty.ac.uk/community/community-collaboration

4   See: http://poverty.ac.uk/living-poverty

References

Arnold, D. and Bongiovi, J.R. (2013) 'Precarious, informalizing and flexible work: transforming concepts and understandings', *American Behavioural Scientist* 57:3, 289–308.

BBC (2015) *Thinking Allowed*, 20 May, www.bbc.co.uk/programmes/b006qy05/episodes/guide

BBC (2016a) 'Met Police deputy chief links Brexit vote to hate crime rise', 20 July, www.bbc.co.uk/news/uk-england-london-36835966

BBC (2016b) 'Too poor to stay warm', *Panorama*, 21 March, http://www.bbc.co.uk/programmes/b0756g0x

BBC (2016c) *Thinking Allowed*, 20 April and 20 July, www.bbc.co.uk/programmes/b006qy05/episodes/guide

Beatty, C. and Fothergill, S. (2014) 'The local and regional impact of the UK's welfare reforms', *Cambridge Journal of Regions, Economy and Society* 7:1, 63–79.

Bradshaw, J. (2013) 'Consultation on child poverty measurement', PSE Policy Response Series 8, http://poverty.ac.uk

Calder, G. (2016) *How inequality runs in families*, Bristol: Policy Press.

Cameron, D. (2013) Speaking on *The Andrew Marr Show*. BBC. Transcript available from http://news.bbc.co.uk/1/shared/bsp/hi/pdfs/060113.pdf

Clark, J. and Newman, J. (2012) 'The alchemy of austerity', *Critical Social Policy* 32:3, 299–319.

Clery, E. (2015) 'Welfare', in *British Social Attitudes 33*, www.bsa.natcen.ac.uk/latest-report/british-social-attitudes-33/welfare.aspx

Crossley, S. (2015) 'The Troubled Families Programme: the perfect social policy?', Briefing 13, London: Centre for Crime and Justice Studies.

Daly, M. and Kelly, G. (2015) *Families and poverty: Everyday life on a low income*, Bristol: Policy Press.

Daly, M., Hillyard, P., Kelly, G. and Tomlinson, M. (2011) 'Consultation response: Northern Ireland draft Child Poverty Strategy', PSE Policy Response Series 4, http://poverty.ac.uk

D'Arcy, C. and Kelly, G. (2015) 'Analysing the National Living Wage', Resolution Foundation Briefing, London: Resolution Foundation.

Davies, H. (2015) 'Shared parenting or shared care? Learning from children's experiences of a post-divorce shared care arrangement', *Children and Society* 29, 1–14.

DCLG (Department for Communities and Local Government) (2013) *The cost of troubled families*, London: HMSO.

DWP (Department for Work and Pensions) (2014) *Official statistics: Disability facts and figures*, www.gov.uk/government/publications/disability-facts-and-figures/disability-facts-and-figures#discrimination

DWP (2016) 'Analysis of EEA migrants' access to income-related benefits measures', www.gov.uk/government/uploads/system/uploads/attachment_data/file/548225/analysis-of-eea-migrants-access-to-income-related-benefits-measures.pdf

Fahmy, E. (2012) 'Getting the measure of fuel poverty: Response to the Hills Fuel Poverty Review Consultation', PSE Policy Response Series 7, http://poverty.ac.uk

Gordon, D. (2006) 'The concept and measurement of poverty', in C. Pantazis, D. Gordon and R. Levitas (2006) *Poverty and Social Exclusion in Britain*, Bristol: Policy Press.

Gordon, D. (2010) *Measure of access to quality services for children – consultation response*, PSE Working Paper Policy Response No. 5, http://poverty.ac.uk/working-papers-policy-response-social-exclusion-poverty-measurement-public-services-local-services

Gordon, D. (2011a) 'Consultation response: Social Mobility and Child Poverty Review', PSE Policy Response Series 2, poverty.ac.uk

Gordon, D. (2011b) 'Measure of access to quality services for children – consultation response', PSE Policy Response Series 5, http://poverty.ac.uk

Gordon, D. (2012) 'Consultation response: tackling child poverty and improving life chances: consulting on a new approach', PSE Policy Response Series 1, http://poverty.ac.uk

HM Treasury (2015) 'Spending review and Autumn statement 2015', Policy paper, www.gov.uk/government/publications/spending-review-and-autumn-statement-2015-documents/spending-review-and-autumn-statement-2015

Ipsos MORI (2015) 'NHS continues to be top issue for British voters', *Ipsos MORI Political Monitor*, April.

Ipsos MORI (2016) 'Immigration is now the top issue for voters in the EU referendum', *Ipsos MORI Political Monitor*, June.

ITV (2013) 'Breadline Britain', *Tonight*, 28 March, www.itv.com/news/2013-03-28/breadline-britain/

Joyce, R. and Sibieta, L. (2013) 'Observations: Labour's record on poverty and inequality', Institute for Fiscal Studies, 6 June, www.ifs.org.uk/publications/6738

Lansley, S. and Mack, J. (2015) *Breadline Britain*, London: Oneworld.

Levitas, R. (2012) 'There may be "trouble" ahead: what we know about those 120,000 "troubled" families', PSE Policy Response Series 3, http://poverty.ac.uk

Lewis, P. (2011) 'Upskilling the workers will not upskill the work: why the dominant economic framework limits child poverty reduction in the UK', *Journal of Social Policy* 40:3, 535–56.

Lupton, R., Hills, J., Stewart, K. and Vizard, P. (2013) 'Labour's social policy record: policy, spending and outcomes 1997–2010', Social Policy in a Cold Climate Research Report 1, London: LSE, Centre for Analysis of Social Exclusion.

Mack, J. (2015) 'Explaining poverty to the public', Third Peter Townsend Memorial Conference, London, 19–20 June.

Mack, J. and Lansley, S. (1985) *Poor Britain*. London: George Allen and Unwin.

Metcalf, D. (2016) 'Work immigration and the labour market', Report to the Migration Advisory Committee, www.gov.uk/government/publications/migration-advisory-committee-mac-report-immigration-and-the-labour-market

Patrick, R. (2016) 'Living with and responding to the "scrounger" narrative in the UK: exploring everyday strategies of acceptance, resistance and deflection', *Journal of Poverty and Social Justice*, Online first, doi: 10.1332/175982716X14721954314887.

Piachaud, D. (1987) 'Problems in the definition and measurement of poverty', *Journal of Social Policy* 16:2, 147–64.

Resolution Foundation (2016) 'Budget 2016 response', Briefing, London: Resolution Foundation.

Statham, J. (2011) 'Grandparents providing child care', Childhood Wellbeing Research Centre Briefing Paper, www.gov.uk/government/uploads/system/uploads/attachment_data/file/181364/CWRC-00083-2011.pdf

Tarr, A. and Finn, D. (2012) *Implementing Universal Credit: Will the reforms improve the service for users?* London: Centre for Economic and Social Inclusion.

Tomlinson, M. and Kelly, G. (2011) 'Response to Northern Ireland's Draft Budget', PSE Policy Response Series 6, http://poverty.ac.uk/

Townsend, P. (1979) *Poverty in the United Kingdom*, London: Allen Lane and Penguin Books.

UNCERD (2016) 'Concluding observations on the twenty-first to twenty-third periodic reports of United Kingdom of Great Britain and Northern Ireland', http://tbinternet.ohchr.org/Treaties/CERD/Shared%20Documents/GBR/CERD_C_GBR_CO_21-23_24985_E.pdf

Walker, R. (2014) *The shame of poverty*, Oxford: Oxford University Press.

Technical appendix

Survey details

The Poverty and Social Exclusion study is based on two surveys conducted in 2012.

Necessities of Life survey

The Necessities of Life survey was carried out between May and June 2012 and is based on a random sample of 1,447 adults aged 16 or over in Britain and 1,015 in Northern Ireland. The response rate was 51% in Britain and 53% in Northern Ireland. The survey was carried out by the National Centre for Social Research (NatCen) in Britain and by the Northern Ireland Statistics and Research Agency (NISRA) in Northern Ireland as part of their Omnibus surveys. The full Necessities of life questionnaire can be downloaded from the PSE website at: http://www.poverty.ac.uk/pse-research/questionnaires

The PSE Necessities of Life survey micro-data and the survey technical reports can be downloaded from the UK Data Service website at: https://discover.ukdataservice.ac.uk/catalogue/?sn=7878&type=Data%20catalogue

Living Standards survey

The Living Standards survey was carried out between March and December 2012 by the National Centre for Social Research (NatCen) in Britain and by the Northern Ireland Statistics and Research Agency (NISRA) in Northern Ireland. The survey re-interviewed respondents to the 2010/11 Family Resources Survey (FRS) who said they could be contacted again. Every adult living at each address was interviewed.

The sampling frame was designed so as to give a minimum sample in Britain of 4,220 households (including 1,000 households in Scotland overall and an additional 220 households in rural Scotland) and a minimum sample in Northern Ireland of 1,000 households. Both low income and ethnic minority respondents were oversampled. The final sample size achieved was 5,193 households (4,205 in Britain and 988 in Northern Ireland) in which 12,097 people were living (9,786 in Britain and 2,311 in Northern Ireland). The response rate was 63% in Britain and 61% in Northern Ireland.

Details about the Living Standards survey sampling frame can be downloaded from: http://www.poverty.ac.uk/sites/default/files/ attachments/WP%20Methods%20No.21%20-%20PSE%20Main%20 Survey%20Sampling%20Frame%20%28Gordon%2C%20Oct%20 2011%29_1.pdf

The full Living Standards questionnaire can be downloaded from the PSE website: http://www.poverty.ac.uk/pse-research/questionnaires

The PSE Living Standards survey micro-data and the survey technical reports can be downloaded from the UK Data Service website at: https:// discover.ukdataservice.ac.uk/catalogue/?sn=7879&type=Data%20 catalogue

Index

References to figures and tables are in *italics*